The Gifted Learning Disabled Student

D1528381

N 1-881622-10-X

Table of Contents

Introduction 1

Contrary to many people's view of what it means to be gifted or learning disabled, the two "conditions" can occur together – and with greater frequency than one might expect. When a very bright child is unhappy or underachieving in school, it may be the result of an undiagnosed learning disability. A learning disability in a child who is also intellectually gifted can be very frustrating and confusing to the child, the parents, and the school personnel.

In this book, we have attempted to provide the reader with information on how to recognize and understand the gifted child who may have a learning disability, strategies and programs that can meet the needs of these students, and resources for additional help. Some of these articles have been published in educational and psychology journals, while others were written by CTY staff and colleagues. From our library of resources, we selected what we felt were some of the best writings on this topic. We selected articles that would be helpful and informative to parents, students, and school personnel rather than highly technical or research papers.

We have included articles that address issues and concerns from preschool through college. And, we have included a section on Attention Deficit Disorder (ADD) or ADHD since this is often a syndrome that accompanies or gets confused with learning disabilities and/or giftedness. At the end of the section describing these students, as well as after the ADD articles, we have reprinted several articles that present case studies. Reading about "real" people and, in some cases, very successful individuals with exceptional gifts who also had to struggle with a learning problem can be very enlightening and inspiring.

Gifted students who are gifted and have a learning disability are "doubly exceptional". They are often misunderstood or go unnoticed. We at CTY are particularly concerned about these students since they are seldom accurately diagnosed and rarely receive the appropriate and very individualized services they so desperately need to fulfill their academic promise. We hope that in some small way the information contained in this packet will assist in the identification of one or more of these very special students, and will help you in your efforts to be an effective advocate for their needs.

CENTER FOR TALENTED YOUTH (CTY)
THE JOHNS HOPKINS UNIVERSLTY

Introduction

CTY was formally established in 1979 as an educational center for academically able children and youth. In the intervening years, CTY has emerged as an international leader in the field of talent development. Currently, CTY is poised to contribute to the way educational policy is devised and implemented.

Working in concert with select schools who agree to integrate the Center's basic principles with their own agendas, CTY hopes to demonstrate that students learn most effectively when educational opportunities are matched to their abilities. High standards, continual challenges, rigorous liberal arts curricula, a commitment to learning from teachers as well as students, and unwavering attention to the abilities and needs of individual learners will inevitably improve our schools.

The CTY Mission

- To identify, through national and international talent searches, pre-collegiate children who reason extremely well mathematically and/or verbally

- To provide teacher training and support services to schools or other institutions willing to accept the CTY challenge

- To assist parents and concerned citizens in advancing talented students by providing access to useful information and resources

- To investigate the nature of talent development, academic ability, and the effectiveness of program models and curriculum through research and evaluation

3

■ To provide school administrators with the opportunity to examine the adaptability of CTY principles and practices to the total school population

■ To provide talented youth with challenging and invigorating course work and related educational opportunities matching their demonstrated pace and level of learning (the "optimal match").

The Optimal Match

An "optimal match" is the adjustment of an appropriately challenging curriculum to match a student's demonstrated pace and level of learning. The "optimal match" must be preceded by an evaluation of a student's interest and ability in a subject. For example, let us take a third-grade student with a demonstrated ability in mathematics extending beyond third grade. This student is bored, frustrated and perhaps exhibiting behavioral problems. Once the degree of ability is ascertained, a variety of educational strategies are available to adjust instruction properly to the child's situation. Among these options are placement in a higher grade for mathematics, relevant enrichment in the third-grade classroom in mathematics, an out-of-classroom mentor in mathematics with the child pursuing other relevant activities during the math period and a summer mathematics program. The option chosen in the optimal match process depends on a number of factors including an accurate assessment of the educational and emotional needs of the child, a consideration of parental support and reinforcement, and the resources of the local school community.

The "optimal match" principle stands in contrast to educational systems that have a pre-established program K-12 and place a child in the course of study without substantial alteration of learning patterns, grade placement, or use of community resources in light of individual needs. While the "optimal match" may be an alien concept to many people today, it is as old as American education itself. The following is a quote from Lawrence Cremin's award-winning book on the history of American education with reference to learning in the North American colonies (17th century):

> *What sometimes clearly indicates that schooling went on anywhere and everywhere, not only in the school rooms, but in kitchens, manses, churches, meeting houses, ...* the content and sequence of learning remained fairly well defined, and each student progressed from textbook to textbook at his own pace. [emphasis added]

The "optimal match" assumes the following:

a. Learning is sequential, developmental, and relatively predictable. One can assess a student's progress in mastery of orderly sets of concepts and skills.

b. Once a learner has mastered a given stage or level of understanding, it is time to proceed to the next. Delay will produce boredom; too rapid a pace will produce confusion and discouragement. An "optimal match" - and appropriate challenge - results in new conceptual depth, intellectual excitement, and growth. This principle tends to argue against "horizontal" enrichment in favor of "vertical" methods which move towards increased levels of complexity in synchrony with the learner's own maturation, whether these be within the standard curriculum or in areas which complement it.

c. Among children of a given age, there are substantial differences in skills and knowledge that primarily reflect differences in rate of learning. Individual differences characterize not only general intelligence but, more importantly for educational purposes, specific subject areas (e.g., mathematics, foreign languages, literature, sciences). One student may be more advanced in some domains than others. Providing for the "optimal match" involves taking these differences into account.

SOURCE: Robinson, N.M., & H.B. (1982). The Optimal Match: Devising the Best Compromise for the Highly Gifted Student. In D. Feldman (Ed.), New Directions for Child Development: Developmental Approaches to Giftedness and Creativity, No. 17. San Fransisco: Jossey-Bass.

Identification Policy

■ CTY focuses upon identifying children who demonstrate high capacity in verbal and/or mathematical reasoning abilities. CTY, of course, recognizes a wide array of other talents, but it has chosen to limit its pursuit. CTY applauds those institutions which focus responsibly on other talent areas and sees them as necessary for providing a complete array of services for youth.

■ Verbal and mathematical reasoning abilities form the focus of CTY activity for the following reasons:

– They are core abilities, central to almost all areas of learning and pursuit.

– They represent talents essential for success in learning, both in school and in life.

- They can be efficiently and economically developed within the institutional setting of most schools regardless of location or cultural resources.

- They are more identifiable and less elusive than other types of talent.

■ To identify students with high capacity for verbal and/or mathematical reasoning abilities, CTY recommends a two-stage process: general screening and in-depth differentiation. The initial screening at grade level determines the areas of talent; the latter stage determines the degree of talent within each individual by "out-of-level" testing. Testing up to very high levels (as opposed to grade-level testing) permits a sufficient ceiling to discriminate degrees of ability among extremely bright students.

Academic Program Policy

■ CTY believes in schooling as a principal form of advancing a youth's education and strives to ensure that schooling is responsive to a maturing talent. CTY does not offer a prescription for success in life; rather, it advocates responsive and appropriate educational opportunities.

■ CTY does not use the word "gifted" when referring to the young people with whom it deals. The word "gifted" should be reserved for individuals who have made significant contributions to the advancement of knowledge or practice.

■ Students proceed educationally according to their own demonstrated pace and level of learning in each subject.

■ Appropriate subject matter (i.e. "enrichment") cannot be provided without appropriate pace (i.e. "acceleration").

■ CTY sees the liberal arts as the most engaging and, in the long run, most valuable curricular embodiment of verbal and/or mathematical reasoning abilities.

■ In a particular subject, students are often examined before instruction begins to determine what they already know in order that the teaching may emphasize new material. Pre- and post-testing can eliminate unnecessary boredom resulting from needless repetition of skills and content.

■ CTY balances rigorous and challenging educational course work with a social experience that encourages the development of a balanced human being.

■ Evaluation and accountability are essential components of all educational efforts on behalf of children.

■ CTY demonstrates both descriptively and empirically that a difference is made in a person's education by its intervention.

Implications of CTY Policy upon Schools

In its summer and weekend programs, CTY has worked with thousands of academically able children and youth from public, independent and parochial schools; thus, its observations could have important implications for the conduct of American education.

■ While CTY concentrates for reasons of organization, economy, and efficiency upon academically able children, it believes strongly that with appropriate adaptation and adjustment, its policy and practice are applicable to a much more diverse group of students.

■ Schools should not bear sole responsibility for the nurturing—both educational and emotional—of children. The imaginative use of other institutions, including the family, museums, universities, clubs and churches, contributes decisively to meeting the challenge.

■ There is no one program that meets the needs of all academically able youth. Given the diversity of human minds, a variety of approaches will maximize each child's opportunity to learn.

■ The artificial lock-step of education (kindergarten through graduate school in discrete units and in predetermined progression) should give way as much as possible, so each student can progress at his own speed in each area of study. Depending upon development of talent in each subject area, students could be placed simultaneously at various levels of instruction.

■ Talent needs intellectual tools, including the ability to define terminology and symbols; recall facts, names, examples, rules and categories; recognize trends, causes and relationships; and acquire principles, procedures, implications and theory. High level cognitive skills including evaluation, synthesis, and analysis are also important. Disciplining highly able children in the complete range of cognitive abilities renders them prepared for sustained contribution in later life.

■ Such attributes as creativity, problem solving, risk taking and critical thinking, are often associated with the unfolding of high level verbal and/or mathematical reasoning abilities and are worthy of emphasis when serving highly capable children and youth. They are best taught embedded in appropriate subjects rather than as a separate course.

■ Courses for highly capable students should not be of a "make-more-work" nature. Ideally, they should either help such students to move more efficiently through a subject or expand the intellectual terrain in a relevant and challenging manner.

Who Are These Students? 3

Conceptions and stereotypes of what constitutes giftedness have made it difficult for many people to accept the notion that a child can be gifted and also have learning disabilities. As a result, few such students are systematically identified. Yet, as an educator or a parent you may be aware of a child who appears to have a great deal of potential but isn't achieving at a high level in school. How can you determine whether that child has high academic ability but has difficulty achieving in one or more areas because of a learning disability? While a diagnostic evaluation by a trained psychologist is desirable, there are many clues that can alert you to this possibility.

The articles in this section are intended to help parents and educators understand the characteristics of children who are gifted and have learning disabilities. Students who exhibit these characteristics can then be referred for additional testing. Included are articles that present definitions of learning disabilities, list some of the behavioral traits of children who are gifted and have learning disabilities, and discuss ways to identify these children. Since early identification is so important to the successful remediation of learning disabilities, we include information that focuses on the preschool child who might be both gifted and learning disabled. Finally, an article is included that presents case studies of eminent individuals who exhibited reading and other problems at a young age. Knowing that these individuals overcame learning difficulties can be inspirational to others working to overcome such problems.

Since remediation is so related to the specific traits identified, several of these articles also include some discussion of strategies to help these children. However, strategies will be explored more fully in the next section.

Gifted Learning Disabled Students

Contrary to many people's view of what it means to be gifted or learning disabled, the two "conditions" can occur together – and with greater frequency than one might expect. When a child is unhappy or underachieving in school, it may be the result of an undiagnosed learning disability. A learning disability in a child who is also intellectually gifted can be very frustrating and confusing to both the child and the parents. Some common signs of a learning disability are:

- widely different test scores from one administration of a test to the next;

- very different test scores on one test versus another (e.g., an ability test versus an achievement test) or from one section of a test to another (e.g., verbal skills that are significantly lower than math scores);

- unexplained differences between standardized test scores and actual classroom performance (e.g., the child with a high IQ who is experiencing difficulty in reading, written language, or math; or when a teacher says "I don't understand why Susie's test scores are so low. She's one of my brightest students. She probably had a bad day when she took the test.");

- very slow, laborious handwriting that persists beyond first or second grade and that is inferior to other children the same age;

- noticeable inability to attend to classroom work or teacher's instructions, or to inhibit inappropriate behavior in a school setting;

- noticeable difficulty organizing work, belongings, and/or self (e.g., constantly loses books or homework; forgets to take books or homework to school; clothes, room, notebooks and locker at school are a total disaster); always late, even for things that are important to him/her;

- persistent problems figuring out what others expect, appropriate behavior in a given situation (e.g., laughs in serious situations or always fails to "catch on" to jokes or teasing; misses the point in books or movies; poor social awareness);

- constantly gets into trouble in school (e.g., teacher says things like "uncooperative, doesn't listen, or lazy");

- has great difficulty with puzzles, gets lost often gets disoriented in new places, very poor at all sports;

- inability to spell, punctuate, or capitalize even with normal instruction;

■ problems with organizing thoughts in written form or expressing oneself according to the usual written language conventions.

A student may have a learning disability and not show any of the above behaviors. Likewise, a student may exhibit several of the above signs and still be happy and productive.

There are many different types of learning disabilities and all degrees of severity. Some problems are so mild that they go unattended for years until the student begins experiencing serious difficulty in school or the problem persists for so long that someone finally decides to seek professional help. Gifted children in particular, are often able to compensate for weaknesses by relying on their strengths.

It is very important to identify a true learning disability as soon as possible so that the appropriate remediation and programming can be started. The earlier the problem is diagnosed, the easier it is to deal with and the greater the success for the child. Left unattended, a learning disability will only get worse. It will not go away and children do not outgrow it. And, if a child struggles with a learning problem throughout grade school, his/her self-esteem, learning style, and motivation may all begin to deteriorate. By the time a child with a learning disability is identified in late adolescence, the problem is much more complex and difficult to work with because it is no longer just an academic problem. It is also a social, emotional, and family problem.

There are other reasons for unhappiness or underachievement in school. Very gifted children are often inappropriately placed in educational programs where they are underchallenged and frustrated. Certain temperament and/or family interaction patterns can set the stage for negative academic attitudes and behavior. Emotional upsets in a child's life are also a possibility. Finally, a mismatch between a child's particular learning style (especially if it a strong preference that is inflexible) and the classroom situation can result in academic underachievement.

A Gifted and Learning Disabled Child is...

■ A student with an overall IQ score in the superior range or a score on one section of an individually administered IQ test in the superior range . . .**OR**

■ A student with an exceptional ability in one area (e.g., mathematics: SAT math score of 500 at 12 years of age) . . .**AND**

■ Who exhibits a significant discrepancy between achievement and identified intellectual potential . . .(not due to emotional problems or motivational problems caused by inappropriate placement and/or learning style)

What to Do

1. Talk to your child. Find out more about what is making him or her unhappy. What do they like most and least about school/their teacher?

2. Watch your child as he/she does schoolwork. Spend some time observing your child while doing homework. Does he balk on beginning certain things? Does he get frustrated easily when working on certain subjects? When left to her preferences, does she choose brightly lit areas for study or dim corners? Does she need to hear music or have people around? Does she lie on her bed or the floor, or does she sit at a desk? Does she continually seek assistance and feedback from you or your spouse?

3. Go to your child's class for a visit. Observe the teacher, the classroom atmosphere and routine. You may be able to find the key to your child's problems. For example, he may need more individual attention than he is currently receiving (some children do). Or, she may prefer to work with other children and this kind of learning is not allowed in her present classroom.

4. Talk to your child's teacher. Try to establish a working relationship to solve the "problem." Ask for feedback and performance reports on a regular basis. Ask for help.

5. Ask your school for special testing if you suspect a learning problem. This is your right and it will not cost you anything. You should be aware, however, that not all schools have personnel trained in diagnosing mild learning disabilities, or even a moderate one in a very gifted child. In gifted children, a learning disability is often masked by good oral skills, good thinking skills, and the ability to compensate for average performance. Most schools will not label anything less than complete failure (one to two years below grade level) as a learning disability. So, the gifted learning disabled child is often caught in a system that is unwilling to provide the necessary remediation for weaknesses and often refuses to recognize gifts.

6. Finally, get professional help. A professional trained in identifying learning disabilities and intellectual giftedness can, with an extensive testing battery, diagnose a disability if one exists. A professional also should be able to set up an appropriate program to help your child achieve his/her potential.

Who Should Do the Testing?

1. A person trained and experienced in administering and interpreting psychological and educational tests. (A learning disability in the intellectually gifted is difficult to diagnose; there is a need for complete assessment of psychological processes, personality, as well as educational levels).

2. A person trained and experienced in testing children/adolescents (depending on the age of the child in question) - the condition manifests itself in very different ways depending on the age of the child.

3. A person with training and experience with both gifted and learning disabled students. (A one-sided and incomplete diagnosis can sometimes be worse than none at all).

4. A person who will help you plan a program based on the test results (ask).

What You Should Expect

1. Names of tests administered; something about the tests and why they are being used.

2. A complete diagnosis. This will necessitate a full and comprehensive testing battery (see the section below on "A Comprehensive Testing Battery"). Adequate testing will take time, usually several testing sessions. And, it may be expensive. Check with your health insurance company about coverage for psychological testing. (Mention that there is a problem and that you were referred for testing).

3. That the examiner ask for background information. (You can help by providing your observations if you are a teacher; by gathering information on other testing and reports from teachers if you are a parent).

4. A verbal and a written interpretation of test results.

5. Specific recommendations and follow-up.

A Comprehensive Testing Battery

■ Test of overall ability (individually administered IQ test: A specific ability test may also be helpful)

■ Achievement measures (a complete battery plus specific tests for specific problems)

■ Tests to identify underlying cognitive processing (individually administered IQ test; perceptual motor tests; memory tests; auditory processing test; visual discrimination test)

■ Tests to assess emotional stability, self-concept, learning style

Three Definitions of Learning Disabilities

Definition #1
(Canadian Association for Children and Adults with Learning Disabilities)

Learning disabilities is a generic term that refers to a heterogeneous group of disorders due to identifiable or inferred central nervous system dysfunction. Such disorders may be manifested by delays in early development and/or difficulties in any of the following areas: Attention, memory, reasoning, coordination, communicating, reading, writing, spelling calculation, social competence, and emotional maturation.

Learning disabilities are intrinsic to the individual and may affect learning and behavior in any individual including those with potentially average, average, or above average intelligence.

Learning disabilities are not due primarily to visual, hearing, or motor handicaps; to mental retardation, emotional disturbance, or environmental disadvantage; although they may occur concurrently with any of these.

Learning disabilities may arise from genetic variations, biochemical factors, events in the pre- to per-natal period, or any other subsequent events resulting in neurological impairment.

Definition #2
(National Joint Committee on Learning Disabilities, 1988).

Learning disabilities is a general term that refers to a heterogeneous group of disorders manifested by significant difficulties in the acquisition and use of listening, speaking, reading, writing, reasoning, or mathematical abilities. These disorders are intrinsic to the individual, presumed to be due to central nervous system dysfunction, and may occur across the life span. Problems in self-regulatory behaviors, social perception, and social interaction may exist with learning disabilities but do not by themselves constitute a learning disability. Although learning disabilities may occur concomitantly with other handicapping conditions (for example, sensory impairment, mental retardation, serious emotional disturbance) or with extrinsic influences (such as cultural differences, insufficient or inappropriate instruction), they are not the result of those conditions or influences.

Definition #3
(ACLD, 1984)

Specific learning disabilities is a chronic condition of presumed neurological origin which selectively interferes with the development, integration, and/or demonstration of verbal and/or non-verbal abilities.

Specific learning disabilities exist as a distinct handicapping condition in the presence of average to superior intelligence, adequate sensory and motor systems, and adequate learning opportunities. The condition varies in its manifestations and in degree of severity.

Throughout life the condition can affect self-esteem, education, vocation, socialization, and/or daily living activities.

GIFTED BUT LEARNING DISABLED
A PUZZLING PARADOX

Susan Baum

How can a child learn and not learn at the same time? Why do some students apply little or no effort to school tasks while they commit time and considerable effort to demanding, creative activities outside of school? These behaviors describe students who are simultaneously gifted and learning disabled. For many, however, the terms *learning disabilities* and *giftedness* are at opposite ends of a learning continuum. Indeed, because of funding regulations, in some states a student may be identified and assisted with either learning disabilities or giftedness, but not both.

Uneasiness in accepting this seeming contradiction in terms stems primarily from faulty and incomplete understandings of each term. This is not surprising because the "experts" in each of these disciplines have difficulty reaching agreement. Some still believe that giftedness is equated with outstanding achievement across all subject areas. Thus, a student who may be an expert on bugs at eight years old, who can name and classify a hundred species of insects, and who studies picture books on the topic for hours, but cannot read, is automatically excluded from consideration for the gifted program. Many educators view below-grade-level achievement as a prerequisite to a diagnosis of a learning disability. Thus, when an extremely bright student is struggling to stay on grade level, he may slip through the cracks of available services because he is not failing.

Who Are The Learning Disabled/Gifted?

Recent advances in both fields have alerted professionals to the possibility that both sets of behavior can exist simultaneously (Fox, Brody, and Tobin, 1983; Whitmore and Maker, 1986; Baum and Owen, 1988). Who, then, is the student who is both gifted and learning disabled? Simply spoken, the LD/gifted child exhibits remarkable talents or strengths in some areas and disabling weaknesses in others. Three general varieties have been recognized: identified gifted students who have subtle learning disabilities, unidentified students whose gifts and disabilities may be masked by average achievement, and identified learning disabled students who are also gifted.

Identified Gifted Students
Who Have Subtle Learning Disabilities

This group is easily identified as gifted because of high achievement or high IQ scores. As they grow older, discrepancies widen between expected and actual performance. These students may impress teachers with their verbal abilities, while their spelling or handwriting contradicts the image. At times, they may be forgetful, sloppy and disorganized. In middle school or junior high, where there are more

17

long term written assignments and a heavier emphasis on comprehensive, independent reading, some bright students find it increasingly difficult to achieve. Comments from concerned adults assert, "if the student would only try harder...." While increased effort may be required for these students, the real issue is that they simply do not know how! Because these students may be on grade level and are considered gifted, they are likely to be overlooked for screening procedures necessary to identify a subtle learning disability. The identification of a subtle disability would help students understand why they are experiencing academic difficulties. More importantly, professionals can alter learning strategies and compensation techniques to help these learning disabled gifted students deal with their duality of learning behaviors.

A word of caution is necessary at this point. A learning disability is not the only cause of a discrepancy between potential and achievement. There are a number of other reasons why bright children may be underachieving. Perhaps expectations are unrealistic. Excelling in science, for example, is no assurance that high level performance will be shown in other academic areas. Motivation, interest, and specific aptitudes influence the amount of energy students are willing to apply to a given task. Social or emotional problems can interfere with achievement. Grades and school are simply unimportant to some students. Some youngsters have not learned how to study because, during primary grades, school was easy and success required minimal effort.

Unidentified Students

The second group of youngsters in which this combination of learning behaviors may be found are those who are not noticed at all. These students are struggling to stay at grade level. Their superior intellectual ability is working overtime to help compensate for problematic weaknesses caused by an undiagnosed learning disability. In essence, their gift masks the disability and the disability masks the gift. These students are often difficult to find because they don't flag our attention by exceptional behavior. Their hidden talents and abilities may emerge in specific content areas or may be stimulated by a classroom teacher who uses a creative approach to learning. The disability is frequently discovered in college or adulthood when the student happens to read about dyslexia or hears peers describe their learning difficulties.

Identified Learning Disabled Students Who Are Also Gifted

Unlike the first group mentioned, these bright children, discovered within the identified learning disabled, are often failing miserably in school. They are first noticed by what they cannot do as opposed to the talent they are demonstrating. This group of students is most at risk because of the implicit message that accompanies the LD categorization - there is something wrong with the student that must be fixed before anything else can happen. Parents and teachers alike become totally focused on the problem. Little attention, if any, is paid to the student's strengths and interests other than to use them to remediate weaknesses.

Interestingly, these are the very children who have high level interests at home. They may build fantastic structures with Lego bricks or start a local campaign to save the whales. The creative abilities, intellectual strength and passion they bring to their hobbies are clear indicators of their potential for giftedness (Renzulli, 1978). Because these students are bright and sensitive, they are more acutely aware of their difficulty in learning. Furthermore, they tend to generalize their feelings of academic failure to an overall sense of inadequacy. Over time, these pessimistic feelings overshadow any positive feelings connected with what they accomplish on their own at home. Research has shown that this group of students is often rated by teachers as most disruptive at school. Gifted/LD students have been found to be frequently off task. They may act out or daydream, or complain of headaches and stomachaches. They are easily frustrated and use their creative abilities to avoid tasks (Whitmore, 1980; Baum and Owen, 1988). Since school does not offer these bright youngsters much opportunity to polish and use their gifts, these results are not surprising.

Curricular Needs

Although each of these subgroups has unique problems, they all require an environment that will nurture their gifts, attend to the learning disability and provide the emotional support necessary for LD/gifted students to deal with inconsistent abilities. Four general guidelines emerge to assist professionals in developing programs that will meet the needs of these students. These guidelines are discussed below with specific examples of how the guidelines may be implemented.

Attention Focused on the Development of the Gift

As was mentioned previously, remediation of basic skills historically has been the single focus of efforts to serve students once they have been classified as learning disabled. Few opportunities exist where bright LD students can demonstrate gifted behaviors. Research has shown that a focus on weaknesses at the expense of developing gifts can result in poor self esteem, a lack of motivation, depression and stress (Baum, 1984; Whitmore & Maker,1985). In addition to remediation, focused attention on the development of strengths, interests, and superior intellectual capacities is necessary. The students need a stimulating educational environment which will enable them to fully develop their talents and abilities. Enrichment activities should be designed to circumvent problematic weaknesses and to highlight abstract thinking and creative production.

Over the last six years, the state of Connecticut has funded a variety of special programs for gifted/LD students. All the programs emphasized the development of gifts and talents of these students. The results of the projects showed dramatic improvement in student self-esteem, motivation, and productive learning behaviors. Improved achievement in basic skills for many students was an unexpected bonus (Baum,1988). In fact, Whitmore and Maker (1986) claim that more gains are seen when intervention focuses on the gift rather than the disability.

A Nurturing Environment
That Values Individual Differences

According to Maslow's Hierarchy of Needs (1962), individuals must feel like they belong and are valued in order to reach their potential or self-actualize. How valued can a student feel if the curriculum must be continually modified, or assignments watered down, to enable the student to achieve success? Currently, only certain abilities are rewarded by schools, primarily those that involve strong verbal proficiency. Indeed, according to Howard Gardner (1983), schools spend much of their time teaching students skills to become college professors. Success in the real world depends on skills or intelligences in other areas besides reading and writing.

A nurturing environment, one that shows concern for developing student potential, values and respects individual differences. Students are rewarded for what they do well. Options are offered for both acquiring information and communicating what is learned. The philosophy fosters and supports interdependence; students work in cooperative groups to achieve goals. Multiple intelligences are acknowledged–developing a well produced video production about life in the Amazon is as valued as the well written essay on the same topic. In such an environment no child will feel like a second class citizen and the gifted/LD student can excel.

Compensation Strategies

Learning problems connected with a learning disability tend to be somewhat permanent through life. A poor speller will always need to check for errors in spelling before submitting a final draft. Students who have difficulty memorizing math facts may need to use a calculator to assure accuracy. Thus, to simply remediate weaknesses may not be appropriate or sufficient for the gifted learning disabled student. Remediation will make the learner somewhat more proficient but probably not excellent in areas of weakness. For instance students who have difficulty with handwriting will ultimately fare much better if allowed to use a computer to record their ideas on paper than they will after years of remediation in handwriting. The following checklist outlines suggestions for providing compensation techniques to assist the student in coping with problematic weaknesses typical of the learning disabled student.

1. Find sources of information that are appropriate for students who may have difficulty reading. Some examples are visitations, interviews, photographs, pictorial histories, films, lectures, or experimentation. Remember these children do not want the curriculum to be less challenging or demanding. Rather they need alternative ways to receive the information.

2. Provide advanced organizers for both receiving and communicating information to students who have difficulty organizing and managing time. These include outlines of class lectures, study guides, and a syllabus of topics to be covered so families can provide support. Teach students who have difficulty transferring

ideas to a sequential format on paper to use brain-storming and webbing in order to generate outlines and organize written work. Resources are listed at the end of this article. Provide management plans in which tasks are listed sequentially with target dates for completion. Last, but equally important, provide a structure or visual format to guide the finished product. A sketch of the essay or science project board will enable these students to produce a well organized product.

3. Use technology to promote productivity. Technology has provided efficient means to organize and access information, increase accuracy in mathematics and spelling, and enhance the visual quality of the finished product. In short, it allows the gifted/LD student to hand in work of which he can feel proud. Preventing an LD student from using a word processing program to complete all written assignments is like prohibiting the blind child from using texts printed in Braille!

4. Offer a variety of options for communication of ideas. Writing is not the only way to communicate. All learning can be expressed and applied in a variety of modes. Slides, models, speeches, mime, murals, and film productions are examples. Remember, however, to offer these options to all children. These alternate modes should be the rule rather than the exception.

5. Help students with problems in short-term memory to develop strategies for remembering. The use of mnemonics, especially those created by students themselves, is one effective strategy to enhance memory. The use of visualization techniques has also proved to be effective in improving memory. Resources are listed at the end of this article.

Awareness of Individual Strengths and Weaknesses

It is imperative that gifted/LD students understand their abilities, strengths, and weaknesses so that they can make intelligent choices about their future. If a goal important to them will require extensive reading and, if reading is a weak area, they will have to acknowledge the role of effort and assistance they may need to achieve success. "Rap sessions," where these students can discuss their frustrations and learn how to cope with their strange mix of abilities and disabilities, are helpful. Mentoring experiences with LD/gifted adults will lend validity to the belief that such individuals can succeed.

Closing Thoughts

This article, a brief overview of some issues involved in working with students who are both gifted and learning disabled, is intended to create an awareness of who these students are and what they need. In reality, however, we must teach these students how to be their own advocates. They must ultimately choose a career that will accentuate their strengths. In doing so they will meet others who think, feel, and create as they do.

One gifted/LD student, after years of feeling different and struggling to succeed, was finally able to make appropriate decisions about what he truly needed in his life. He was an outstanding amateur photographer and always loved music. He had also started several "businesses" during his teenage years. In his junior year at college he became depressed and realized that he was totally dissatisfied with his course work, peers, and instructors. He wondered if he should quit school. After all, he was barely earning C's in his courses. His advisor suggested that he might like to create his own major, perhaps in the business of art. That was the turning point in this young man's life. For the first time since primary grades he began to earn A's in his courses. He related that he finally felt worthwhile. "You know," he said, "finally I'm with people who think like me and have my interests and values. I am found!"

Resources

Webbing and Mind-Mapping

Heimlich, J. E. & Pittleman, S. D. (1986). *Semantic mapping: Classroom applications.* Newark, DE: International Reading Association.

Large, C. (1987). *The clustering approach to better essay writing.* Monroe, NY: Trillium Press.

Rico, G. L. (1983). *Writing the natural way.* Los Angeles: J. P. Tarcher.

Visualization Techniques to Improve Memory.

Write to Trillium Press, P. O. Box 209, Monroe NY 10950 for information on the following materials.

Bagley, M. T. *Using Imagery to Develop Memory.*

Bagley, M. T. *Using Imagery in Creative Problem Solving.*

Bagley, M. T. & Hess, K K. *Two Hundred Ways of Using Imagery in the Classroom.*

Hess, K. K. *Enhancing Writing Through Imagery.*

References

Baum, S. (1984). Meeting the needs of learning disabled gifted children. *Roeper Review, Z,*16-19.

Baum, S. (1988). An enrichment program for gifted learning disabled students. *Gifted Child Quarterly, 32.* 226-230.

Baum, S. & Owen, S. (1988). High Ability/Learning Disabled Students: How are they different? *Gifted Child Quarterly , 32.* 321-326.

Fox, L. H., Brody, L. & Tobin, D. (Eds.) (1983). *Learning disabled gifted children: Identification and programming.* Baltimore, MD: Allyn & Bacon.

Gardner, H. (1983). *Frames of mind: The theory of multiple intelligences.* New York: Basic Books, Inc.

Maslow, A. (1962). *Toward a psychology of being.* Princeton, NJ: Van Nostrum.

Renzulli J. (1978). What makes giftedness: Reexamining a definition. *Phi Delta Kappan, 60*, 180-184.

Whitmore, J. (1980). *Giftedness, conflict, and underachievement.* Boston: Allyn and Bacon.

Whitmore, J. & Maker, J. (1985). *Intellectual giftedness among disabled persons.* Rockville, MD: Aspen Press.

Note. From *Preventing School Failure,* (Fall 1989), 34 (1) 11-14. Reprinted with permission of the Helen Dwight Reid Educational Foundation, published by Heldref, 4000 Albemarle St. N.W., Washington, D.C. 20016. Based on *Being Gifted and Learning Disabled...From Definition to Practical Intervention,* by S. Baum (in press) published by Creative Learning Press. Dr. Susan Baum is an assistant professor at the College of New Rochelle in New York.

ERIC Clearinghouse on Handicapped and Gifted Children/ Council for Exceptional Children

WHAT ARE SPECIFIC
LEARNING DISABILITIES?

Larry B. Silver

Many people think of learning disabilities as a single condition, which causes a person to reverse letters and read words backwards, but this is only one way these problems may show themselves. Learning disabilities may occur in reading, spelling, math, organization, or motor performance, such as handwriting. They may appear in one area or several. It is important to remember that the pattern for each person is different.

Steps to Learning:
Input, Integration, Memory, and Output

Information is recorded in the brain through the five senses. This "input," once recorded in the brain, is organized and comprehended, a process called integration. Once integrated, the information may be used or stored so that it can be retrieved (memory). Finally, one must be able to communicate this information to others. In the person with learning disabilities, something interferes with one or more of these steps. Although any learning task requires more than one of these functions, it is helpful to look at each function separately.

INPUT DISABILITIES

We take in most of our information by seeing (visual input) and hearing (auditory input). Although a person's eyes and ears may function correctly, the brain may not record accurately what the eye sees or the ear hears. When that happens, a person is said to have a **visual perception** or an **auditory perception** disability. Some individuals have difficulty with one or the other or both areas of input. Others might have difficulty when both visual and auditory perception are needed at the same time.

Visual Perception Disabilities
Those with learning disabilities may have difficulty distinguishing subtle differences in shapes, reversing letters like "e" for "e" or "E" for "3," or may have trouble visually organizing what they see on paper, confusing "d" and "b" and "p" and "q." This confusion with spatial positioning may show up in written work, in copying designs, or in doing visual motor tasks. A common problem, a visual-motor disability may occur when the eyes have to tell the hands or legs what to do, such as catching, hitting, or kicking a ball, jumping rope, working a puzzle or striking a nail with a hammer. Activities such as these may be difficult for those with learning disabilities.

Those with visual perceptual problems also may have trouble organizing their body's position in space, or may confuse left and right. They may have a visual "figure-ground" problem: a difficulty in focusing on the important figure in the midst of all the other images in the background. When reading, for example, they may skip words or jump lines. Some may have problems with depth perception, and bump into things or fall off chairs. Some may misjudge distance; they will be the "careless" ones who always knock over drinks.

Auditory Perception Disabilities

Some have difficulty distinguishing subtle differences in sound. They may confuse words such as "blue" and "blow," or "ball" and "bell." Because they misunderstand what is said, they answer incorrectly. For instance, a person who is asked "How **are** you?" may hear "How **old** are you?" and answer "Twelve."

There are auditory figure-ground problems, too, that show up in common scenarios such as this one: A child is watching TV in the family room, where others are playing. Mother calls out instructions to the child from the kitchen, but gets no response, because the child may not pick out her voice from background sounds.

Some may have an auditory lag, and cannot process spoken messages as fast as most people. They are likely to miss some of what is spoken at a normal rate. The person who speaks more slowly makes it possible for them to follow.

INTEGRATION DISABILITIES

Much of the information recorded in the brain must be sequenced, or put in the right order. Then it must be abstracted, or understood. Those with learning disabilities may have problems with either or both. Difficulties with visual or auditory input may make integration even more problematic.

Sequencing Disabilities

The person with learning disabilities may hear or see a story and understand it. But in retelling it, or in writing it down, that person may mix up the sequence of events, beginning in the middle, moving to the end, going on to the start. That person may read "was" for "saw" or "dog" for "god." An inability to sequence accurately is one possible cause of difficulty with spelling.

Abstraction Disabilities

Some individuals may have trouble understanding the concepts behind words or images. For example, a student may be able to say what it is to vote, yet not understand the concepts of representative government or democracy.

MEMORY DISABILITIES

Information received, recorded and integrated in the brain must be stored to be retrieved later. Two kinds of memory serve this function. Short-term memory holds information as long as you pay attention to it: for instance, when you get a phone number from the information operator, hold it in your head, and dial. But if you are interrupted, you are likely to forget the number. Long-term memory stores frequently repeated material, which comes back when you think about it, such as a home address. Short-term or long-term memory can be a problem, and it can be associated more with either visual or auditory information.

For instance, the child who knows all his spelling words at night, but can't remember them in the morning may have a short-term memory problem. That same child may be capable of perfectly accurate long-term memory, recalling the specific details of a vacation made three years before. Most children are able to learn with repetition, but the child with short-term memory deficits must repeat something many, many times (making it long-term memory) to learn it.

OUTPUT DISABILITIES

We communicate what we know through words – language output – or through muscle activity, such as gesturing, drawing, or writing – motor output. Either can be dysfunctional.

Language Disabilities
Oral language occurs either spontaneously, as when one initiates a conversation, or on demand, when one responds to a question. With spontaneous language, one can organize thought and find the right words before one speaks; with demand language, one has to do all three at once, and that's where disability can occur. It's confusing, because the person with demand language disability may sound normal when speaking spontaneously, and may even talk incessantly to keep others from asking a question. Yet, that same person, when asked "How was your day?" may respond "Huh? What did you say?" Often the person with demand language problems rambles and has trouble finding the right words in answering.

Motor Disabilities
The person who has trouble using large groups of muscles in a coordinated way has a gross motor disability. These are the clumsy ones who stumble, and have trouble walking, running, climbing, or riding a bike. Those who have trouble getting the smaller muscles to act as a team have fine motor disability. For instance, before you write, information in your brain must be sent to the many muscles of your dominant hand. If you watch your hand as you write, you will notice the many detailed, fine motor (muscle) activities needed. Slow, poor handwriting may be the result of a fine motor disability.

REMEMBER: Any problem with learning may involve one or more of the learning disabilities described above. It is important that each individual have a psychoeducational evaluation to assess which disabilities, if any, exist.

LIGHTING A CANDLE RATHER THAN CURSING THE DARKNESS ...
The essential thing to remember is that each person with learning disabilities has learning strengths as well. Areas of strength are often highly developed in the learning disabled. It is important to recognize those strengths and build on them rather than be frustrated by the weaknesses.

"What Are Specific Learning Disabilities?", adapted from The Misunderstood Child by Larry B. Silver, M.D., is part of Topics in Learning Disabilities. This rainbow series of factsheets for parents was produced and distributed by the Information and Communications Program of TRI-Services' National Institute of Dyslexia. This Institute is no longer in operation.

Issues in the Identification and Programming of the Gifted/LearningDisabled Child

Donna P. Suter
Joan S. Wolf

Gifted/learning disabled children have received little attention. There are several reasons for this lack of attention, the most important of which becomes clear when the characteristics of the gifted/learning disabled are examined. These children exhibit a significant discrepancy between potential and achievement. Depending on the level of intellectual ability and the severity of the learning difficulties, the gifted/learning disabled may either be identified as learning disabled with the giftedness masked by the handicapping condition, or may be functioning at or near grade level, in which case both the learning disability and giftedness go undetected. Because identification is difficult, little empirical research has been reported and the need for special services has been overlooked.

As data have become available, several characteristics of this population have been discussed. These children may exhibit any number of deficits in cognitive ability. Long and short term memory is often impaired, making tasks such as spelling and math computation difficult, and memorization of multiplication tables nearly impossible. There may be visual or auditory processing difficulties and/or visual motor integration problems (Maker, 1977; Whitmore, 1980). Strengths in cognitive functioning most frequently mentioned include good problem solving skills, abstract thinking abilities, and good communication skills (Daniels, 1983; Hadary, Cohen, & Haushalter, 1979; Whitmore, 1980). Behavioral problems often revolve around poor self-concept. It is difficult for gifted/learning disabled children to understand the discrepancy between their higher level thinking ability and their inability to master basic academic skills. This leads to high levels of self-criticism. Other behavioral difficulties that may characterize these students are withdrawal or aggression, short attention span, difficulty following directions, and poor peer relations (Maker & Udall, 1983; Tannenbaum & Baldwin, 1983). These characteristics, which could be indicative of a number of different handicapping conditions, make the process of identifying the gifted/learning disabled difficult.

Identification

How do educators go about finding these students? They may be found in classes for the gifted and identifiable because of weaknesses in some area, in special classes for the learning disabled, or in the regular classroom where they appear as average ability students perhaps with some mild behavioral difficulties. In any case, the most important step in identification involves both parents and teachers, and is based on our knowledge of gifted/learning disabled students which can be used to analyze a child's strengths and weaknesses. Phrases such as "he seems bright but he's doing poorly in class" or "she knows a great deal about subjects which interest her, but is unmotivated by classroom tasks" may be helpful as preliminary indicators.

A number of researchers (Fox & Brody, 1983; Maker & Udall, 1983; Rosner & Seymour, 1983) have suggested a flexible multidimensional approach to identification which includes an individual test of intelligence such as the Wechsler Intelligence Scale for Children-Revised (WISC-R) (Wechsler, 1974), academic tests, an informal reading inventory, teacher and parent report, a test of creativity, and a child interview. Fox and Brody (1983) discuss the advantages of using creativity tests such as the Torrance Tests of Creativity (1966), in order to assess abilities which may not emerge on cognitive ability measures such as the WISC-R. However, because of the problems inherent in the appropriateness and validity of creativity tests, the authors are somewhat equivocal about their use. The key to identification may lie in the attention to performance characterized by great variability across tasks (Wolf & Gygi, 1981). Oral language skills, problem solving abilities, conceptual knowledge, and creative production may be superior while basic academic skill levels are far less advanced (Whitmore & Maker, 1985).

Much of the work with gifted/learning disabled children has employed the WISC-R in the identification process because of the availability of subtest comparisons to identify both strengths and weaknesses, and variability across tasks. However, at this point there does not appear to be a clear cut pattern of performance for this group. Schiff, Kaufman, and Kaufman (1981) reported Verbal-Performance discrepancies are greater ($M = 18.5, p$ .001) for learning disabled students with superior-tested intelligence than for learning disabled and non-handicapped students who have average scores ($M = 13$).

Maker and Udall (1981) collected WISC-R data on nine third, fourth, and fifth grade students participating in a gifted/learning disabled program. The majority had higher Performance than Verbal scores and most had a significant discrepancy with wide subtest scatter. The lowest subscale scores were Digit Span, Information, Block Design, and Coding. The highest were Picture Arrangement, Arithmetic, Comprehension, and Vocabulary. Discrepancies ranged from 1 to 30 points with a mean difference of 18.0. Academically weak areas were handwriting, spelling, and mathematics while strengths included good verbal abilities, good social skills with adults, a sense of humor, creativity, and imagination. Listening and concentration skills were poor and attention span was short. This group also had difficulty with peer relationships.

Fox (1981) examined the case histories of 17,000 children referred to the Temple University Reading Clinic from 1952-1979 and found 322 children (246 boys and 76 girls) who were both gifted and learning disabled on the basis of WISC and reading achievement scores. Large Verbal-Performance discrepancies (15 points or more) were evident for 50% of this sample with approximately 22% having higher

Verbal scores and 28% higher Performance scores. The Similarities and Comprehension subscales were found to be highest for these students. Digit Span and Arithmetic, both measures of attention and concentration (Sattler, 1982) tended to produce the lowest scores (Fox, 1981).

Schiff et al. (1981) examined the WISC-R scores of 30 gifted and learning disabled white children of predominantly high socioeconomic status, ages 6 to 13. They found higher Verbal than Performance scores with a mean discrepancy of 14.7 points. This sample of children scored well on the four Verbal Comprehension subtests (95th percentile), moderately well on the five Perceptual Organization tasks (80th percentile), and average on the Freedom from Distractibility subtests (64th percentile) (Kaufman, 1975). In examining Bannatyne's categories (1974), Verbal Conceptualization (Comprehension, Similarities, Information) was highest with Acquired Knowledge (Information, Arithmetic, Vocabulary) next, then Spatial (Picture Completion, Block Design, Object Assembly), with Sequencing (Arithmetic, Digit Span, Coding) last. Weaknesses are basically the same for this sample as for average intelligence learning disabled students but the strengths of the learning disabled gifted are more like average non-learning disabled children from high socioeconomic backgrounds which typically show higher Verbal than Performance scores (Schiff, et al., 1981).

Several common findings can be discerned from these studies (see Table 1).

1. Large Verbal-Performance discrepancies are frequently seen;

2. Subscales that assess verbal reasoning abilities (Comprehension, Similarities) tend to yield high scores; and

3. Scores on Digit Span, Arithmetic, and Coding reflecting attention and concentration tend to be low.

Although the research with the WISC-R is promising, there are not sufficient data available to draw any conclusions concerning WISC-R patterns for this population. Thus, careful evaluation of the quality and nature of responses is important.

To summarize the identification process:

1. A multidimensional approach to identification is necessary to determine areas of strength and weakness.

2. The WISC-R is helpful in identifying strengths and weaknesses as well as overall performance.

3. Academic testing is necessary to determine the discrepancy between potential and performance.

4. Important information can be obtained from parents and teachers about abilities that may not be demonstrated on standardized tests.

5. Evaluators should spend time interviewing and assessing the quality of children's responses for signs of giftedness.

Table 1
A Comparison of Findings on WISC-R IQ's for Gifted/Learning Disabled Students

	Maker & Udall (1981) n = 9	Fox (1981) n = 322	Schiff et al. (1981) n = 30
	Higher Performance than Verbal	Both patterns reported Higher Performance than Verbal Higher Verbal than Performance	Higher Verbal than Performance
High Loads	Arithmetic Comprehension Vocabulary Picture Arrangement	Similarities Vocabulary	Vocabulary Information Comprehension Similarities
Low Loads	Digit Span Information Block Design Coding	Digit Span Arithmetic	Digit Span Coding Arithmetic
Mean Discrepancy	18.0		14.7

The Case of Aaron

The following case study is illustrative of the kinds of strengths, weaknesses, and variability in skill level that characterize gifted/learning disabled students. "Aaron" is a fifth grade boy who was referred to the school psychologist by his teacher because of withdrawn behavior and mild learning difficulties, particularly in spelling and math computation. During the initial referral interview with his teacher, it became apparent that Aaron had strong skills in creative writing and understanding math concepts. However, it was difficult for the teacher to convince Aaron to share his talents with other children. He preferred to remain aloof and often sat in class with his jacket on, with the hood over his head. His parents reported that many hours had been spent drilling on multiplication tables and weekly spelling lists with little success. Aaron spent much of his free time at home designing elaborate Lego structures and expressed an interest in architecture as a career choice.

Testing showed a WISC-R Full scale intelligence score of 132 with a 19 point discrepancy between the Performance (138) and Verbal (119) scales. Subtest scores ranged from 10 to 17 with above average scores in Block Design, Picture Arrangement, and Object Assembly,
and low scores in Arithmetic, Coding, Digit Span, and Information. Scores on the Stanford Achievement Test ranged from the 30th to the 70th percentile with the exception of spelling (20th percentile). On the Woodcock Reading Mastery Test, Aaron also scored within the average range (44th percentile), with strengths in Word Comprehension and Passage Comprehension. The KeyMath test score of 4.8 (grade equivalent) was only slightly below his grade placement although wide subtest scatter was evident. The overall academic functioning of this student was within the average range, however, it was far below his expected achievement as measured by the WISC-R. Aaron's performance was typical of youngsters with high ability who present a learning disability (see Table 2). There are several programming implications for children like Aaron.

Programming

An important consideration for serving gifted/learning disabled youngsters is that of the appropriate setting in which to serve them. Resource classes typically focus on weaknesses and attempt to remediate by drilling and practicing basic skills. This setting may not provide opportunities for exposure to higher level material of interest to gifted students. Regular class instruction may better meet the need for intellectual stimulation, but provide little assistance in dealing with the students' learning difficulties. Placement in programs for the gifted would allow access to higher level material as well as interaction with other gifted students but often involves independent work and high level reading tasks which may be too advanced for the gifted/learning disabled student.

Table 2
Diagnostic Profile for a Gifted/Learning Disabled Student

Name "Aaron"   Grade 5.4   Age 10.5

Intellectual Functioning	Standardized Achievement				Visual	Behavioral
	Reading	Spelling	Mathematics	Comprehensive		
WISC-R S.S.	Woodcock Reading Mastery Test	Wide Range Achievement Test	Wide Range Achievement Test	Stanford Achievement Test	VMI	Teacher and Parent Report
	%ile	%ile	%ile	%ile	%ile	
Verbal = 119						
Perform. = 138						
F.S. = 132	Letter Ident. 31	Spelling 16	Arithmetic 61	Read. Comp. 58	82	Unmotivated
Verbal Subtests			KeyMath	Word Study 48		
Information 13	Word Ident. 36		Grade Equiv.	Total Read. 52		
Similarities 14	Word Attack 42		4.8	Vocabulary 30		Difficulty
Arithmetic 10	Word Comp. 65			List. Comp. 34		completing
Vocabulary 14	Pass. Comp. 68			Audit. Comp. 30		tasks
Comprehension 15	Total 44			Spelling 20		Excessive
Digit Span 10				Language 40		withdrawal
Performance Subtests				Math. Con. 70		Poor peer
Picture Comp. 15		Reading 50		Math Comp. 46		relations
Picture Arr. 16				Total Math 46		
Block Design 17				Social St 42		
Object Assem. 16				Science 56		
Coding 13				Total 40		

Another option for many of these children is the formation of a class for students with dual exceptionalities (Daniels, 1983; Tannenbaum & Baldwin, 1983; Whitmore & Maker, 1985). This type of setting would eliminate the movement from classroom to classroom and teacher to teacher that occurs when services are provided separately in regular gifted and special education programs. The gifted/learning disabled class would provide a more cohesive educational program and better meet the emotional needs by accessing other students with similar learning patterns. Because of the small numbers of children identified as gifted/learning disabled, special classes could be formed across grade levels (grades 1-3, 4-6, 7-9).

Whatever the choice of service pattern, teaching methods would need to accommodate the students' strengths and weaknesses by using alternative strategies for instruction and evaluation. Strategies that have been shown to be useful with gifted students having specific learning disabilities include the following:

- tape recorded lectures

- opportunities for experiential learning

- oral presentations

- use of students or others to read complex material orally

- a multisensory approach to learning

- opportunities for choices in modes of presentation

- the use of alternative evaluation methods; i.e., spelling tests given orally, taping reports

- use of criterion referenced testing to identify areas of mastery and deficiencies.

The use of microcomputers as an aid to learning has been suggested by Tobin and Schiffman (1983). Computers help meet the need for individualized instruction in both strength and weakness areas by providing rapid presentation of material easily learned or allowing for many repetitions in a unique and interesting manner if needed. Immediate feedback and reinforcement are also possible when using this technology. Using the computer as a word processor for students who have difficulty writing and spelling can be extremely helpful in decreasing the frustration that is experienced when students need to revise their work.

It is generally agreed that, in addition to academic instruction, these children need help with adaptive behavior skills and self-esteem (Cruikshank, Morse, & Johns, 1980; Daniels, 1983; Wolf & Gygi, 1981). A strong counseling component should address the nature of the child's talents and areas of difficulty, social skills with peers, goal setting, and self-concept. Counseling services to help parents understand their child's exceptionalities would also be helpful as families are an important source of academic and emotional support for the gifted/learning disabled child.

For Aaron, recognition of his areas of strength is a first step in addressing his academic needs. Opportunities for creative writing and situations in which he can be paired with another child to work through a math task would capitalize on his abilities. Providing alternative modes of responding to spelling assignments by adjusting the task demands and output mode would be other aspects of programming for this student. Additionally, counseling for Aaron and his parents is recommended so that they might increase their understanding of Aaron and his strengths and weaknesses, and improve skills in areas of need.

Summary

Students who exhibit superior intellectual ability and yet are having difficulty mastering basic academic skills may be gifted/learning disabled. Performance is characterized by considerable variability across tasks. Strengths frequently lie in reasoning and problem solving skills while weaknesses may be evident in areas involving long and short term memory. Additional characteristics that may be present are mild behavioral difficulties, such as low motivation and task completion, difficulty following directions, withdrawal or aggression, and poor peer relations.

Because identification is difficult, a multidimensional approach is necessary to fully assess patterns of strength and weakness. The case of Aaron illustrates the variability often found in this population that becomes apparent during the identification process. While there is not one representative pattern, variability is often a key to identification.

Identification is further complicated by the variety of settings in which these students may be found, i.e., classes for the gifted, resource programs for learning disabled students, or regular classroom settings. Successful programming must be based on the individual needs of each child and the setting in which services are provided. Important components include instruction in compensation strategies, exposure to higher level concepts and materials, and a counseling program for students and parents.

The educational community is becoming more aware of children who are both gifted and learning disabled. However, because the incidence is low and identification difficult, there is little empirical data available. Given the societal contributions of people such as Albert Einstein, George Patton, Thomas Edison, Hans Christian Anderson, George Washington, and Nelson Rockefeller (Mauser, 1981), it is imperative that the knowledge base continue to grow through research in identification, instructional strategies, and program evaluation.

References

Bannatyne, A. (1974). Diagnosis: A note on recategorization of the WISC scaled scores. *Journal of Learning Disabilities, 7*, 272-274.

Cruikshank, W., Morse, W., & Johns, J. (1980). *Learning Disabilities: The Struggle from Adolescence toward Adulthood.* Syracuse: Syracuse University Press.

Daniels, D. (1983). *Teaching the Gifted/LD Child.* Rockville, MD: Aspen Systems.

Fox, L. (1981). Identification of the academically gifted. *American Psychologist, 36*, 1103-1111.

Fox, L., & Brody, L. (1983). Models for identifying giftedness: Issues related to the learning-disabled child. In L. Fox, L. Brody, & D. Tobin (Eds.), *Learning Disabled Gifted Children* (pp. 101-116). Boston: University Park Press.

Hadary, D., Cohen, S., & Haushalter, R. (1979). Out of darkness and silence. *Science and Children, 16*, 40-41.

Kaufman, A. (1975). Factor analysis of the WISC-R at eleven age levels between 6 1/2 and 16 1/2 years. *Journal of Consulting and Clinical Psychology, 43*, 135-147.

Maker, C. (1977). *Providing Programs for the Gifted Handicapped.* Reston, VA: The Council for Exceptional Children.

Maker, C., & Udall, A. (1983). A pilot program for elementary-age learning disabled/gifted students. In L. Fox, L. Brody, & D. Tobin (Eds.), *Learning Disabled/Gifted Children* (pp. 141-152). Baltimore: University Park Press.

Mauser, A. (1981). Programming strategies for pupils with disabilities who are gifted. *Rehabilitation Literature, 42*, 270-275.

Rosner, S. (1983). Diagnosis: A case-typing approach. In L. Fox, L. Brody, & D. Tobin (Eds.), *Learning Disabled/Gifted Children* (pp. 141-152). Baltimore: University Park Press.

Rosner, S., & Seymour, J. (1983). The gifted child with a learning disability: Clinical evidence. In L. Fox, L. Brody, & D. Tobin (Eds.), *Learning Disabled/Gifted Children* (pp. 77-97). Baltimore: University Park Press.

Sattler, J. (1982). *Assessment of Children's Intelligence and Special Abilities* (2nd ed.). Boston: Allyn and Bacon.

Schiff, M., Kaufman, A.S., & Kaufman, N.L. (1981). Scatter analysis of WISC-R profiles for learning disabled children with superior intelligence. *Journal of Learning Disabilities 14*, 400-404.

Tannenbaum, A., & Baldwin, L. (1983). Giftedness and learning disability: A paradoxical combination. In L. Fox, L. Brody, & D. Tobin (Eds.), *Learning Disabled/Gifted Children* (pp. 11-36). Baltimore: University Park Press.

Tobin, R., & Schiffman, G. (1983). Computer technology for learning-disabled/gifted students. In L. Fox, L. Brody, & D. Tobin (Eds.), *Learning Disabled/Gifted Children* (pp.195-206). Baltimore: University Park Press.

Torrance, E. (1966). *Torrance Tests of Creativity*. Princeton, NJ: Personnel Press.

Wechsler, D. (1974). *Manual for the Wechsler Intelligence Scale for Children-Revised*. New York: Psychological Corporation.

Whitmore, J. (1980). *Giftedness Conflict, and Underachievement*. Boston: Allyn and Bacon.

Whitmore, J., & Maker, C. (1985). *Intellectual Giftedness in Disabled Persons*. Rockville, MD: Aspen Systems Corporation.

Wolf, J., & Gygi, J. (1981). Learning disabled and gifted: Success or failure? *Journal for the Education of the Gifted, 4*, 199-206.

Donna P. Suter is a doctoral candidate, Department of Educational Psychology, University of Utah. Joan S. Wolf is Assistant Professor, Department of Special Education, University of Utah, Salt Lake City, Utah.

Reprinted with permission from the Journal for the Education of the Gifted, vol. 10, no. 3, 1987, pp. 227-237. Copyright 1987. The Association for the Gifted, Reston, Virginia 22091.

Learning Disabilities and the Preschool Child

A Position Paper of the National Joint Committee on Learning Disabilities

The passage of Public Law 99-457, which will eventually mandate services for handicapped children birth-to-age-five, is the most significant legislation for the handicapped since the advent of PL 94-142. The fall implications of this legislation for LD children have yet to be determined. However, the DLD executive board has begun discussion and is gathering appropriate information. As an organization, we have already taken a stand on learning disabilities in the preschool years on. (See *DLD Times*, Vol. 3, No. 1.)

As the implementation of PL 99-457 continues, we are certain there will be implications for public schools, headstart programs, university training programs, and others. We will keep you abreast of such developments and DLD's positions as regards these issues. Meanwhile, as each state is establishing its main agencies and making plans for the birth-through-five population, DLD members should get involved. We urge each of you to advocate for the interests of preschool LD children in your various states.

The National Joint Committee on Learning Disabilities (NJCLD) is concerned about the early identification, assessment, planning, and intervention for those preschool children who demonstrate specific developmental delays or deficit patterns that often are early manifestations of learning disabilities.[1] These manifestations include atypical patterns of development in cognition, communication, motor abilities, and/or social and personal behaviors that adversely affect later academic learning. Development in each of these areas is characterized by individual differences as well as variability in rates and patterns of maturation.

It is during the preschool years that developmental disorders of different types and degrees are first suspected or recognized. Because the preschool years represent a critical period during which essential prevention and intervention efforts are most effective, professionals and families must attend to the needs of preschool children whose development is characterized by patterns of specific deficits.

Learning Disabilities in Children During the Preschool Years

Learning disabilities is a term that refers to a heterogeneous group of disorders[2] of presumed neurological origin manifested differently and to varying degrees during the life span of an individual.[3] These disorders are developmental in nature and must be viewed as problems not only of the school years, but also of preschool years and continuing into adult life. During the preschool years, learning disabilities frequently are manifested as specific deficits in language and speech development, reasoning abilities, and other behaviors requisite to early academic achievement. These deficits may occur concomitantly with problems in self-regulation, social interaction, or motor performance. Various manifestations of learning disabilities may be seen in the same child at different ages and as a result of learning demands. This perspective is especially important to maintain when dealing with the preschool child.

Indiscriminate premature labeling of the preschool child as learning disabled is not warranted. Normal development is characterized by broad ranges of individual and group differences, as well as by variability in rates and patterns of maturation. During the preschool years, this variability is marked. For some children marked discrepancies in abilities are temporary and are resolved during the course of development and within the context of experiential interaction. For other children, there is a persistence of marked discrepancies within and among one or more domains of function, necessitating the child's referral for systematic assessment and appropriate intervention.

Issues in Early Identification[4]

The purpose of identification programs is to find children who are suspected of having handicapping conditions. The early identification of learning disabilities in preschool children includes the examination of at-risk indicators,[5] systematic observations of the child, and the use of screening tests and other procedures. All early identification programs should be based on procedures that are reliable and valid. Once children are identified they will require comprehensive assessment and systematic follow-up services.

An effective identification program must take into account the numerous biological and environmental factors that influence the course of a child's development during the preschool years. Procedures used for initial identification or screening are not a substitute for comprehensive assessment. Furthermore, identification programs that are not followed by assessment, intervention, and follow-up services are futile.

At-Risk Indicators

Professionals often use indicators that are acknowledged to be associated with adverse developmental outcomes as a basis for deter mining that a child is at-risk for learning disabilities. The use of at-risk indicators should be only one step in determining the status and needs of the child and serves as an initial basis for referral and continued monitoring of a child's growth and development.

At-risk indicators do not always predict which child is in jeopardy of future developmental deficits or which aspects of development will be delayed or disordered. Caution should be used when informing parents about the presence of these indicators. For example, some children with a history of perinatal complications may develop normally, while other children without such histories may demonstrate specific patterns of deficits that will require careful assessment and intervention. Children whose histories suggest that they are at-risk for learning disabilities should be observed carefully by means of frequent and periodic examinations, in order to ascertain whether growth and development follow expected patterns.

Systematic Observations

Reliance on at-risk indicators is not a substitute for systematic observations of the child's behaviors and abilities. These observations should provide a description of the presenting concerns as well as information regarding the frequency, persistence, and severity of the behaviors causing concern. When a question is raised about the integrity of development, the family should be so advised and the child should be referred to the primary care physician and to other qualified professionals, to a community health facility, or to a preschool assessment team for clarification of these observations. This is an essential activity if effective planning and implementation of appropriate treatment is to occur.

Screening Tests and Other Procedures

A third approach to early identification is the use of screening instruments and procedures, such as testing, teacher rating scales, and locally constructed measures. Careful consideration of reliability, validity, and standardization of the screening instruments and procedures is essential in their selection, use, and interpretation. Although the predictive validity of total scores for certain screening tests has been established, the use of individual items to predict later developmental status or plan remedial programs cannot be justified. Screening tests and other procedures are not to be used for diagnosis, planning, placement, or treatment. All children who have been identified as a result of screening and who are suspected of having a specific learning disability should be referred to appropriately qualified professionals for assessment, evaluation, and follow-up services.

Assessment of Children During the Preschool Years

Referral of the child for assessment of developmental status depends on data and information collected during the screening process. When a specific developmental problem is suspected, the family and the child should be referred to appropriately qualified professionals who will conduct an integrated assessment of cognition, communication, motor abilities, sensory functions, and social-emotional development. Determination of the child's status and needs depends on a comprehensive assessment of the child's functioning in the following domains:

(1) sensory functions, including haptic, auditory, and visual systems;
(2) motor function, including gross and fine motor abilities;
(3) cognition, including perceptual organization, concept formation, and problem solving;
(4) communication, including language comprehension, production, a nd use; and
(5) behavior, including temperament, attention, self-regulation, and social interaction patterns.

An interdisciplinary approach must be used in obtaining and interpreting assessment information that is derived from a wide variety of sources, including direct observations of the child. The specific patterns of abilities and disabilities must be determined.

In some cases, an extended period of assessment and observations will be necessary to determine a child's status and needs. Time limited placement in a diagnostic preschool setting can be a useful means for addressing diagnostic questions, determining the child's developmental age, abilities, and deficits, and evaluating various methods of intervention for the individual child. Responsible professionals should ensure the orderly transfer of the child to the appropriate setting as soon as a decision concerning the child's status and needs has been reached.

The child's developmental age and accomplishments as well as previous opportunities and experiences will determine the extent to which early academic skills are present on entering school. The variability seen in a child's readiness for academic learning and instruction reflects cognitive, communicative, social, and emotional growth as well as physical and neurological maturation. Readiness for academic instruction is more related to differential rates of development than to chronological age. An integrated perspective on the child's functioning in various areas of growth and development is essential. This perspective must be maintained when interpreting assessment results and planning educational placement and instructional approaches that are appropriate to the child's status and needs.

Delivery of Preschool Services

Selection of the appropriate program and specific intervention strategies for the preschool child with specific patterns of deficits is predicated on the clear understanding of how these deficits influence overall learning and development. Program selection and the choice of intervention strategies must be determined following a comprehensive and integrated interdisciplinary assessment.

Decisions pertinent to program selection and placement are influenced by many factors. Among these factors are the following:

■   the types of disabilities and the degree of severity;

■   the philosophy of the service provider or agency;

■   the professional preparation, experience, and attitudes of service personnel;

■   the kinds of intervention strategies and resources available within public or private preschool programs;

■   the ability of the family to facilitate the child's development in the home environment; and

■   geographic constraints.

Various agencies and professionals are responsible for services to the child during the pre school years. Consequently, cooperation among those agencies and professionals who plan and implement preschool education and intervention programs is critical. As the child is moved from one service setting to another, coordination and orderly transfer of information among agencies and professionals are essential to ensure continuity of services.

Preschool programs for the child with specific deficits must provide periodic review of the child's status, including a review of the placement, curriculum, and intervention approaches. Only careful monitoring of the child's progress can lead to a determination of the effectiveness of the child's program.

No single approach to intervention can be expected to serve as a panacea for the different needs presented by preschool children with specific deficits. Alternative and modified methods of intervention must be available. Appropriate consultative and direct services by professionals from different disciplines should be used as necessary.

The primary focus of intervention should be on activities appropriate for the child's developmental age and directly related to the enhancement of functioning in the area(s) of the child's disability. Traditional readiness activities in preschool programs often are not sufficient to ensure later school success. Early intervention programs should focus on ameliorating the deficits that affect the current functioning of the child as well as facilitate the development of abilities, skills, and knowledge considered to be requisites for later academic, linguistic, and social functioning.

A continuum of program and service options must be available if preschool children with specific developmental deficits are to be served appropriately. Programs should be mandated through appropriate federal and state legislation. State agencies need to enforce a continuum of service options, provide appropriate funding, and promote interagency cooperation between the public and private sectors.

The Family

In some cases, parents are the first to suspect that their child may have a problem and should address their concerns by consulting with a physician or other qualified professional. In other cases, some families initially may deny the existence of a problem because they are fearful of or threatened by its possibilities and consequences. Because family acceptance and cooperation are both critical to effective intervention, differences in family responses must be recognized and appropriate support services provided.

The family serves as an important source of information about the child's status and needs. Similarly, it is essential that the family under stand and help to implement the programmatic goals established for their child. Family members should have access to a range of support services, including the following:

- assistance in recognizing, understanding, and accepting the child's problems;

- assistance in developing effective ways to manage and facilitate the child's development in the home environment;

- assistance in program selection; and

- assistance in locating parent support networks and programs.

Direct family involvement in the preschool program is a major factor in effectiveness. The family has responsibility for the application and generalization of learned skills and adaptive behaviors into the home environment and will consequently require open communication with professionals who provide services to the child. They also need to be included in the development of program policy and advocacy efforts.

Issues in Personnel Preparation

Qualified personnel are necessary to meet the needs of preschool children, especially those with suspected learning disabilities. Competency standards for personnel providing these preschool services are required. Professional education programs must provide an under standing of the principles of normal child development and disorders in the domains of cognition, communication, motor development, sensory function, social-emotional adjustment, and academic development.[6,7]

Physicians, nurse practitioners, allied health professionals, and other related service providers should receive systematic preparation in the identification and referral of preschool children with suspected deficits. These individuals should be knowledgeable about the range of programs and services available to the child and family. Similarly, education personnel and day-care providers should receive systematic instruction about normal development, indicators of learning disabilities and other developmental disorders, methods of screening, and procedures for referral. In this way, assessment and appropriate intervention can be initiated as early as possible. Similarly, all individuals concerned with services for the preschool child must develop appropriate strategies to achieve effective interaction with the child's family.

Needs and Recommendations

Based on the foregoing discussion, the NJCLD recommends the following:

(1) *Systematic identification programs for all preschool children should be instituted.*

    a. Individuals who work directly with preschool children must learn to identify those children with suspected deficits and must know how, as well as to whom, these children should be referred for assessment.

    b. Procedures for developmental review and early identification of disabilities must be validated, developed, and implemented on a cost-effective basis.

    c. Technically adequate instruments for screening of preschool children must be developed.

(2) *Assessment procedures should be based on an interdisciplinary approach that explores all possible sources of the child's present problems and provides an integrative statement of the child's status and needs.*

This requires that:

    a.   professional preparation programs provide multiple theoretical bases for understanding the contributions of various factors to children's development as well as to their problems; and that

    b.   professionals from various disciplines work in collaboration to ensure that comprehensive evaluations are provided as necessary.

(3) *Early intervention programs should be available to all preschool children with identified developmental deficits.*

    a.   Federal and state agencies must mandate, fund, and monitor the development and implementation of preschool diagnostic and intervention programs for children with patterns of specific deficits for the ages 0-6 years.

    b.   There must be validation of public and private sector delivery models in urban, suburban, or rural areas that are appropriate to the needs of children with various developmental deficit.

(4) *Qualified personnel are necessary to meet the needs of preschool children who demonstrate patterns of specific deficits.*

    a.   Professional preparation programs for personnel who will work with preschool children with developmental deficits should include instruction in normal child development as well as its disorders.

    b.   Preschool teachers, early childhood specialists, and daycare providers must be knowledgeable about identification and appropriate referral of preschool children suspected of developmental delays or deficits.

    c.   Preschool and daycare programs must be staffed by qualified personnel who have learned to use a variety of intervention strategies appropriate to the needs of the children enrolled within these settings.

(5) *Families should be assisted in participating fully in all phases of identification and treatment of a preschool child with specific patterns of deficits.* In order to accomplish this, certain needs must be met.

    a.   Parental participation must be encouraged and welcomed.

    b.   Parents must be provided with support services that will enable their full and active participation.

c. Efforts must be made to develop parent education materials and programs that explain the child's needs and detail the intervention strategies to be implemented by the family.

(6) *Professionals should provide information to the public concerning issues about child development and its disorders.*

a. Guidelines should be developed that will provide the public with information about the roles and responsibilities of various professionals in the identification, assessment, and treatment of children with developmental disorders.

b. Professionals should develop and use networks that will facilitate referrals of children and their families to appropriate service providers and agencies.

(7) *All professionals and agencies responsible for the identification, assessment, and treatment of children with developmental disorders must recognize and respond to the unique requirements necessary to meet the needs of the non-English or limited-English speaking population.*

a. Individuals involved in the identification, assessment, and treatment of non-English or limited-English speaking preschool children must ensure that neither language barriers nor cultural differences will influence findings and recommendations.

b. Programs that provide services to non-English or limited-English speaking preschool children with developmental disorders must have available qualified personnel who can provide appropriate services to these children.

c. Assessment instruments and instructional materials should be developed to ensure adequate assessment and treatment of non-English speaking or limited English speaking children with developmental disorders.

d. Information about child development and its disorders must be developed for use with non-English speaking or limited English speaking families to enhance their understanding of their children and their special needs when present.

(8) *Systematic research must continue to address issues related to identification and provision services for preschool children with suspected learning disabilities.*

a. What refinements are necessary in the use of at-risk indicators in order to maximize their prognostic value?

b. What indices of early behavior best predict or correlate with later personal and social adjustment?

c. What indices of early behavior predict or correlate with later academic learning?

d. What factors contribute to the success of various intervention programs and strategies?

[1] As used in this paper, the word preschool includes the period from birth through kindergarten age.

[2] Learning disabilities: Issues on definition (1981, January 30). A position paper of the National Joint Committee on Learning Disabilities, The Orton Dyslexia Society, Baltimore, MD.

[3] Adults with learning disabilities: A call for action: (1985, February 8). A position paper of the National Joint Committee on Learning Disabilities, The Orton Dyslexia Society, Baltimore, MD.

[4] As used in this paper identification refers to any and all initial steps taken to select children who are suspected of having handicapping conditions.

[5] As used in this paper, at-risk indicators refers to biological, genetic, and perinatal events as well as adventitious diseases or trauma that are known to be associated with adverse developmental outcomes.

[6] Learning disabilities: Issues in the preparation of professional personnel (1983. September 16). A position paper of the National Joint Committee on Learning Disabilities, The Orton Dyslexia Society, Baltimore, MD.

[7] Inservice programs in learning disabilities. (1981, September 27) A position paper of the National Joint Committee on Learning Disabilities. The Orton Dyslexia Society, Baltimore, MD.

The National Joint Committee on Learning Disabilities. Learning Disabilities and the Preschool Child. A position paper of the National Joint Committee on Learning Disabilities, February 10, 1985. The Orton Dyslexia Society Baltimore, MD. Reprinted with permission from the Orton Dyslexia Society.

HOW DOES YOUR SCREENER
STACK UP?

The following is an excerpt from a position statement prepared in March 1989 by the Illinois Association for Supervision and Curriculum Development (IASCD). We thank the Association for permission to reprint.

With the passage of P.L. 99-457 in 1986, P.L. 94-142 was amended to (a) provide mandatory early childhood special education services to 3-5 year olds throughout the country, and (b) allow states to develop comprehensive service delivery systems for the birth to 2-year-old population of children with special needs. Identification has become an even greater priority.

Simultaneously, however, identification has increased in complexity as states struggle with the issues of developing varied approaches and measures which can serve a screening function across the wide range of ages, ethnic diversity, and needs included in the population to be served. As the population to be screened becomes younger, emphasis moves away from identifying existing academic or preacademic problems, disabilities, or delays to identifying potential problems. For young infants with a limited repertoire of behaviors, screening information must come from an even more specific, qualitative assessment of the behavior. Methods and instruments available within any state or community must cover this wide range of children and needs. In addition, these efforts must be coordinated across multiple agencies, particularly at the birth to 2-year level. In all instances, it is critical that screening: (a) be seen as a first step in the assessment process; (b) be seen as yielding information that must be further substantiated; and (c) not be seen as a diagnosis of delay, handicap, or justification for exclusion or retention from chronological age appropriate programs.

Definitions of the Assessment Process

The assessment process is a series of sifting activities with children. The first step is a large mesh screen through which most children will pass. For those children who are caught by the screen; that is, those who do not pass, a fines meshed screen is in order. This finer screen is a comprehensive diagnostic assessment. For some children, such a procedure will establish eligibility for special programs. It may also help to identify individual strengths and weaknesses as a basis for planning broad intervention programs and strategies. For many children, a third step in the assessment process will be necessary to determine more specific strengths and needs.

As the first step in an assessment program, screening is the step that should be available to all children. Screening provides an opportunity to look at the developmental skills of a large number of children in a limited amount of time. Most children will be able to demonstrate skills at an average developmental level as defined by the screening instrument. If the results of the screening indicate that a child has not passed or performed within an average developmental range, then that child should be seen individually by an experienced diagnostician. It is through this process that children in need of services are identified.

Selection of Screening Procedures

As screening activities become standard practice for young children, the selection of the most effective instrument is a major responsibility demanding great care. Screening can provide many benefits and there is significant research to support the establishment of criteria by which this selection is made.

Some questions to consider in setting criteria include the following:

1. Do manuals report validity and reliability measures for the test?

2. Will all aspects of development and multiple problems be considered in the plan for screening?

3. Do the test procedures reflect the needs of the age levels and do the components appeal to young children?

4. Can the procedures be conducted in a limited amount of time?

5. Will the test results be easily used by teachers, nurses, home visitors, and public health workers?

6. Will the measures used support correct decisions or will they over-identify or under-identify the population needing assistance?

7. Are referral and programmatic services available and accessible for infants/young children who fail the screening?

8. Young children change rapidly; therefore, will the screening results be treated as tentative information subject to periodic follow-up?

9. How will parents be included in the screening procedures? Are the results shared with parents in a personal, confidential manner?

10. Does the screening procedure take cultural diversity into account? What plans have been made to screen children with primary languages other than English?

11. Will those who administer the test be properly trained, sensitive to socio-cultural factors and able to document appropriate experiences with young children? Are there appropriate staff for limited English proficient children and their families?

Guidelines for Appropriate Screening Procedures

1. Screening activities should be perceived as play by the child.

2. Allowances should be made for the parent to remain with the child during screening, if necessary. Parents should be given a written explanation of the purpose and limits of the screening.

3. The screener needs to approach all child interactions in a positive manner.

4. The younger the child, the more critical it is that the activities involve the manipulation of concrete toys and materials rather than pictures and paper/pencil tasks.

5. Components of the screening process need to include a range of activities which allow the screener to observe and record:

    Child: Physical health
             Fine/gross motor skills
             · Social interactions
             Emotional expressions
             Vocabulary and communication competence
             Levels of concept development
             Adaptive skills

    A parent interview should, at minimum, obtain the following information:

             Medical history
             General health
             Family health concerns
             Serious or chronic illness
             Family composition
             Parent perception of child's social/emotional and cognitive development

6. The screener must have prior experience with infants/young children in order to score the measure accurately and support the validity of the results.

If possible, feedback to parents is best immediately following the screening event. Parents should be an integral part of the process and fully informed of their rights. It is not appropriate for parents to wait long periods of time for the results of screening. Therefore, the screening team should analyze the data promptly and communicate the final results to parents.

SPECIFIC READING DISABILITY
IN FOUR HISTORICAL MEN

P.G. Aaron
Scott Phillips
Steen Larsen

THOMAS ALVA EDISON

Thomas Alva Edison was born on February 11, 1847. A few years earlier, his parents had migrated from Canada and his father, Samuel Edison, operated a lumber mill on the banks of a canal in Milan, Ohio. Edison's mother, Nancy, was the daughter of the Reverend John Elliott, and according to Josephson (1959) she had taught in a two-room school in Vienna, Ontario. With the coming of railroads, Milan lost much of its canal business and the Edison family was obliged to move again. According to Josephson, they moved during the spring of 1854, when Edison was 7 years old, and settled in Port Huron, Michigan. It is not known whether the Edisons owned or rented their house in Port Huron, but it was a substantial two-story, six-bedroom house (Conot,1979) with columned balconies and four fireplaces, set amidst a grove of pine trees in a 10-acre tract. This information is significant because in the present context, it is important to know whether the limited schooling Edison received was because of financial difficulties or some other reason.

In the fall of 1855, when he was 8 years old, Thomas Edison was enrolled in the one-room school of Reverend Engle (Josephson, 1959). If this date is accurate, there was a 1-year gap between the family's move to Port Huron and Edison's entering school. Since biographers have attached little importance to this unaccounted year, it is difficult to ascertain the reason for Edison's late entry into school. According to Wachhorst (1981), nearly 5% of the nearly 2,100 anecdotes about Edison's boyhood refer to the story that his teacher called him "addled." Although it is unlikely that this single episode was responsible for the termination of young Edison's education, it appears certain that Edison's first encounter with school was neither pleasant nor long-lasting.

After Edison left school, his mother apparently took up the responsibility of tutoring him (Josephson, 1959). Even though most biographers have reported that Edison had no more than 3 months of formal education, according to Conot (1979), he not only went to three schools at Fort Gratiot and Port Huron but also attended classes at Cooper Union. By the time he was 9 years old, Edison must have been exposed to sufficient reading instruction because he inscribed on the cover page of Parker's *Natural and Experimental Philosophy*, which he later donated to the Ford Museum in Greenfield Village, "Parkers [sic] Philosophy was the first book in science that I had when [sic] a boy 9 year's old I picked out [sic] as it was the first one I could understand" (see Figure 1). Parker's book has 470 pages in fine print and has chapters on such topics as mechanics, hydraulics, acoustics, optics, astronomy, electricity, and magnetism. In addition, it has a chapter on electromagnetic telegraphy. One can raise the question, "How can a 9-year-old boy read such a big book, let alone a reading disabled boy?"

There are two possible answers to this question. One is that Edison exaggerated his accomplishment; the inelegant autographic inscription he wrote on the book he presented to Ford indicates such a possibility. The second possible answer is that Parker's book is profusely illustrated, and thus the reader does not have to depend much on reading to understand the book. Being "visually talented," Edison might have relied more on diagrams and illustrations than on written language to figure out the information in the book.

Between the ages of 12 and 15, when Edison was a vendor on the railroad, he had a layover of about 4 hours in Detroit, which he spent in the Detroit Public Library. Later on he stated: "I started with the first book on the bottom shelf and went through the lot, one by one. I didn't read a few books. I read the library" (Runes, 1948, p. 48). Edison probably meant the Young Men's Society, whose library was later organized into the Detroit Free Library. There is evidence that Edison obtained membership in this library by paying a fee of $2. In his introduction to the collected works of Thomas Paine, Edison wrote:

My father had a set of Tom Paine's books on the shelf at home. I must have opened the covers about the time I was 13. And I can still remember the flash of enlightenment which shone from his pages. It was a revelation, indeed to encounter his views on political and religious matters. (Runes, 1948, p. 154)

Given these observations, Edison's early life can be summarized by stating that even though he had only a limited amount of formal education, he was exposed to reading more than an ordinary child of his age would have been.

Biographical Information

1. Descriptive accounts by biographers: Edison's biographers have used phrases such as "wayward" and "different from other boys" (Josephson, 1959, p. 25) to describe him as a boy. The most frequently used epithet is "addled," allegedly used by his first teacher.

2. School records: School records from which the nature of Edison's academic performance could be surmised are nonexistent.

3. Self-reports: Edison's descriptions of his own performance at school come from the biographical notes he dictated to Meadowcroft (Dyer, Martin, & Meadowcroft, 1929) and from newspaper articles written by reporters who had interviewed Edison. According to Josephson (1959), Edison said, "I remember I used never to be able to get along at school. I was always at the foot of the class. I used to feel that the teachers did not sympathize with me and that my father thought I was stupid" (p. 20).

Cognitive Characteristics

1. Written spelling errors: In July 1885, Edison spent about a week in the beachside house of his friend and associate Ezra Gilliland, located in Woodside, Massachusetts. Being on vacation and having plenty of time on hand, he decided to put his thoughts down in a diary. By this time, Edison was 38 years old and had become well known for his improvement of the telephone and the establishment of the Pearl Street electricity station. By the time he wrote the diary, he had read numerous articles and books on applied science. For these reasons, the diary, although short, is of great value for studying Edison's language. Rune published a version of the diary, with the errors removed, in 1948. The spelling and syntax errors described in the following section are from Edison's original diary, which is preserved in the Edison National Historic site, West Orange, New Jersey. The correct spelling and the date of the diary entry are shown in parentheses: tartr (tartar), Macauley (MaCaulay, July 12), inexhaustable (inexhaustible), receeding (receding), dasies (daisies), Daisie's (Daisy's), anaethized (anaesthetized, July 14), articutating (articulating), receeding (receding), progedy (prodigy), beleivear (believer), marvellous (marvelous, July 18), shreik (shriek, July 21), insectiverous (insectivorous), disect (dissect), innoculated (inoculated), tenticles (tentacles, July 22).

The following spelling errors were found after a random search of a few letters deposited in the Edison Institute, Greenfield Village, Dearborn, Michigan: peice (piece, Oct. 30, 1970), beleiver (believer, April 7, 1871), reccommendation (recommendation, February 23, 1878), adjument (adjustment), mouthpeice (mouthpiece, March 1878), interferance (interference, October 13, 1917). In view of the fact that Edison had read Parker's 470-page book at the age of 9, and an entire library soon thereafter, one cannot argue that these errors were due to limited reading experience.

Numerous spelling errors can be seen in the *Weekly Herald*, the newspaper Edison published on board a train when he was 15 years old. According to Professor Reese Jenkins (personal communication, 1984), director of the Edison Papers Project, Rutgers University, the evidence of the *Weekly Herald* is fraught with problems. Nevertheless, Edison, at the age of 15 when he published the two-page news bulletin, had been exposed to books such as the ones by Parker and Paine and also had been visiting at least one library. Furthermore, the spelling errors found in the *Weekly Herald* are "phonetic" and are similar to the ones found in his diary written almost two decades later, which suggests that the spelling errors persisted over the years in spite of additional reading experience. The misspelled words also indicate that his vocabulary was larger than that of an average 15-year-old boy. Thus, there is a marked discrepancy between the range of his vocabulary and his spelling skill. The errors seen in one page of the news bulletin are as follows: intellengence (intelligence), obligeing (obliging), profiesser (professor), seams (seems), leaveing (leaving), supprise (surprise), stateing (stating), villians (villains), posession (possession), quantitys (quantities), delayid (delayed), oppisition (opposition), propietor (proprietor), accommadation (accommodation).

2. Errors of syntax in the written language: Josephson (1959, p. 22), in support of his statement that Edison never learned how to spell and that up to the time of his adulthood his grammar and syntax were appalling, quotes, without mentioning the source, the following letter written by Edison to his mother when he was about 19 years old:

DEAR MOTHER—

Started the Store several weeks I have growed considerably I dont look much like a Boy now—Hows all the folks did you receive a Box of Books from Memphis that he promised to send them—languages.

Your son AL

Edison's diary, which he wrote when he was 38 years old, also contains errors of syntax. In the following examples, dates and words that he omitted are enclosed in parentheses; words that are incorrect are italicized: I didn't hear (a) word he said (July 14, 1885), Put my spongy mind at work on life (of) Goethe (July 14), Boston ought to be buoyed and charts furnished (for) strangers (July 15), This removed the articulat*ing* upholstery (July 15), Hell will get *up* a reputation as a summer resort (July 16), It would stagger the mind of Raphael *in a dream* to imagine a being comparable to the Maid of Chautaqua (July 17), Last night room was *very* close(d) (July 18), Bug proof windows seem*s* to repel obtrusiveness (July 18), Mrs. Roberts caught cold in her arm [and] *its* cough is better (July 18), I would strike*n* them (July 19), I am getting caloric*ly* stupid (July 20).

3. Deficits in processing sequential information: One diary entry, dated July 18, 1885, implies that Edison was not skilled in recalling information in the order in which it was presented. He wrote:

Went out yachting, all the ladies in attendance...Ladies played game called memory-scheme. No. 1 calls out name of prominent author, No. 2 repeats this name and adds another and so on. Soon one has to remember a dozen names, all of which must be repeated in the order given. Miss Daisy had the best and I the poorest memory.

If mathematics could be viewed as a form of analytical language, Edison could not be considered as being particularly strong in it. Arithmetic errors could be seen in Edison's laboratory worksheets (Conot, 1979, p. 73). Even when the need was great, Edison worked around the use of mathematics by adopting the trial-and-error method. He reportedly said, "I do not depend on figures at all, I try an experiment and reason out the result, somehow by methods which I could not explain" (Conot, 1979, p. 32). He also wrote that he tried to read Newton's *Principia Mathematica* and "came to the conclusion that Newton could have dispensed his knowledge in a much wider field had he known less about figures. It gave me a distaste for mathematics from which I never recovered" (Runes, 1948, p. 45). Later on, however, while working on the electricity distribution system, he was obliged to hire Francis Upton, a mathematical physicist from Princeton, because "it is just as well to have one mathematical fellow around, in case we have to calculate something out" (Josephson, 1959, p. 136).

4. Superior ability in simultaneous processing of information: According to Jenkins (Byrnes, 1978), Edison was basically nonmathematical; he thought in a visual and tactile way with the aid of little drawings, sketches, and models. In fact, Edison's sketches have a striking resemblance to those of Leonardo da Vinci. Josephson quotes one of Edison's sons as saying, "He [Edison] had really very little power of abstraction and had to be able, above all, to visualize things" (1959, p. 123). Thus, there is consensus among these writers that Edison's cognitive style was visuospatial and gestalt rather than analytic and linear.

Edison's simultaneous-gestalt style of solving problems is evident nowhere more than in his development of the incandescent light bulb into a commercially lucrative enterprise. Edison did not invent the light bulb; Joseph Swan of England had an incandescent lamp in operation when Edison began to tackle the problem; Sigfried Marcus of Vienna had already filed a patent for an incandescent lamp. These prototype incandescent lamps, however, required thick carbon rods in order to withstand intense heat; to light up a block, this system would have needed copper cables of gigantic proportions. Edison was creative in solving several problems all at once, thus making the incandescent lamp a commercial success. He saw that because voltage, resistance, and amperage (current) were inversely related, he could reduce the amount of current required by increasing the resistance of the filament in the bulb with the use of thin carbon filament. Edison also simultaneously adopted the parallel circuit instead of the serial circuit. In fact, he had a seven-point plan that included the high resistance filament, parallel distribution, the constant output dynamo, underground conduction network, insulation, and lighting fixtures with switches. Edison could see the forest whereas his competitors were lost in the woods because they could see only the trees.

Neuropsychological
Characteristics

Other than the fact that Edison was right handed we have very little information in this regard.

Biological Characteristics

1. Genetic predisposition in the family: The information available that would allow any meaningful pedigree analysis is meager. According to Edison's biographers, his father, Sam Edison, was a political radical who supported a movement for representative government for Canada. This is in accord with Edison's statement that his father possessed books such as the one by Thomas Paine. In light of this, the following brief message written by Sam Edison to his son Alva is significant: "This Packedg contains all mast entr Discription of Dockaments know to the civilised world" (Conot, 1979, p. 79). Edison had four sons and two daughters. It is difficult to determine whether the poor academic performance of three of Edison's four sons was the result of any form of learning disability or could simply be attributed to other factors.

    Edison's poor hearing is given as a possible reason by Adelman and Adelman (1987) for his learning disability. It is known that Edison could receive telegraphic messages even under the noisiest conditions. There is no evidence that he was even partially deaf. Edison himself wrote, "The things that I have needed to hear I have heard" (Runes, 1948, p. 48).

2. Immune system disorders: Several biographers note that there was a family history of bronchial problems. It is not certain, however, if such health condition was immunological in nature.

In summary, Edison's biographers appear to be unanimous in recognizing his superior visuo-spatial mode of imagination. The meager evidence available from his boyhood days shows that Edison experienced problems with spelling and syntax. These errors of spelling and syntax, however, persisted well into his late thirties in spite of his extensive reading of scientific journals. This suggests that these errors could be remnants of a basic reading disability.

WOODROW WILSON

Thomas Woodrow Wilson, the 28th President of the United States of America, was born on December 28, 1856, in Staunton, Virginia. His father, Dr. Ruggles Wilson, started his career as a pastor of a small church in Pennsylvania but moved to Jefferson College to become *professor extraordinary* of rhetoric. Janet Woodrow, Wilson's mother, attended the female seminary in Chillicothe, Ohio, where her father, the Reverend Thomas Woodrow, was pastoring a Presbyterian church. According to Baker (1927), the official biographer of Wilson, Janet Woodrow "had received a better formal education than most of the women of her day" (p. 32).

There is no evidence that Woodrow Wilson had formal schooling until he was 8 years old. Wilson's father, however, read aloud passages from literature to the family, and then "he and Tommy (Woodrow Wilson) would set to work to pick it apart" (Baker, 1927, p. 38).

Biographical Information

1. Descriptive accounts by biographers: According to Baker (1927), Wilson did not have systematic early education and his parents seemed to be in no hurry to send him to school, even though he was more than 8 years old. Baker goes on to say that "he was somewhat slow of development" (p. 37). Wilson himself, at one time, commented on his slow maturation. When he was 33 years old, he wrote to his wife, "It may be all imagination...but...Woodrow Wilson...always a slow fellow in mental development...long a child, longer a diffident youth, now at last, perhaps, becoming a self-confident man..." (Weinstein, 1981, p. 101). Additional evidence as to Wilson's delay in the acquisition of reading skill comes from Eleanor, one of his daughters, who attributes the delay to a cause other than reading disability. According to her, "father loved to hear grandfather read and sat by the hour listening to him. As a result, he did not learn to read easily himself until he was 12" (McAdoo, 1937, p. 40). And again, according to Baker (1927), in Sunday school Wilson had to learn the shorter form of catechism because "he committed to memory with difficulty" (p. 48).

   These instances of Wilson's slow maturation, and the fact that many preschool children from homes that value reading (as was Wilson's home) learn how to read without formal instruction (Soderberg, 1977), render environmental explanations of Wilson's slow acquisition of reading skill unlikely.

2. School records: Information regarding Wilson's academic achievement at school is meager. We have, however, reasonably well-preserved records of his performance in college. In the fall of 1873, Wilson entered Davidson College, near Charlotte, North Carolina. The records show that during both semesters he was there, Wilson experienced difficulty with Greek. According to Baker, Wilson entered his mathematics and Greek classes on probation and at the end of the year he was near physical breakdown. After a year at Davidson, Wilson

returned home and stayed with his parents for the next 15 months, and then entered Princeton University as a freshman. Thus, he was obliged to repeat his freshman year. Wilson was 18 years and 9 months when he entered Princeton and the then-president of the University, Dr. McCosh, was a friend of Wilson's father. The acquaintance probably went back to the days when Wilson's father attended Princeton Theological Seminary and President McCosh used to stop to see Dr. Wilson whenever he made trips to the South (Baker, 1927). Thus, Wilson being able to get into Princeton need not be considered as out of the ordinary.

Wilson's first year in Princeton was difficult. His correspondence with his friends and parents reveals several problems. In one of his letters to Robert Bridges he wrote: "My report was eminently unsatisfactory, bringing me down to 37th in consequence of my nonattention to Physics and the injustice of old Guyot, Pscych [sic]" (Link, 1966, p. 385). In October 1879, after graduating from Princeton, Wilson entered law school at the University of Virginia where he also encountered academic difficulties. His father wrote, "the law is, I see, trying your mettle, and alas! occassionally you have been tempted to cry out, you are too hard for me, away with your iron limbs" (Link, 1966, p. 597). There is no apparent reason why Wilson left the University without obtaining a law degree. The vast amount of material to be read at the law school might have had an adverse effect on him. Whatever it was, Wilson's letters to his parents indicate that his leaving was not due to lack of interest or dedication.

3. Self-reports: While at Princeton, Wilson maintained a diary, written intermittently and mostly in shorthand. Some of these entries contain more or less precise information about his reading accomplishments. For instance, one of the entries reads: "Read Macaulay all the evening, finishing the 12th chapter of history" (Link, 1966, p. 135). The previous entry shows that Wilson had already read the 11th chapter. Again he noted, "Spent most of the rest of the day from 12 to 5 in reading Macaulay's History of England" (Link, 1966, p. 138). The particular volume of MaCaulay's *History of England* that Wilson read has about 13 words per line and 55 lines per page. Since normal reading speed is about 300 words per minute (Carver, 1982), simple computation shows that the average reader can cover a typical chapter from MaCaulay's book in about 2½ hours. Wilson's diary entries show that he took about twice this amount of time.

Wilson's remarks about his own reading behavior are also revealing. He wrote in his diary: "I read very slowly and enjoy immensely as I go along. I sometimes wish that I could read a little faster" (Link, 1966, p. 137). Several years later he wrote to his fiancee: "Steady reading always demands of me more expenditure of resolution and dogged energy than any other sort of work; and it, consequently, tells upon me sooner" (Link, 1967, p. 496).

Cognitive Characteristics

1. Written spelling errors: Considering the prolific amount of written material
    Wilson has left behind, the number of spelling errors he committed is rather
    small. His writings during his early college career, however, contain many
    spelling errors. Some examples of spelling errors are: Tursday (Thursday),
    origonal (original), ocasional (occasional), correspondants (correspondents).
    Spelling errors found in Wilson's later writings are: Shakspere (Shakespeare),
    appeals (appalls), dos n't (doesn't), dicease (disease), disapline (discipline),
    discource (discourse), develope (develop), embrionic (embryonic).

    A curious fact about Wilson's writing is that he often relied on shorthand
    notation. Wilson learned shorthand, apparently on his own, and continued the
    use of it all his life. Why Wilson undertook the tedious task of mastering the
    shorthand system is intriguing. Perhaps there is some reason for Wilson's
    preference for shorthand of which he himself was not aware. By transforming
    the alphabetic notation into an ideographic form such as the shorthand
    notation, he was able to avoid the phonemic analysis of the written word;
    many potential spelling errors could also be avoided. Rozin, Poritsky, and
    Sotsky (1971) found that English-speaking dyslexic children learned to read
    better when taught to read in Chinese ideographic scripts. Gloning, Gloning,
    and Tschabitscher (cited in Regard, Landis, & Graves, 1985) report that the
    ability to read shorthand script could be lost through stroke while the ability to
    read longhand is preserved. This shows that reading of shorthand and
    longhand scripts is mediated by two different neurological systems and that
    reading shorthand probably involves the simultaneous processing strategy.

2. Errors of syntax in written language: Wilson's writings reveal a few errors of
    syntax; he also had a tendency to omit or substitute articles.

3. Deficits in processing sequential information Wilson was not particularly strong
    in arithmetic, which involves sequential processing. As a student in Princeton,
    he complained about Wednesdays because they were math days. In later years,
    he joked about this weakness as "an infirmity" (Weinstein, 1981, p. 18). His
    daughter Eleanor described how he frowned at the prospect of adding even a
    short column of figures and sometimes called to the children from the next
    room, "Children, what is seven times eight?" (McAdoo, 1937, p. 12). It should
    be noted that even though many dyslexic children are poor in carrying out a
    sequence of arithmetic operations, they may have adequate or even superior
    mathematical logic (Steeves, 1983).

4. Superior ability in simultaneous processing of information: Wilson's primary
    interest was writing and speech making, and he did not show any special
    interest in drawing or painting. The few casually drawn sketches that are found
    in his notebook, however, reveal a good deal of sophistication and talent.
    These drawings show that Wilson, indeed, did possess a superior ability to
    visualize and represent three-dimensional objects accurately on paper. His first
    book, *Congressional Government*, published in 1885, contains passages that

can evoke in the reader's mind vivid pictures of scenes of the Capitol. Wilson wrote this book without having made a single trip to see Congress in action.

Wilson was good at expressing himself in metaphoric language. For example, when he heard that Senator Carter Glass was made an important figure in the Methodist Church, Wilson expressed surprise that "the Methodists would raise a glass so high" (Weinstein, 1981, p. 137). On hearing that two men who happened to live in Morvan, the estate of Richard Stockton, one of the signers of the Declaration of Independence, had applied for a liquor license on behalf of Princeton, Wilson is reported to have said, "Morvan has produced three signers, one for liberty and two for license" (Weinstein, 1981, p. 137).

Neuropsychological Characteristics

1. Evidence of incomplete cerebral lateralization: Wilson suffered his first stroke on May 27, 1896, which resulted in weakness of his right hand and numbness of the fingers. In right-handed individuals, such a cerebral insult invariably produces aphasic symptoms. Other than the weakness and numbness of his right hand, Wilson apparently suffered few ill effects from the stroke—3 days later he sailed to Glasgow, and the many letters he wrote to his wife during his trip abroad contain no evidence of any language disturbance. Obviously, language functions were represented atypically in Wilson's brain. Wilson suffered a second stroke in 1904 that caused weakness of the right upper extremity, and again, it had little effect on his speech. According to Weinstein, during the course of Wilson's life, he might have suffered as many as nine strokes in the left hemisphere, and none of them impaired his language ability. A right hemisphere stroke, sustained during his trip west after his return from the Peace Conference, however, had a devastating effect on him, including his language. These clinical observations suggest a diffuse cerebral organization.

2. Handedness: For all practical purposes, Wilson used his right hand, even though it is quite likely that he was not strongly right handed. Three days after his first stroke in 1896, which left his right hand weak and numb, he set sail for Glasgow. While on ship, he wrote letters to his wife with his left hand. He appeared to have made the switch without much effort, for his letters reveal that the quality of his handwriting was good. In individuals with a normal pattern of cerebral lateralization, such a switching of hands for writing is not typically accomplished with such ease (Levine & Sweet, 1983).

Biological Characteristics

1. Genetic predisposition in the family: There is no evidence that Wilson's parents had reading disabilities. However, a letter written to Wilson by his younger brother Josie, when the latter was about 11 years old, contains spelling and syntactical errors that are suggestive of developmental dyslexia. The strongest evidence of dyslexia in Wilson's family comes from a book written by Fleming (1984), Wilson's uncle's great-granddaughter. Fleming

writes that one of Wilson's grandsons, as well as she and her five children, is dyslexic.

2. Immune system disorders: According to Weinstein's (1981) medical biography of Wilson, contrary to what many of his biographers have said, Wilson must have had an exceptionally strong constitution to withstand the ravages of cerebral vascular disease for as long as he did. Nevertheless, the letters written by his mother to Wilson reveal her perennial concern about his health. The periodicity of his recurring illness (usually occurring during the spring season), the nature of his illness (undefined gastrointestinal disorder), and the conditions under which he became ill (usually when under stress), all suggest the possibility of immunological disorder.

In summary, the nature of the errors of Wilson's written language, his own revelations of his slowness in reading, his preference for shorthand for writing, and the biographical accounts of his slow start, all can be parsimoniously explained by a weakness in the use of phonological-sequential processes for reading.

HANS CHRISTIAN ANDERSEN

Even though in English-speaking countries Andersen is associated with fairy tales and children's stories, he published five major novels. According to Bredsdorff (1975), his most authoritative biographer, Andersen was accepted in the past as a writer of great literary distinction both in Britain and in America, and his first biography was written not by a Danish writer but by Nisbet Bain, an Englishman. To quote Bredsdorff, "Andersen is considered a very great writer whose appeal is as great to adults as it is to children, in some cases even more so, and...he is not only a great master of style but also a great humorist" (1975, p. 9).

Hans Christian Andersen was born in Odense, Denmark, on April 2, 1805. His father was a cobbler with very little education, although Andersen writes that he could read. Andersen's mother was an illiterate washerwoman. Even as a very young boy, Andersen was possessed with a vision of one day becoming a "digter" (i.e., an actor-writer-poet). Because Odense was a small, provincial town, it became necessary for him to seek his fortunes as a playwright elsewhere, and he left for Copenhagen at the age of 14. While in Copenhagen, he could get only minor roles in the theater and, at the end of the third year, even this became impossible because he was dismissed from the theater. A play he submitted to the Royal Theater was also rejected. The members of the board of directors, however, were sympathetic to Andersen. Impressed by his youthful ambitions but dismayed by the number of mistakes in spelling and grammar found in his manuscript, they recommended that he attend grammar school and acquire the elements of education. They asked Jonas Collin, one of the members, to make the necessary financial arrangements, and Collin eventually became Andersen's chief benefactor and mentor.

At the age of 17, Andersen joined the grammar school at Slagelse, a small town near Copenhagen, and was admitted into the second form (seventh grade). According to Bredsdorff (1975), all other boys in his class looked at him with astonishment because they were only 11 years old and Andersen towered above them. The headmaster of the school was Dr. Simon Meisling, a name that haunted Andersen all his life. Even though at the end of the first year he managed to pass from second to third form, he was detained during the subsequent year. As his letters to Jonas Collin and his diary entries show, this was not for want of effort on his part—he still nourished the dream of becoming a playwright and strove toward attaining that goal. After 5 years of struggle, Andersen left the grammar school without a diploma, partly because of his difficulties in learning Latin and Greek and partly as a result of interpersonal difficulties with the headmaster, Dr. Meisling. He returned to Copenhagen and with the help of private tutors finally passed the "Examen Artium," which qualified him to enter the university (even though he never did).

Biographical Information

1. Descriptive accounts by biographers: According to Keigwin (1976), Andersen sprinkled his writings with every kind of conversational touch—little bits of Copenhagen slang, much grammatical license, and above all, a free use of particles. Molbech, a contemporary literary critic of Andersen, asked, "When will such a prolific writer, already quite well-known in his native country, learn to write his mother-tongue correctly?" (Bredsdorff, 1975, p. 347). This question was raised in spite of the fact that Andersen's manuscripts were corrected by Edvard Collin, the son of his benefactor Jonas Collin and a close friend.

   Some comments written by Charles Dickens, with whom Andersen spent 5 weeks during 1857, are pertinent here. Andersen had visited Dickens 10 years earlier and had come to consider him as a close friend. Even before Andersen arrived in his house in 1857, Dickens wrote to a friend, Miss Burdett-Coutts: "Hans Christian Andersen may perhaps be with us, but you won't mind him—especially as he speaks no language but his own Danish, and is suspected of not even knowing that" (Bredsdorff, 1975, p. 214). During Andersen's visit, Dickens again wrote: "We are suffering a good deal from Andersen...I have arrived at the conviction that he cannot speak Danish" (Bredsdorff, 1975, p. 214). The reason for these statements, Bredsdorff speculates, is that Dickens relied on the information given by Mary Howitt, who translated some of Andersen's earlier fairy tales into English, but was refused a monopoly to translate all his writings. These comments, however, cannot be easily dismissed as malicious gossip spread by a jealous translator inasmuch as similar comments have been made by others, perhaps in a subtle way. Edvard Collin, who read many of Andersen's manuscripts before they went to press, wrote in his book (1882): "He was diligent, he read much;...he learned many things, but he never learned to learn properly" (Bredsdorff, 1975, p. 69). Bredsdorff (1975) himself writes, "Andersen never learnt to spell properly and if he had lived in our time he would probably have been dubbed dyslectic" (p. 19). Ten years later, Bredsdorff was still "completely convinced that Andersen suffered from dyslexia" (personal communication, May 1985).

2. School records: As noted earlier, in spite of his diligence, Andersen barely passed from seventh to eighth grade and had to repeat the eighth grade. Available records show that his most difficult subjects were Latin and Greek.

3. Self-reports: While at grammar school in Slagelse, Andersen kept a diary, and some of the entries reveal clearly the agony he went through while at the school. The following diary excerpts are from Bredsdorff's (1975) biography of Andersen: Sept. 19, 1825—"Unfortunate person!—did badly in Latin, You won't get into the fourth, will have to leave school" (p. 54). Dec. 5, 1825—"Yes, he [Dr. Meisling] treats me kindly, O God! if only I could show some progress but I'm scared of the exam, I'm balancing somewhere between the two bottom marks" (p. 57).

Andersen's letters to his friends also reveal his difficulties at school. In one letter he wrote, "I wish my father had burnt every book I ever got hold of and had forced me to make shoes, then I would never have become mad" (p. 64). In a letter to Edvard Collin he wrote on July 2, 1826, "Something restless and hasty in my soul which makes it twice as difficult for me to get to grips with languages" (p. 61). These excerpts from his diary and letters leave little doubt that Andersen had difficulty in learning languages; more importantly the excerpts give an insight into the pain and agony a highly motivated and intelligent youth could go through in his efforts to overcome learning disability.

Cognitive Characteristics

1. Written spelling errors: Andersen's manuscripts contain numerous spelling errors. Rosendal (1975), after rejecting potential explanations such as Andersen's Funen dialect, lack of diligence and interest, and late education, concludes that "he must have been a constitutional dyslexic" (p. 160). The numerous spelling errors Andersen committed cannot be attributed to lack of experience in writing, because he started writing poetry at the age of 11. A small poem titled "Maria," written in 1816, is preserved in the Andersens Hus in Odense. The first four lines of this poem are quoted below; the spelling errors are italicized.

> Henslumret er en Munter *Sabning*
> Som *segnet* bort i *Ungdom* Aar
> Hun knap *for* Oie paa *Jodisk* Ting
> For hun *sin Sende budskab faar*...

These spelling mistakes are reported not to discredit the creative, 11-year-old budding poet, but are presented to show that such errors persisted and did not disappear from Andersen's later writings. A formal letter written by Andersen in 1824, when he was 19 years old, to Mr. Hempel, an editor, has six spelling errors on one page; correct spellings are in parentheses: Desippel (Discipel), Gulberg (Guldberg's), Indtaekten (Indtaegten), tilfald (tilfaldt), sadt (sat), Olenhlaeger (Oehlenschlaeger). Occasionally, Andersen misspelled even his benefactor's name, Collin, as Colin.

2. Errors of syntax in written language: Rosendal (1975) notes that Andersen experienced difficulties expressing himself in writing, which is presumably one of the reasons he adopted an *oral* style, which was his special contribution to Danish literature. Literary critic Molbech frequently commented about Andersen's "nasty grammatical errors and orthographic carelessness" (Bredsdorff, 1975, p. 346).

A small sample of errors of syntax taken from a few pages of Andersen's diaries, dated 1825 and 1826, are shown below. The incorrect spellings are followed by the correct spellings, and the English translations are in parentheses:

deklameret; declamerede (declaimt instead of declaimed)

repeteret; repeterede (repead instead of repeated)

brang; bragte (brang instead of brought)

for mig Taenker jeg; for jeg Taenker mig (for myself I wish to instead of I wish to myself)

anbefale; anbefalede (recommend instead of recommended). (Laurisden, 1980)

mit; min (mine instead of my)

kom; komme (came instead of come)

og talte vi om (and talked we about instead of we talked about)

antog man sig mig (accepted one them me instead of one accepted me). (Andersenhus, Odense, Manuscript No. 40)

3. Deficits in processing sequential information: No pertinent information regarding deficit in sequential processing of information is available.

4. Superior ability in simultaneous processing of information: Andersen made numerous pencil and pen sketches of sceneries during his frequent trips away from Denmark. In spite of the fact that he did not have any formal training in art, the sketches are artistically pleasing and have a quality of elegant simplicity. Some of his pencil drawings resemble those of Vincent Van Gogh. Indeed, Van Gogh was aware of Andersen's drawings and wrote to his brother Theo, "Don't you find Andersen's fairy tales very fine? It's certain that Andersen also draws illustrations" (Heltoft, 1969, p. 5). Andersen wrote to a friend: "I often feel a desire to sketch on paper what I think I cannot render in words" (Bredsdorff, 1975, p. 302). One of his friends, H.C. Orsted, the discoverer of electromagnetism, is reported to have said that if Andersen had not become a writer he would have become a painter. The number and quality of his sketches warranted their publication in the form of a book, titled *Hans Christian Andersen as an Artist*, by Kjeld Heltoft in 1969.

Another creative outcome of Andersen's superior simultaneous ability is seen in the hundreds of paper-cuttings he has left behind. According to one eyewitness, as he was talking, Andersen would fold a large sheet of paper several times, run big scissors through the paper, make several effortless cuts, and then unfold the paper. Suddenly the plain paper was transformed into a stencil filled with little figures of elves, gnomes, fairies, and animals reminiscent of the ones seen in his fairy tales. In order to create such figures, Andersen must have been able to visualize the finished product even before he started producing it.

Neuropsychological and Biological Characteristics

No direct neuropsychological information is available to enable us to make meaningful inferences regarding Andersen's cerebral organization. There is, however, evidence to suggest that Andersen could be considered a visual person. He was able to evoke exotic visual images instantly and effortlessly. Andersen's tales are full of metaphors and allegories. It is said that Andersen wrote more self-portraits than Rembrandt painted. He was the swan mistaken for an ugly duckling by the world; he was the little boy who found that the emperor had no clothes; he was the beautiful top whereas the Riborg Voigt, who did not consent to marry him, was the worn-out ball. Andersen excelled in this form of analogical thinking.

Andersen died without marrying; other available biological information is too meager to support any conclusions.

Andersen's diary entries and his letters indicate that he did try his best to do well at school. His learning difficulties seem to have been intrinsic rather than external in origin.

LEONARDO DA VINCI

Leonardo da Vinci was born out of wedlock on April 15, 1452, in the small village of Vinci, which lies in the Tuscan hill country of modern Italy about 20 miles from Florence. Information regarding Leonardo's birth is contained in a tax return statement submitted by his grandfather, the notary Ser Antonio da Vinci, and is preserved along with state documents in Florence (Payne, 1978). The document attests that Leonardo was baptized by a local priest and the ceremony was attended by nine family friends. Another tax return filed by Leonardo's father, Ser Piero, includes young Leonardo's name as a member of the household. It is, therefore, reasonable to assume that Leonardo was accepted and raised by members of his father's family. When he was about 12 years old, Leonardo was sent to work as an apprentice under Verrocchio, who was a talented sculptor, goldsmith, and painter. The intent, apparently, was to make an artist out of Leonardo.

Leonardo came from a family of notaries of many generations. One of his stepbrothers continued the family tradition by becoming a notary. In Renaissance Italy, notaries functioned much like lawyers and acted as agents and legal advisers to ecclesiastical institutions, guilds, and wealthy citizens. In contrast, artists of that period, unless they had proved they had extraordinary talents, were considered craftsmen. More often than not they were of humble origin and came from undistinguished families. In view of these observations, it is reasonable to question why Leonardo did not choose to become a notary.

Biographical Information

1. Descriptive accounts by biographers: That Leonardo was an illegitimate child is sometimes advanced to explain the fact that he did not pursue formal education. Although illegitimacy carried a stain of some sort in Italian Renaissance society, power and position or money and special dispensation could lessen the stigma (Martines, 1968).

    According to Payne (1978), Leonardo "had difficulty in learning languages; it was not that he could not apply himself to the task, for at one time he made a serious attempt to learn Latin" (p. 238). It is also known that curriculum pursued in medieval grammar schools placed heavy emphasis on the learning of languages and required a great deal of reading and memorization of Italian and Latin. A lack of aptitude for learning languages, therefore, emerges as a possible reason for Leonardo not choosing to become a notary.

2. School records: Information available regarding Leonardo's childhood is meager, and nothing is known about his early formal education.

3. Self-reports: Starting from about the age of 37, Leonardo recorded most of his thoughts by writing them down. A good many of his ideas were jotted down on loose sheets of paper in a haphazard, unsystematic fashion. In his will, he bequeathed all his diaries and papers to Francesco Melzi who was his faithful

disciple and companion for more than 10 years. Hidden among this jumble of information could be found a few self-deprecatory remarks made by Leonardo about his own lack of formal education, for example, "I being not a man of letters"; "having a lack of literary training" (Reti, 1974, p. 293). Marinoni (1974), who has translated the two manuscripts discovered in Madrid in 1965 (Codex Madrid, and), quotes additional examples: "They will say that being without letters I cannot say properly what I want to say" (p. 77); "The painter is a man without letters who does not possess to the full the contemporary linguistic instruments" (p. 80). In a curious statement that could be viewed as a fragment of self-portrait, Leonardo describes the painter along the following lines: "He is well dressed...he wears the clothes he likes...and his house is full of delightful paintings and is spotlessly clean. He is often accompanied by music and by men who read from a variety of beautiful works and he can listen to these with great pleasure" (MacCurdy, 1958, p. 853). Why should other men have read to the painter so that he could listen with great pleasure? Is it because the artist was not proficient in reading or because he was engaged in painting and, consequently, could not read? An affluent artist like Leonardo was likely to do his paintings in his studio, not in his house.

Cognitive Characteristics

1. Written spelling errors: Unlike English orthography, Italian orthography is shallow; no complex rules are involved in phoneme-grapheme conversion; and words are spelled the way they are pronounced. Such a highly regular orthography minimizes the opportunities for making spelling errors. There exists, however, a possibility for committing errors of parsing, segmentation, and blending in written Italian. Such errors frequently result in nonwords. For example, *la radio* (the radio) could be incorrectly parsed as "I 'aradio" or blended as "laradio." In addition, spelling errors could also occur as a result of consonant doubling (casa—ccasa); letter substitutions (ipocrito—ipoclito); letter additions (queglj—quelglj); and letter deletions (contrastare—contastare).

Leonardo often "wrote haphazardly...spelling arbitrarily, skipping words and phrases" (Marinoni, 1974, p. 60). Santillana (1966), who was personally involved in translating some of Leonardo's treatises, makes the following observation:

The spelling proves to be a pure chaos, one that far exceeds the irregularities of the day...the words are severed and broken, and also amalgamated...the spelling is that of the servant girl...he uses archaic verbal forms which have disappeared from contemporary [i.e., Renaissance] literature. (p. 191)

One need not search far to find such errors in Leonardo's writings; the following examples, selected from Sartori (1987), illustrate. Incorrect parsing and blending: ino ccidente (in occidente), na tura (natura), cicommette (chi commette), cinon (chi non); consonant doubling: allevan te (a levente), quessto (questo); letter substitution: che s'alluminava (chessallumj nava), audacia (aldacia); and letter deletion: voc (voce), acqe (acque).

Sartori (1987), who has examined Leonardo's writings from the perspective of dyslexia, notes that his orthography has been described as "capricious and peculiar; inconsistent and unusual" (p. 2). Sartori also points out that normal readers, living or historical, do not typically commit such errors. In contrast, the errors committed by Leonardo are similar to the ones committed by a 15-year-old dyslexic boy studied by Sartori (see Table 1).

TABLE 1
Written Spelling Errors of Leonardo and Those of a 15-Year-Old Dyslexic Subject

Type of Error	Leonardo	Correct Spelling	Dyslexic Subject	Correct Spelling
Blending	cicommette	chi commette (who makes)	pergliamici	per gli amici (for the friend)
Segmenting	muta tionj	mutationj (mutations)	in chiostro	inchiostro (ink)
	lumj nosa	lumjnosa (luminous)	i nizio	inizio (beginning)
	aritro vare	a rit rovare (at finding again)	a dogni	ad ogni (at every)
	ino ccidente	in occidente (in the west)	lanno scorso	l'anno scorso (the last year)
Consonant Errors	quelqlj	queglj (those)	tacquini	taccuini (notebook)
	sciatta	schiatta (sons)	lanno	l'hanno (have)
	tottare	toccare (touch)	socquadro	soqquadro (topsy-turvy)

Alternate hypotheses could be advanced to account for the idiosyncrasies of Leonardo's orthography, and these deserve to be examined. One such possibility is that, during the Renaissance, firm rules of spelling were not laid down and Italian spelling was inconsistent. Another hypothesis is that spelling varied from region to region within Italy; Tuscany, the region Leonardo came from, could have had its own peculiarities of spelling. A final possibility is that, having had no formal schooling, Leonardo was not acquainted with many words. Even though all these could have contributed to Leonardo's erratic spelling, none seems to be a major factor. Sartori (1987) compared the spontaneous writings of Michelangelo Buonarroti and Francesco Melzi with those of Leonardo. Both Michelangelo and Melzi were Leonardo's contemporaries, and came from the same region. Examining the 133 words Michelangelo used in one of his letters, Sartori could not find a single error that was similar to the ones committed by Leonardo Melzi, who inherited Leonardo's manuscripts, rearranged and copied some of the pages in order to compile the Treatise on painting. A comparison of Leonardo's original manuscript and the copy made by Melzi (Marinoni, 1974, p. 63) shows that he corrected all the spelling and punctuation errors found in Leonardo's original manuscript. It is obvious, therefore, that even at the time of the Renaissance, the errors committed by Leonardo were considered unusual. The incorrect word segmentation and blending could not be explained by the fact that Leonardo lacked formal schooling, since these errors resulted in nonwords that are not found in spoken language. Furthermore, while copying other manuscripts, Leonardo committed the same kinds of errors seen in his spontaneous writing.

2. Errors of syntax in written language: Some of Leonardo's narratives are reduced to mere strings of words that were freed from rhetorical encumbrances and are devoid of grammatical connections (Marinoni, 1974). In addition to making errors of syntax, dyslexic individuals frequently use incorrect punctuation in written language. According to Richter (1939), Leonardo gave little attention to punctuation, and did not use accents or apostrophes at all.

3. Deficits in processing sequential information: As noted earlier, dyslexic individuals encounter difficulties in processing information sequentially. Such difficulties can be seen in Leonardo's processing of sequences of words and phrases, remembering days and dates, and carrying out arithmetic operations. For example, in one of his diary entries, he added 25, 2, 16, 6, and 1 and arrived at the figure 48. In a geometric problem, he inscribed a section of a hexagon in a circle and proceeded to divide the area outside the hexagon into submultiple portions. He then constructed a table of two columns, one with numbers 1 through 50, and the other with the product of each number in column 1 multiplied by 6. In the construction of this multiplication table of 6, he made a simple error by entering 104 as the product of 6 x 34. He continued this mistake with all of the subsequent figures and ultimately arrived at the multiplication, 50 x 6. Leonardo entered the answer as 200 (Reti, 1974).

Among Leonardo's errors of sequence, two in particular are of relevance in the present context. He recorded Caterina's (who was possibly his mother) arrival by writing, "On the 16th day of July Caterina came on the 16th day of July 1493" (MacCurdy, 1958, p. 1156). His diary entry on his father's death reads: "On the ninth day of July 1504, on Wednesday at seven o'clock, died, at the Palace of Podesta, Ser Piero da Vinci, notary, my father, at seven o'clock; he was eighty years old, he left ten sons and two daughters (MacCurdy, 1958, p. 1159). In addition to the repetition of the phrase "seven o'clock," several other errors can be detected. The day of death was Tuesday and not Wednesday as he had written; his father's age was 77 instead of 80. It is also possible that the number of children is incorrect; Payne (1978) states that Ser Piero had three daughters. It may be noted that all these errors involve sequential information.

4. Superior ability in simultaneous processing of information: Leonardo relied a great deal on drawings and sketches to communicate his ideas; his diaries and notebooks are filled with rebuses, sketches, and drawings. When copying Euclid's theorems, Leonardo did not transcribe the Latin text word for word, but often translated and recorded the theorems in a series of drawings. For him, drawings and sketches constituted the primary medium of expression and communication.

Leonardo's painting of the Virgin and Child with St. Anne provides further evidence of his superior spatial visualization ability. Portraying the personal relationship among the three figures (Christ, Mary, and Mary's mother St. Anne) without violating the importance attributed to each one of them by religious tradition had, for artists, posed a tremendous problem in composition. Leonardo solved it through a gestalt-like fusion of the figures into a pyramidal arrangement. A similar fusion of figures is also seen in the Last Supper. The celebrated Mona Lisa has been the object of great many analyses. Stites, Stites, and Castiglione (1970) present evidence that Mona Lisa was actually the remarkable Isabella d'Este, daughter of the Duke and Duchess of Ferrara and the wife of the Marquis Francesco Gonzaga of Mantua, and not the wife of Francesco del Giocondo, the Florentine merchant, as is commonly believed. Isabella reputedly had a strong and compelling personality and, in all likelihood, this was captured and accurately portrayed by Leonardo.

Leonardo's manuscripts from 1496 through 1499 devote more space to geometry than to any other subject, an indication of his preoccupation with the field during those years. Leonardo's illustrations of complex three-dimensional designs in solid geometry are extraordinary for their depth and accuracy.

Neuropsychological Characteristics

1.   Evidence of incomplete cerebral lateralization: As noted earlier, there appears to exist some association between diffuse cerebral organization, incomplete lateralization, and specific reading disability. During the last year of his life, when he was the resident artist at the court of the French king Francis at Amboise, Leonardo suffered a stroke. Evidence of this illness comes from a record made by Antonio de' Beatis, secretary of the Cardinal of Aragon, who visited Leonardo on October 10, 1517. The secretary's observation that Leonardo's right arm was paralyzed indicates that the lesion was localized in the left cerebral hemisphere. In right-handed persons, a lesion in the left cerebral hemisphere that causes paralysis of the right arm is usually accompanied by aphasic symptoms. Since the Cardinal's secretary had had conversations with Leonardo but still did not make reference to any speech problems, it has to be inferred that Leonardo, in spite of a left hemisphere stroke, was free from aphasic symptoms. Furthermore, on April 23, 1518, about 6 months after the Cardinal's visit, Leonardo went to the chambers of the royal notary at Amboise and made his last will. An intricate document with 18 separate clauses, it was made in the presence of five witnesses. The information contained in the will is private, for the most part, which indicates that Leonardo was able to communicate to the panel of witnesses his intent and describe his relatives as well as details regarding his personal possessions and properties. The fact that Leonardo was able to make a complex deposition suggests that his language remained relatively unimpaired in spite of the left-sided cerebral lesion.

2.   Handedness: Analysis of his handwriting as well as sketches reveals that Leonardo wrote, drew, and painted with his left hand (Marinoni, 1974). A well-known characteristic of Leonardo was his tendency to write in the mirror-reversed form. According to his biographer, Vasari (1959), Leonardo wrote backwards, in rude characters, and with his left hand. A plausible explanation of this tendency to mirror-write is that Leonardo felt comfortable with this style of writing. Probably because he perceived each word holistically as a gestalt, the directional orientation of the word, right to left or left to right, was not an impediment. In all likelihood, Leonardo processed the word as a picture rather than as a string of graphemes, and this cognitive style might explain his preference to write in mirror-reversed form. Such a cognitive strategy is also associated with a diffuse cerebral organization and specific reading disability (Corballis, 1980).

Biological Characteristics

Little information is available about Leonardo regarding genetic predisposition or immune system disorders.

CONCLUDING REMARKS

Biographical, neuropsychological, and biological evidence presented in this paper indicates that the four historic men in question had certain characteristics traditionally associated with developmental dyslexia. The resolution of the issue whether these men had learning disability or not also depends partly on one's definition of learning disability. If one adopts a definition based on *dysfunction model*, in which the presence of neurologic and physiologic symptoms is the basic criterion of LD, securing posthumous evidence is difficult. If, on the other hand, one adopts a definition based on the *difference model*, in which LD is viewed as representing an extreme position within the normal range of variation in human information processing strategies, then post hoc analysis of historic evidence is quite possible. Further, LD is compatible with an exceptionally high level of intelligence and creativity.

Even though not addressed in this paper, the question "How did these men manage to overcome or circumvent their learning disabilities?" is perhaps the most useful facet of psychohistoric investigation. An examination of the lives of the four historic men points to two important contributing factors. One is the unusually intense interest each one of these men had in a particular area, even from a very young age. This consuming interest drove them to books. The second factor is a positive and supportive parental attitude, which can be readily documented in the case of Woodrow Wilson, who maintained extensive correspondence with his parents. The letters between Wilson and his parents reveal a fascinating aspect of parent-son relationship that is worth studying in itself.

ABOUT THE AUTHORS

P.G. Aaron *has a master's degree in biology from Madras University, India, and a PhD in educational psychology from the University of Wisconsin. Currently he is a professor of educational and school psychology at Indiana State University.* **Scott Phillips** *received his master's degree in education from Indiana State University. Presently he is a doctoral candidate in the Department of Educational and School Psychology, Indiana State University.* **Steen Larsen** *is the head of the Department of Education and Psychology at the Royal Danish School of Education Studies, Copenhagen. He has published a number of books in Denmark, Sweden, and Finland concerning the following issues: neuropsychological and cognitive function in children, cerebral laterality and dyslexia, and the possible impact of new technology on children's cognitive development and education. Address: P.G. Aaron, Department of Educational and School Psychology, Indiana State University, Terre Haute, IN 47809.*

ACKNOWLEDGMENTS

1. Research reported in this paper was supported by a grant from the Research Committee, Indiana State University.

2. Our indebtedness to the following organizations for making the original manuscripts available for study and for granting permission to reproduce them is gratefully acknowledged: The Edison Institute, Henry Ford Museum and Greenfield Village; Edison National Historic Site, West Orange, NJ; Firestone Library, Princeton University; Library of Davidson College, North Carolina; Det Kongelige Bibliotek, Copenhagen; and Hans Christian Andersenhus, Odense, Denmark.

REFERENCES

Aaron, P.G. (1978). Dyslexia, an imbalance in cerebral information processing strategies. Perceptual and Motor Skills, 47, 699-706.

Aaron, P.G., Baxter, C.F., & Lucenti, J. (1980). Developmental dyslexia and acquired alexia: Two sides of the same coin? Brain and Language, 11, 1-11.

Aaron, P.G., Olsen, J., & Baker, C. (1985). Dyslexic college student: Is he also dysphasic? Cognitive Neuropsychology, 2, 115-147.

Aaron, P.G., & Phillips, S. (1986). A decade of research with dyslexic college students: A summary of research. Annals of Dyslexia, 36, 44-65.

Adelman, K., & Adelman, H. (1987). Rodin, Patton, Edison, Wilson, Einstein: Were they really learning disabled? Journal of Learning Disabilities, 20(5), 270-279.

Annett, M., (1981). The right shift theory of handedness and developmental language problems. Bulletin of the Orton Society, 31, 103-121.

Artley, A.S. (1980). Learning disabilities versus reading disabilities: A vexing problem. In C. McCullough (Ed), Persistent problems in reading education (pp. 119-124). Newark, DE: International Reading Association.

Baker, R.S. (1927). Woodrow Wilson: Life and letters (Vol. 1). Garden City, NY: Doubleday.

Barron, J., Treimen, R., Wilf, F. & Kellman, P. (1980). Spelling and reading by rules. In U. Frith (Ed.), Cognitive processes in spelling (pp. 159-194). New York: Academic Press.

Benton, A.L. (1984). Dyslexia and spatial thinking. Annals of Dyslexia, 34, 69-85.

Blank, M., & Bruskin, C. (1984). The reading of content and noncontent words by dyslexics. In S.J. White & V. Teller (Eds.), Discourses in reading and linguistics (pp. 59-70). New York: New York Academy of Sciences.

Bradshaw, J.L., & Nettleton, N.C. (1981). The nature of hemispheric specialization in man. The Behavioral and Brain Sciences, 4, 51-91.

Bredsdorff, E. (1975). Hans Christian Andersen. New York: Charles Scribner.

Bryant, P.E., & Bradley, L. (1980). Why children sometimes write words which they do not read. In U. Frith (Ed.), Cognitive processes in spelling (pp. 355-372). New York: Academic Press.

Bryden, M.P. (1982). Functional asymmetry in the intact brain. New York: Academic Press.

Brynes, S. (1978, Fall). The Edison papers: A report on research at Rutgers. Matrix, pp. 10-12.

Carver, R. (1982). Optimal rate of reading prose. Reading Research Quarterly, 18, 56-88.

Conot, R. (1979). A streak of luck. New York: Seaview Books.

Cook, L. (1981). Misspelling analysis in dyslexia: Observation of developmental strategy shifts. Bulletin of the Orton Society, 31, 123-134.

Corballis, M. (1980). Laterality and myth. American Psychologist, 35(3), 284-295.

Das, J.P., Kirby, J.R., & Jarman, R. (1979). Simultaneous and successive cognitive processes. New York: Academic Press.

DeFries, J.C., & Decker, S.N. (1982). Genetic aspects of reading disability: A family study. In R.N. Malatesha & P.G. Aaron (Eds.), Reading disorders: Varieties and treatments (pp. 255-280). New York: Academic Press.

Denckla, M.B., & Rudel, R.G. (1976). Rapid automatized naming: Dyslexia differentiated from other learning disabilities. Neuropsychologia, 14, 471-479.

Dyer, F.L., Martin, T.C., & Meadowcroft, W.H. (1929). Edison, his life and inventions. New York: Harper & Row.

Finucci, J.M. (1978). Genetic consideration in dyslexia. In H.R. Myklebust (Ed.), Progress in learning disabilities (Vol. 4, pp. 41-64). New York: Grune & Stratton.

Fisher, P., & Frankfutter, A. (1977). Normal and disabled readers can locate and identify letters: Where's the perceptual deficit? Journal of Reading Behavior, 9, 31-43.

Fleming, E. (1984). Believe the heart. San Francisco: Strawberry Hill Press.

Gaskins, I. (1982). Let's end the reading disabilities/learning disabilities debate. Journal of Learning Disabilities, 15(2), 81-83.

Gerber, M.M. (1984). Orthographic problem-solving ability of learning disabled and normally achieving students. Learning Disability Quarterly, 7, 157-164.

Geschwind, N. (1983). Biological association of left-handedness. Annals of Dyslexia, 33, 29-40.

Geschwind, N. (1984). The brain of a learning-disabled individual. Annals of Dyslexia, 34. 319-327.

Geschwind, N., & Behan, P. (1982). Left-handedness: Association with immune disease, migraine, and developmental learning disorder. Proceedings of the National Academy of Sciences, 79, 5097-5100.

Gibson, E.J., & Guinett, L. (1971). Perception of inflexions in brief visual presentation of words. Journal of Verbal Learning and Verbal Behavior, 10, 182-189.

Guyer, B., & Friedman, M. (1975). Hemispheric processing and cognitive styles in learning disabled and normal children. Child Development, 3, 658-668.

Hammill, D., Leigh, J., McNutt, G., & Larsen, S. (1981). A new definition of LD. Learning Disability Quarterly, 4(4), 336-342.

Heltoft, K. (1969). Hans Christian Andersen as an artist. Copenhagen: The Royal Danish Ministry of Foreign Affairs.

Herschel, M. (1978). Dyslexia revisited: A review. Human Genetics, 40, 115-134.

Jolly, H. (1981). Teaching basic function words. Reading Teacher, 35, 136-140.

Josephson, M. (1959). Edison. New York: McGraw-Hill.

Keen, M.L. (1977). The linguistic interpretation of aphasic syndromes: Agrammatism in Broca's aphasia, an example. Cognition, 5, 9-46.

Keigwin, R. (1976). Hans Christian Andersen: Eighty fairy tales. New York: Pantheon.

Kershner, J.R. (1977). Cerebral dominance in disabled readers, good readers, and gifted children: Search for a model. Child Development, 48, 61-67.

Kirby, R., & Robinson, G. (1987). Simultaneous and successive processing in reading disabled children. Journal of Learning Disabilities, 20(4), 243-252.

Laurisden, H. (1980). (ED.). H.C. Andersen's Dagboger. Copenhagen: Lademann.

Leong, C.K. (1974). An investigation of spatial-temporal information-processing in children with specific reading disability. Unpublished doctoral dissertation, University of Alberta, Canada.

Levine, D., & Sweet, E. (1983). Localization of lesions in Broca's motor aphasia. In A. Kertesz (Ed.), Localization in neuropsychology (pp. 185-208). New York: Academic Press.

Liberman, I.Y., Liberman, A.M., Mattingly, I., & Shankweiler, D. (1980). Orthography and the beginning reader. In J.F. Kavanaugh & R.L. Venezky (Eds.), Orthography, reading, and dyslexia (pp. 137-154). Baltimore: University Park Press.

Link, A.S. (1966). The papers of Woodrow Wilson (Vol). Princeton, NJ: Princeton University Press.

Link, A.S. (1967). The papers of Woodrow Wilson (Vol.). Princeton, NJ: Princeton University Press.

MacCurdy, E. (1958). The notebooks of Leonardo da Vinci. New York: George Braziller.

McAdoo, E.W. (1937). The Woodrow Wilsons. New York: Macmillan.

Marinoni, A. (1974). Leonardo the writer. In L. Reti (Ed.), The unknown Leonardo (pp. 56-85). New York: McGraw-Hill.

Martines, L. (1968). Lawyers and statecraft in Renaissance Florence. Princeton, NJ: Princeton University Press.

Mitterer, J. (1982). There are at least two kinds of poor readers: Whole-word poor readers and recoding poor readers. Canadian Journal of Psychology, 36, 445-461.

Orton, S. (1937). Reading, writing, and speech problems in children. New York: W.W. Norton.

Payne, R. (1978). Leonardo. Garden City, NY: Doubleday.

Perfetti, C.A., & Hogaboam, T. (1975). Relationship between single-word decoding and reading comprehension skill. Journal of Educational Psychology, 67, 461-469.

Porac, C., & Coren, S. (1981). Lateral preferences and human behavior. New York: Springer.

Reti, L. (1974). The unknown Leonardo. New York: McGraw-Hill.

Regard, M., Landis, T., & Graves, R. (1985). Dissociated hemispheric superiorities for reading stenography vs. print. Neuropsychologia, 23, 431-435.

Richter, J.P. (1939). The notebook of Leonardo da Vinci (Vol.). New York: Dover.

Rosendal, A. (1975). The causes of H.C. Andersen's spelling difficulties. Anderseniana, 3, 160-184.

Rozin, P., Poritsky, S., & Sotsky, R. (1971). American children with reading problems can easily learn to read English represented by Chinese characters. Science, 171, 1264-1267.

Runes, D.D. (1948). The diary and sundry observations of Thomas Alva Edison. New York: Philosophical Library.

Santillana, G.D. (1966). Man without letters. In M. Philipson (Ed.), Leonardo da Vinci: Aspects of the Renaissance genius (pp. 77-109). New York: George Braziller.

Sartori, G. (1987). Leonardo da Vinci: Omo sanza lettere. A case of surface dyslexia. Cognitive Neuropsychology, 4(1), 1-10.

Snowling, M.J. (1980). The development of grapheme-phoneme correspondence in normal and dyslexic readers. Journal of Experimental Child Psychology, 29, 294-305.

Soderberg, R. (1977). Reading in early childhood: A linguistic study of a pre-school child's gradual acquisition of reading ability. Washington, DC: Georgetown University Press.

Stanovich, K. (1980). Toward an interactive compensatory model of individual differences in the development of reading fluency. Reading Research Quarterly, 16, 32-71.

Steeves, K.J. (1983). Memory as a factor in the computative effciency of dyslexic children with high abstract reasoning ability. Annals of Dyslexia, 33, 141-150.

Stites, R.S., Stites, E.M., & Castiglione, P. (1970), The sublimations of Leonardo da Vinci. Washington, DC: Smithsonian Institution Press.

Thompson, L.J. (1969). Language disabilities in men of eminence. Bulletin of the Orton Society, 14, 113-120.

Vasari, G. (1959). Lives of the most eminent painters, sculptors, and architects (G.D. DeVere, trans.). New York: Modern Library.

Wachhorst, W. (1981). Thomas Alva Edison: An American myth. Cambridge, MA: MIT Press.

Weinstein, E.A. (1981). Woodrow Wilson: A medical and psychological biography. Princeton, NJ: Princeton University Press.

Witelson, S. (1977). Developmental dyslexia: Two right hemispheres and none left? Science, 195, 309-311.

Reprinted with permission from Journal of Learning Disabilities, vol. 21 no. 9, November 1988. Pro-Ed, 8700 Shoal Creek Blvd, Austin, TX 78758-6897

How Can We Meet Their Needs? 4

Gifted students who also suffer from learning disabilities need individualized programs to address their strengths and weaknesses. Specifically, they need (a) high level for "gifted" programming in their areas of strength, (b) developmental instruction in subjects of average growth, (c) remedial teaching in areas of disability, and (d) adaptive instruction in areas of disability. This can best be done by using a variety of strategies based on recommendations that result from a thorough assessment of the student's abilities, achievement, and processing deficits. In this section, we include articles that describe some of the strategies that have proven to be effective with this population.

The first few articles focus on intervention techniques for children with learning disabilities. We then include several articles that focus specifically on the child with learning disabilities who is also gifted. While the techniques that benefit children with learning disabilities are useful for this population, these articles emphasize the importance of focusing primarily on the gifted child's strengths in an effort to develop the gift or talent. The authors offer suggestions for doing this effectively in a number of settings.

We also include an article that addresses the issue of testing the child who is learning disabled. This is a particularly important concern for the student who is gifted and has high aspirations with regard to college and career goals but who may not score high on standardized tests because of learning disabilities if the tests are administered in traditional formats. The last articles in this section address some of the counseling needs of students who are gifted with learning disabilities and the importance of helping such students develop self-esteem.

For additional assistance in locating or modifying a program to meet the needs of gifted learning disabled students, be sure to investigate the many references, organizations, and schools included in the Resources section.

Treating Learning Disabilities

Larry B. Silver

The Role Of The Parent: Advocacy

Specific learning disabilities are not just an academic problem. A child with learning disabilities is affected at school, but that child is also affected anywhere interaction with others is necessary: in the family, in religious settings, in social groups, on teams. As a parent, you are the one person who plays a part in all of your child's experiences. You must become your child's advocate in each of these arenas, a very difficult task. Your reward is knowing that you are doing everything you can to help your child become a happy, competent adult. As the child's advocate, your job is to work with the child, teachers, professionals, and activities leaders so that the child will have as many positive experiences as possible. There is one guideline for doing that: Emphasize strengths while compensating weaknesses.

The Role Of The School

Federal law states that your child is entitled to an appropriate public education. Hopefully, your child's school is staffed with professionals trained to recognize and treat specific learning disabilities. They may have pinpointed the need for testing in the first place, and can advise you on the best plan for supporting your child academically. If your school system has not recognized or evaluated your child, you must push for identification of your child's disability and needs in a polite but persistent way, and see that those needs are met.

Once your child has been tested, you and your child's teachers should know the child's learning strengths and weaknesses. The school will want to establish an Individual Education Plan (IEP) to treat your child in "the least restrictive environment."

The **Individual Education Plan** is a written statement of the instruction and expectations appropriate for your child. It should also include a system for monitoring the child's progress. Even the simplest IEP should contain the following statements:

1) The child's level of educational performance

2) Academic goals for the school year

3) The short-term objectives, stated in instructional terms, that will lead to the achievement of the yearly goals

4) The specific special education and support services the child will receive

5) The amount of time the child will spend in regular educational programs and justification for special placements recommended

6) Initiation dates and length of services;

7) Criteria and methods for evaluating the achievement of short-term objectives–annually, if not more often.

The "least restrictive environment" will vary with the child, but will usually take one of three forms:

1) The child may remain in the regular classroom, supplemented with a daily hour or half-hour of tutoring by a special educator. In this situation, you have two tasks: First, make sure that the special educator and the classroom teacher communicate regularly to determine ways to emphasize the child's strengths and correct or compensate for weaknesses. Second, monitor the program carefully to insure that, as the year goes by, your child continues to get the amount of special help specified at the beginning of the school year. You should be consulted if change is to occur.

2) The child may be assigned to a special educator's resource room, but fed in, or "mainstreamed" into a regular classroom for subjects the child can handle: perhaps only gym and art at first, but eventually, English, science or math. Again, your role is to make sure all the educators involved are talking to each other regularly about the child.

3) The child may be assigned full-time to a self-contained classroom designed specifically for learning disabled students. These usually consist of eight to twelve students, a special educator, and an aide.

Whatever the placement, be a pleasant but alert monitor of the services your child receives. Ask if teachers are trained and certified in special education for the learning disabled. Request regular progress reports. Think ahead. Spring is not too soon to ask about plans for your child for the following September.

The Role Of The Classroom Teacher

The classroom teacher may not be trained to provide remedial therapy, but he or she can provide important positive learning experiences daily. The classroom teacher must always remember two things: that a child with learning disabilities has a real, if invisible, handicap; and that such children usually have compensating talents. A child with a broken leg cannot sprint, but he may be a fine singer. Similarly, the child with fine motor problems, who cannot write legible answers on the board, may be quite articulate when asked verbal questions. The child with demand language problems can write on the board but should not be asked to answer questions in class. Sensitive teachers who recognize that there is more than one way to learn can teach a child to use strengths and compensate for weaknesses. There is no better way to build a child's self-esteem.

Support: Academic Therapy

If the school system is unwilling or unable to provide the specialized help your child needs, you may wish to seek the help of a private tutor, often available through university or hospital-centered clinics, or through private centers for special learners. Again, you must be an informed consumer and an advocate for your child. The tutor may see your child one to five times a week for special help; three to five times a week is preferable. This adult should be a warm, supportive person with specialized training in teaching basic skills and the child's best ways of learning to the child with learning disabilities. Ask what methods the tutor will use, and what experience he or she has. Ask for references, and after hiring someone, listen to what your child tells you about the learning experience. Ideally, the parent, the classroom teacher, and the tutor will act as a cooperative team. At a minimum, you should make sure that each knows what the other is doing.

The Child with Learning Disabilities and Others

A child, of course, is a person, not just a student. The most effective treatment will be carried out not only in school, but in the family and in social groups as well. Although there is no specific formula for every person, some ways of thinking and problem-solving are more productive than others. Once again, the general principle for parents is to emphasize the child's strengths while compensating for weaknesses. As the child experiences success, he or she will begin to feel competent, and then more confident.

In The Family

In order to feel like a competent member of the family, every child must make a contribution to it, usually in the form of household chores and responsibilities. It's wise to assign these with careful thought for what your child is able to do. The child with gross motor problems who is asked to carry out the trash is likely to spill it, but that same child may be able to feed the cat. Whatever tasks you set for your child, remember that the question is not whether the child can do a task, but how the child can do the task.

Children with learning disabilities need to reinforce what they learn over and over in order to retain it. If you feel inclined to help in this, household activities such as cooking provide practice in reading, measuring, counting, and following instructions in sequence. Chopping and stirring are good gross motor exercises.

Thinking about your child's strengths and weaknesses will help you see other ways to reinforce the child's abilities and practice at home the skills the child lacks.

Homework

Schoolwork is a child's job, and a child needs to feel competent at it to have self-respect. Children with learning disabilities may have difficulty or take excessive time completing assignments. Unless informed, the teacher may be unaware of how long it takes the child to do homework. When parents wind up doing it instead of the child, or when homework becomes a nightly battle, it is best to meet with the teacher to identify ways to help the child manage homework. For instance, if the child has poor handwriting or can't copy an assignment in the time allowed, perhaps the teacher will give the child a copy of the homework assignment, or send homework requirements to parents each day so there is a clear understanding of what must be done at home.

Parents can offer the best support by helping the child plan ahead, and by providing structure and organization. Establish a checklist of items needed every morning and go over it with the child at bedtime so that schoolbooks, special assignments, lunch money and locker keys are not forgotten. Provide a notebook system for organizing papers, and a quiet place and a specific time to do homework each day. If conflict persists, despite good communication between parents and teacher, parents may wish to seek help from a mental health professional.

At Play

Learning disabilities may interfere with a child's success at sports or play. By knowing the child's strengths and weaknesses, you can help your child choose sports, activities, and crafts where he or she has a better chance to perform adequately. Not only does it save the child from failure, it provides a setting where the child can make friends. For example, a child with visual perceptual and visual motor difficulties may have problems with baseball or basketball, but may be very good at sports that do not require much eye-hand coordination, such as swimming, diving, rowing, sailing, horseback riding, soccer, skiing, bowling, or photography. Clumsy children who have fine motor ability might be good at art, or playing certain instruments. Discuss these concepts with the special educator so you can help select activities where the child has the greatest chance of success.

In social activities, as in school, you must be your child's advocate. Explain to group leaders, as you have to teachers, your child's learning strengths and weaknesses. Whether they are relatives, neighbors, coaches, religious instructors or scout leaders, help the other adults in your child's life understand that the child's disability, although invisible, is nonetheless real. Enlist their support; work together to pick positive experiences and to anticipate and avert possible problems so the child can do reasonably well.

The Possible Role Of Psychotherapy

If your child's problems are particularly complex, and your efforts are not working, you may want to consult a mental health professional. Choose someone, if possible, who is knowledgeable about learning disabilities and the personal and family problems it can cause. If the clinician is not familiar with the special problems of someone with learning disabilities, offer some reading material. In any case, the therapist should be well-trained, experienced, and skilled in using more than one kind of therapy. The therapist you choose should also be someone with whom you feel comfortable.

Seeing that a child with learning disabilities gets what he or she needs from others is not an easy job, but it is the necessary first step to competence, success, and confidence for your child.

"Treating Learning Disabilities," adapted from The Misunderstood Child *by Larry B. Silver, M.D., is part of* Topics in Learning Disabilities. *This rainbow series of factsheets for parents was produced and distributed by the Information and Communications Program of TRI-Services' National Institute of Dyslexia. This Institute is no long in operation.*

Strategies for Mainstreamed Students

Fern C. Moskowitz

Classroom teachers are often uncomfortable when special education students are placed in their content area classes. One way to help ensure a successful experience for the learning disabled student is to enlighten the teacher about his needs.

It is not a new concept that students have varying learning styles, and it is especially important that we recognize the unique learning styles of the LD population. The specialist's role with LD students is to help remediate deficits or weaknesses and to provide compensatory education when appropriate. The classroom teacher's role, however, is to use the student's strengths in order to help him learn the content area material. This can be accomplished in several ways. First, the teacher needs to manipulate the classroom environment, including temperature, noise, and lighting. Secondly, the teacher needs to be aware of emotional factors that may influence the student's performance, including motivation, commitment to tasks, and lack of inner structure. Finally, the teacher needs to become sensitive to problems created by the physical or perceptual components of the learning disability that determine if the student is a visual, auditory, or kinesthetic learner.

Attention Deficits

If the student has a developmentally inappropriate attention span and impulsivity that may or may not be accompanied by hyperactivity–

1. Make sure the student is completely attentive when directions are given.

    – turn light off to attract attention
    – have student repeat directions to you
    – break complex directions into uncomplicated one- or two-step tasks
    – establish eye contact

2. Place the student away from any distracting stimuli–windows, doors, etc.

3. Understand and don't dwell on the student's need for physical movement.

    – getting out of seat
    – chewing on a pencil
    – doodling

4. Put a hand on the student's arm or shoulder to gain and maintain attention for orally presented materials.

5. Use concrete and visual materials to help the student attend to the task at hand.

6. Give unmistakable cues to identify and emphasize important information: "This is important."

7. Require the student to provide periodic status reports for long-range projects.

8. When assigning homework, list materials needed for the next class session.

9. Keep extra supplies of pens, paper, and textbooks.

10. Replace one long class activity with several short ones.

11. In order to help the student sustain attention, encourage him to "talk through" the problem.

Organizational Deficit

If the student is unable to provide inner structure and needs extra help to initiate and complete a task successfully–

1. Develop specific routines for the student to follow.

2. Provide the student with a sequentially ordered list of the things he is expected to do.

3. Require a looseleaf notebook with pockets. Encourage the student to punch holes in loose worksheets.

4. Train the student to divide the looseleaf notebook into specific sections for homework assignments, homework, class notes, etc.

5. Encourage the student to line or fold paper into boxes for math examples.

6. Provide time for copying homework assignments from the chalkboard or overhead projector and avoid verbal homework assignments.

7. When lecturing, develop a standard outline or a visual/graphic outline on the chalkboard, overhead projector, or spiritmaster.

8. Have another student act as a helper to

   – take notes using carbon paper
   – check that homework is copied

9. Teach memory strategies (mnemonics).

10. Give unmistakable cues to identify important information: "This is important."

11. Long-term assignments require periodic checking for the LD student. This also provides an opportunity for the teacher to intervene if necessary to ensure adequate organization for a successful outcome.

12. Keep an extra folder with copies of all handouts given in class so that "misplaced" materials can be replaced.

Auditory Processing Deficits

If the student is unable to receive, interpret, organize, retrieve, or express information received through the ears–

1. Avoid multiple verbal directions. Students will follow directions better if shown rather than told what to do.

2. Provide visual outlines/graphic organizers and other pictorial aids (graphs, maps, diagrams, etc.).

3. Encourage the LD student to tape lessons, especially those which you are reviewing for a test. This allows for repeat listening.

4. Avoid giving homework orally. Homework should be placed on chalkboard, overhead projector, or spiritmaster.

5. Ask the student to repeat your question before giving you an answer. (Do we all hear the same thing?)

6. Seat the student in front of the room away from windows, doors, or other locations that may present an auditory distraction.

7. Accept concrete answers.

8. Give ample time for responses.

9. Do not penalize for spelling.

10. When using terminology that involves concepts of time such as "decade," "how many years ago," time lines, etc., do not assume the student can understand or apply them. These may have to be taught.

11. Reinforce all verbal directions with visual cues.

12. Don't give oral tests.

13. Reinforce spelling through writing and looking at words.

14. Encourage the use of a variety of visual learning materials: films, filmstrips, computers, etc.

Visual and Visual-Motor Deficits

If the student is unable to receive, organize, interpret, retrieve, and express information received through the eyes, including fine-motor/handwriting problems—

1. Have the student use tape recorder, typewriter, or word processor (double spacing) for homework.

2. Suggest that the student use an index card for keeping his place when reading.

3. Use testing modifications such as—

    – teacher or helper writes the answers;
    – tests are untimed;
    – student is not required to use separate answer sheet or column to mark answers;
    – the specialist administers test verbally with oral responses from student;
    – the student is permitted to number, underline, or circle responses.

4. In math, encourage the student to use graph paper or lined paper turned on its side to make columns.

5. Have another student use carbon paper when taking notes to share with LD student.

6. Present spiritmasters that are perfectly clear.

7. Seat student in front of the classroom near the center of the chalkboard.

8. Limit the amount of information on each spiritmaster.

9. Eliminate the demands of speed and accuracy in copying.

10. Lower the standards of acceptable handwriting.

11. Be aware that spelling will be phonetic for unfamiliar words.

12. Don't clutter the chalkboard.

13. Reinforce all visual directions with verbal cues.

14. Do not embarrass the student by calling on him to read orally. Check comprehension through participation in discussions.

15. In science, focusing with one eye on a microscope slide might cause difficulty. Use a photograph or a binocular telescope.

16. In social studies, students should be asked to work only on maps and charts that are outlined.

17. Encourage the student to use oral and written rehearsal for material that needs to be memorized.

Language Impaired

If the student experiences problems receiving, organizing, or expressing ideas, including difficulty with word meanings, concept formation, and the learning of grammatical rules–

1. Use linguistically similar words to teach spelling concepts.

2. Explain idioms. They convey meanings not indicated by their wording.

3. When using words with multiple meanings, make sure the student knows which one he is to focus on.

4. Provide the meanings of technical terms which are specific to your content area.

5. Explain vocabulary before assigning a chapter to read.

6. Avoid fill-in tests unless a list of choices is provided as retrieval of technical terms, words, concepts may be difficult.

7. Give simple precise directions.

8. Have students repeat directions in his own words.

9. Try to link all new concepts to previously learned categorical knowledge.

Memory Deficits

If the student is unable to remember what things look or sound like, including problems with short-term, long-term, sequential, visual, auditory, and rote memory–

1. Present new material in short incremental steps.

2. Provide for overlearning, using intensive drill when necessary.

3. Encourage the student to put vocabulary words, concepts, number facts, etc., on index cards for continuous review.

4. In math, provide a calculator, multiplication tables, etc., during instruction in a new process in order to avoid interference with learning the new process.

5. Teach all the strategies for multiplication tables, including rhythm, songs, and finger tricks.

6. Make sure that you have the student's undivided attention.

7. Encourage the use of a multisensory approach (visual–auditory–kinesthetic) to learn vocabulary, spelling, names of cities and states, etc.

The above lists provide a guide for classroom teachers for frequent reference during the school year. They also offer insight into why learning disabled students may experience difficulty learning and how they, as teachers, can be a positive influence in diminishing some of the factors that prevent these students from achieving success.

Reprinted with permission from Academic Therapy, (1988) vol. 23 no. 5.

Gifted and Learning Disabled Students

Practical Considerations for Teachers

Timothy J. Landrum

The task of special educators is indeed a difficult one. Defining areas of exceptionality, locating students with special learning needs, identifying those needs, and programming to address them represent a monumental undertaking given the numerous factors that impact on the educational decision-making process. As the scope of special education continues to broaden, and as educators more closely scrutinize individuals, it is inevitable that students are found whose profiles fall under the definition of more than one area of exceptionality. While the process of tailoring each student's instructional program to a specific set of needs is a complex one for any special educator, it takes on even greater complexity when students are multiply handicapped, or present characteristics of more than one exceptionality.

Many combinations of exceptionality have received considerable acceptance (e.g., behaviorally disordered and learning disabled). Such combinations seem to make intuitive sense for educators; indeed, it has been argued that among the mildly handicapped population, students with different categorical labels are in fact more similar than they are different in terms of learning and behavioral characteristics (Hallahan & Kauffman,1988). The same logic does not hold in considering giftedness and learning disabilities. Perhaps because these two exceptionalities do not seem to share any similarities, the notion that students can be both gifted and learning disabled has been difficult for many educators to accept.

The purpose of this paper is to address several issues surrounding the gifted learning disabled (LD) population. Foremost will be a discussion of whether students can be both gifted and learning disabled. Equally important is consideration of where gifted LD students are currently served and how they might be identified. Finally, if there are students who are gifted and learning disabled, and they can be identified as such, how should educators program for their needs? The focus here will be on providing practical suggestions for teachers who work with gifted LD students, regardless of the setting in which they are served.

Giftedness and Learning Disabilities

Certain combinations of handicapping conditions have received considerable attention, and in many cases programming options have been explored to accommodate these students. For example, behaviorally disordered (BD) and learning disabled (LD) students may be served in cross-categorical BD/LD classrooms. Further, in many school districts students may be labeled as both BD and LD. For many educators, this combination seems reasonable, particularly in light of research that has suggested that in addition to their academic deficits, LD students often experience behavioral difficulties, particularly in social skill areas (Hallahan & Kauffman, 1988; Lerner, 1985), and that BD students are likely to experience academic problems in addition to their behavioral deficits (Coutinho, 1986; Scruggs & Mastropieri, 1986).

Much more difficult to understand and thus to some, more difficult to accept is the student who is both gifted and learning disabled (Wolf & Gygi, 1981). That these two exceptionalities seem oppositional makes the gifted LD child among the most difficult to identify and therefore among the most undeserved (Gunderson, Maesch, & Rees, 1988). Before identification and programming concerns can be addressed, however, a definition of "learning disabled and gifted" must be considered.

Two approaches to the definition of gifted and learning disabled students are evident. Are gifted LD students those who are identified as gifted but who also experience specific disabilities in one or more areas? Or are gifted LD students more likely to be placed in special programs for learning disabled students, because their skill deficits in academic areas have inhibited the development of their giftedness? It seems likely that both are true. The following sections provide a brief examination of the LD gifted concept from each perspective.

Giftedness in Learning Disabled Students

Federal regulations accompanying Public Law 94-142 (P.L. 94-142, 1975), The Education for All Handicapped Children Act, provide an operational definition of specific learning disability. These regulations suggest (in part) that a learning disability might be evident in a discrepancy between a student's achievement and intellectual ability in one or more of the following areas: oral expression, listening comprehension, written expression, basic reading skill, reading comprehension, mathematics calculation, or mathematics reasoning (U.S. Office of Education, 1977). Clearly, a child does not need to present problems in all of these areas to be considered learning disabled; indeed, it seems unlikely that many students would experience problems in every area listed. Using this definition of learning disability, it should also be clear that in spite of deficits in one or more of the areas mentioned, students identified as learning disabled might well possess superior skills or abilities in one or more of the other areas. A similar approach to definitions of giftedness provides a framework in which gifted students might also be found to experience learning disabilities.

Learning Disabilities in Gifted Students

Many definitions of giftedness share a similar structure with definitions of learning disabilities. That is, in both cases, students may be considered exceptional if they present *one or more* of an established set of characteristics. Perhaps the most commonly accepted definition of giftedness is the federal definition, first provided in the Marland report (Marland,1972). This definition states that students may be gifted when they display superior skill or ability in general intellectual ability, specific academic aptitude (e.g., math), creative or productive thinking, visual or performing arts, or psychosocial abilities. As with the definition of learning disability, this definition of giftedness does not suggest that gifted students will possess superior aptitudes in each of these areas. From this perspective, then, it should further be clear that students with particular skill in one area (e.g., mathematical reasoning, a "specific academic aptitude") may or may not display similarly high levels of ability in all areas. Thus a student who is considered gifted by virtue of a particular strength might also be considered learning disabled by virtue of deficits in other areas.

This cursory examination of definitions is far from complete; many issues have not been addressed at all. Readers are referred elsewhere for detailed discussions of definitional issues (cf. Foster 1986; Fox & Brody, 1983; Lerner, 1985; Wallace & McLoughlin 1988). It should be apparent, however, that the concept of gifted *and* learning disabled applies to a real segment of the school population. Once it is accepted that students may display characteristics of both giftedness and learning disability, attention can be shifted from debate regarding definitions of who these students are to concerns regarding how they might be identified and how teachers can best meet their unique needs.

Current Placement of Gifted Learning Disabled Students

In addition to providing a backdrop against which students might be seen as both gifted and learning disabled, the previous discussion of definitions should also suggest that gifted LD students are likely to be served in one of two places. If the superior abilities in specific areas are so far above the norm that they overshadow any deficits the student might experience, the student might be placed in a program for gifted students. Conversely, if the learning problems are so severe that the development of the student's superior aptitude in other areas is inhibited, the student is likely to warrant services for students with LD. While this partitioning of gifted LD students seems to fit well with the common special education practice of serving multiply diagnosed students in programs that address the most predominant handicapping condition, it may be that a large group of gifted LD students, perhaps the largest group, is not served at all. The group most likely to go unserved is that group of LD gifted students that is identified as neither gifted nor learning disabled.

Undetected Gifted Learning Disabled Students

To this point the discussion of gifted and learning disabled has paralleled to some extent any discussion of dual diagnosis (e.g., BD/LD). Unlike other conditions, however, giftedness and learning disabilities are likely to work in opposition, that is, to mask each other, rather than to work in combination to produce deleterious effects as would two handicapping conditions. The nature of these two exceptionalities suggests that many students who are both gifted and learning disabled are not likely to be identified at all.

Tannenbaum and Baldwin (1983) note that gifted students are generally expected to complete assignments quickly and accurately, to have good study habits, to score well on tests of achievement, and to obtain good grades. The learning disabled gifted student, they assert, "rarely exhibits any of the learning and behavioral characteristics that schools look for in gifted students" (p. 20). Similarly, gifted LD students are likely to have developed a series of compensatory strategies that allow them to circumvent their disabilities (Rosner & Seymour, 1983; Whitmore & Maker, 1985). For example, Rosner and Seymour (1983) describe a gifted LD man who had completed a master's degree and most of his doctoral work in spite of a reading rate at the second percentile. He explained that he approached reading tasks by scanning paragraphs for familiar words or concepts, and relied on his own knowledge to fill in details about the passage. Clearly the man's superior abilities allowed him to mask a very significant reading weakness throughout his educational career.

Although this particular individual achieved considerable success, it should be obvious that not all gifted LD students can be expected to reach such levels. Perhaps the most underidentified and therefore most undeserved, group of gift d LD students are those whose superior skills mask their learning disability, yet are not sufficient to distinguish the student as gifted. These students are likely to struggle along in regular class settings where their strengths and weaknesses effectively cancel each other out, leaving them to achieve at only average levels. Thus while LD teachers should be aware of the possibility that their students may possess superior abilities in some areas, and gifted educators should be aware that their students might suffer from particular skill deficits, regular educators, it seems, should also be cognizant of the possibility that among their "normally" achieving students they might well find a group of students that is both gifted and learning disabled.

Practical Considerations for Teachers

Decisions regarding how best to serve gifted LD students must take into account existing placement arrangements. Although many educators have argued that gifted LD students require specialized programming to meet their unique needs (Baum, 1988 Daniels, 1983; Whitmore & Maker, 1985), it is also clear that practical limitations make entirely separate programming an unlikely administrative option. Daniels (1983) notes that separate programming for gifted LD students is difficult in part because of the relatively small numbers of gifted LD students to be found at a given grade level or even in a single building. He suggests that establishing special classes across grade levels (e.g., primary gifted LD class for Grades 1 through 3, etc.) might be more feasible. If small numbers were still a problem, cooperative efforts across several schools might be necessary for the program to reach a critical mass; that is, enough students to justify the establishment of a separate program.

Because separate programming for gifted LD students is not likely to develop on a large scale, attention must remain focused on providing for their needs adequately in the environments in which they are currently placed. Each of the settings discussed earlier is considered in the following sections, and suggestions are offered for teachers who encounter gifted and learning disabled students in those settings.

Recommendations for LD Teachers

LD teachers who are responsible for students who have also been identified as gifted must certainly address the needs those students have. Equally important, though, are the LD students not identified as gifted; their giftedness, or at least their areas of strength, may be masked by their learning difficulties. The following suggestions for LD teachers address both concerns:

While remediation efforts should, of course, be a priority, the gifted LD student whose program consists only of remediation is not being served appropriately. Efforts must also address areas of strength.

Reading ability alone should not form the basis of the teacher's assessment of the student's potential. That is, teachers must not assume that poor readers are lacking in other academic areas. The student's cognitive abilities, reasoning skills, and problem solving ability may be intact in spite of difficulty with the reading process itself (Whitmore & Maker, 1985).

LD teachers should be aware of the following characteristics, which may indicate giftedness (Whitmore & Maker, 1985):

1. Exceptional oral language abilities

2. Exceptional analytical ability

3. Remarkable insightfulness, intuition, or perceptiveness

4. Outstanding memory, though not necessarily in all areas

5. Good problem-solving skills

6. Extreme curiosity, or the desire to know and understand things

7. Creativity

While remedial efforts must continue, such efforts might meet with more success if instructional strategies also incorporate identified areas of strength instead of simply focusing on the deficit to be overcome.

Recommendations for Teachers of Gifted Students

Teachers of gifted students may have difficulty in perceiving learning disabilities in their students. Indeed, for students to have been labeled gifted, they must have developed their superior abilities to such an extent that their areas of deficit are not likely to be apparent at all. Nonetheless, the potential exists for such students to suffer from serious learning disabilities. The following suggestions are offered for teachers of gifted students:

Gifted students should not be expected to be superior in all areas. For example, many gifted students read exceptionally well; teachers have come to assume that all gifted students not only read well but also enjoy reading. In fact, some gifted students show little interest in or motivation toward activities that involve extensive or high-level reading assignments.

Students who are gifted and learning disabled are likely to have extreme difficulty in accepting this discrepancy. They may experience great frustration—for example, they might understand higher level, abstract ideas or problems, yet may not have the skills to solve simple mathematical calculations or be able to express their ideas in writing. Senf (1983), in fact, suggests that gifted LD children are more often referred for assessment not because of skill deficits but rather because of the psychological distress resulting from this extreme discrepancy. All teachers must be sensitive to the self-concepts and the social and emotional needs of the gifted LD student. Parents may also benefit from counseling efforts designed to help the child deal with the unique problems of the gifted LD learner.

Enrichment activities must be designed specifically to work around the student's areas of weakness (Baum, 1988). Students should have access to alternative materials for gathering information (e.g., audio and videotape, films, picture books), and should be allowed to present work in a format that is appropriate to their strengths. Rather than traditional written reports, for example, gifted LD students might present oral reports, slide-tape shows, artwork, or dramatic productions to demonstrate their mastery of objectives.

Recommendations for Regular Class Teachers

Regular class teachers have perhaps the most difficult task in terms of dealing with gifted LD students. Gifted LD students who remain in the regular class may not have been identified as either gifted or learning disabled. The regular teacher's responsibility, then, is to be aware that students may have both learning problems and superior abilities; the difficulty, of course, is that each may hide the other. The following suggestions are offered to help the regular class teacher in identifying and dealing with the learning disabled gifted student:

Regular class teachers must be particularly sensitive to the discrepancies likely to be present in students' performance. For example, they should not assume that a particular weakness is an indicator of overall academic weakness. Poor handwriting, difficulty in math computation, or problems with oral reading, should not lead teachers to assume that the student displaying one of these specific problems is uniformly weak in other areas.

Similarly, teachers must not assume that students displaying particular strengths are equally skilled in other areas, even within the same content area. A student may perform math computations with great ease, for example, yet may have great difficulty with problems requiring mathematical reasoning skills.

In addition to wide variability in performance, gifted LD students may also present mild behavioral problems, seem unmotivated, have difficulty following directions, and have trouble getting along with peers (Suter & Wolf, 1987).

Conclusions

This discussion of the learning disabled gifted student has focused primarily on practical considerations for teachers who deal with these students in a variety of settings. The suggestions above reflect the need for increased awareness among educators working with gifted LD students; a major restructuring of current service arrangements, however, is not called for. As Daniels (1983) points out, the number of students who would qualify as both gifted and learning disabled under conventional classification systems is actually quite small. While students so identified may have educational needs that would best be met in separate specialized programs, it seems that a much larger group of students would be excluded from such programs because their academic discrepancies are not great.

The group of students that would be identified as both gifted and learning disabled clearly presents a unique challenge to educators. The need for further research is great if appropriate procedures for identifying and programming for this group are to be developed. The purpose of this paper, however, has been to address concerns regarding those students who experience extreme discrepancies across performance areas yet who may not be identified as gifted and learning disabled. It is not suggested that such students be removed from their current placements, but rather that educators who work with such students be aware of their unique needs and characteristics.

Debate seems certain to continue regarding the notion that students can be both gifted and learning disabled. Such debate, however, seems focused more on administrative placement criteria than on educationally relevant information for teachers who must work with the students in question. As Whitmore and Maker (1985) state, "The first and foremost need is for all educators in regular classrooms as well as in resource or support services roles, to have a more accurate understanding of the characteristics and needs of this special population" (p. 200). In current practice, then, all teachers must remain open to the possibility that gifted learning disabled students might be served in a variety of settings. Whether or not such students are classified as gifted learning disabled, teachers must become skilled not only at recognizing these students, but also at dealing with their unique needs.

References

Baum, S. (1988). An enrichment program for gifted learning disabled students. *Gifted Child Quarterly, 32*, 226-230.

Coutinho, M.J. (1986). Reading achievement of students identified as behaviorally disordered at the secondary level. *Behavioral Disorders, 11*, 200-207.

Daniels, P.R. (1983). Teaching the learning disabled/gifted child. In L.H. Fox, L. Brody, & D. Tobin (Eds.), *Learning disabled/gifted children: Identification and programming* (pp. 153-169). Austin, TX: PRO-ED.

Foster, W. (1986). Giftedness: The mistaken metaphor. In C.J. Maker (Ed.), *Critical issues in gifted education: Defensible programs for the gifted.* Austin, TX: PRO-ED.

Fox, L.H., & Brody, L. (1983). Models for identifying giftedness: Issues related to the learning-disabled gifted child. In L.H. Fox, L. Brody, & D. Tobin (Eds.), *Learning disabled children: Identification and programming* (pp. 101-116). Austin, TX: PRO-ED.

Gunderson, C.W., Maesch, C., & Rees, J.W. (1988). The gifted/learning disabled student. *Gifted Child Quarterly, 31*, 158-160.

Hallahan, D.P., & Kauffman, J.M. (1988). *Exceptional children* (4th ed.). Englewood Cliffs, NJ: Prentice-Hall.

Lerner, J. (1985). *Learning disabilities: Theories, diagnosis, and teaching strategies* (4th ed.). Boston: Houghton Mifflin.

Marland, S.P. (1972). *Education of the gifted and talented* (Report to the Congress of the United States by the U.S. Commissioner of Education). Washington, DC: U.S. Government Printing Office.

P.L. 94-142, The Education for All Handicapped Children Act of 1975. 20 United States Code, sec. 1400-1420.

Rosner, S.L., & Seymour, J. (1983). The gifted child with a learning disability: Clinical evidence. In L.H. Fox, L. Brody, & D. Tobin (Eds.), *Learning disabled/gifted children: Identification and programming* (pp. 77-97). Austin, TX: PRO-ED.

Scruggs, T.E., & Mastropieri, M.A. (1986). Academic characteristics of behaviorally disordered and learning disabled students. *Behavioral Disorders, 11,* 184-190.

Senf, G.M. (1983). The nature and-identification of learning disabilities and their relationship to the gifted child. In L.H. Fox, L. Brody, & D. Tobin (Eds.), *Learning disabled/gifted children: Identification and programming* (pp. 37-49). Austin, TX: PRO-ED.

Suter, D.P., & Wolf, J.S. (1987). Issues in the identification and programming of the gifted/learning disabled child. *Journal for the Education of the Gifted, 10,* 227-237.

Tannenbaum, A.J., & Baldwin, L.J. (1983). Giftedness and learning disability: A paradoxical combination. In L.H. Fox, L. Brody, & D. Tobin (Eds.), *Learning disabled/gifted children: Identification and programming* (pp. 11-36). Austin, TX: PRO-ED.

U.S. Office of Education. (1977). *Assistance to states for education of handicapped children: Procedures for evaluating specific learning disabilities.* Washington, DC: Department of Health, Education, and Welfare.

Wallace, G.E., & McLoughlin, J.A. (1988). *Learning disabilities: Concepts and characteristics* (3rd ed.). Columbus, OH: Merrill.

Whitmore, J.R., & Maker, C.J. (1985). *Intellectual giftedness in disabled persons.* Austin, TX: PRO-ED.

Wolf, J., & Gygi, J. (1981). Learning disabled and gifted: Success or failure? *Journal for the Education of the Gifted, 4,* 199-206.

Timothy J. Landrum, MEd, is currently a doctoral student in special education at the University of Virginia. Address: Timothy J. Landrum, Department of Curriculum, Instruction, and Special Education, Curry School of Education, 235 Ruffner Hall, 405 Emmet St., Charlottesville, VA 22903.

Reprinted with permission from Academic Therapy, May 1989, Pro-Ed, 8700 Shoal Creek Blvd., Austin, TX 78758-6897.

THE GIFTED LEARNING DISABLED CHILD:
A CHALLENGE AND SOME SUGGESTIONS

Joyce N. French

"Hey do you want to know the difference between a cultural anthropologist and a physical anthropologist?"

"Sure I'd really like to know the difference. Tell me."

Billy did. He established a common frame or reference for the two terms, defined the differences between them in view of function and outcome, and then proceeded to tell me how he was trying to be a physical anthropologist studying about the Indians who used to live in his area, and about what happened to them because of the land, the weather, and *everything* like *that*. He thought he might try being a cultural anthropologist sometime, especially if he ever studied his two teen-age sisters.

Billy brought up this topic in my first session with him, while we were doing some informal diagnostic work on his reading and writing skills. He had been referred to the Learning Center because he was having considerable difficulty in all areas involving reading and writing. "The session took place in March of Billy's third grade year. He was nine years, one month old.

The kind of high level conceptual thinking revealed in this conversation had, in fact, been documented by the school in a psychological report. On the WISC-R (Weschsler Intelligence Scale for Children-Revised) he demonstrated considerable strength in the verbal areas, particularly in subtests dealing with vocabulary, abstract reasoning, and comprehension. Performance areas were substantially lower with weaknesses in picture completion and object assembly. Even with a significant discrepancy between verbal and performance scores, his full scale I.Q. was in the Superior range.

Not gifted, you say. Perhaps, but as Maker (1977) points out there are difficulties with using an inflexible I .Q. score of 130, for example, to identify gifted children where there is a handicap involved for it may affect whether the I.Q. is *"an accurate assessment of his potential"* (p 62). She further suggests that for learning disabled children "the more abstract skills are less likely to be impaired than such abilities as memory and perception"(p. 67).

This certainly seemed to be the case with Billy. His abstract skills, both during testing and in his daily performance, were in no way impaired. School reports repeatedly noted a knowledge of and deep interest in social studies, science and the larger world, and an even and consistent effort to "work conscientiously, trying hard to succeed" However, his very inquisitiveness, one sensed, was a handicap from the school's perspective for a boy lacking so many basic skills.

Perception and memory generally showed up as weaknesses according to the school. Performance scores were significantly lower on the WISC-R than the verbal scores.

The school examiner stated:

> Billy showed specific weaknesses in the visual perceptual area which have direct implications for reading. He had some relative difficulty in identifying missing elements in pictures suggesting a weakness in visualization. Visualization motor manipulative tasks dealing with the part-whole relationship were also a bit for him reflecting some weakness in spatial orientation and in differentiating and reconstructing configurations. In reading, Billy may encounter difficulty in structural analysis of words, seeing the relationships between symbols, and breaking down unfamiliar words into familiar parts.
>
> The visual memory subtest on the Slingerland Screening test showed inversions and transpositions, as well as a weakness in visual memory. The Bender Visual-Motor Gestalt Test yielded results significantly below age expectation with errors of distortion, rotation and integration.

The examiner concluded:

> Billy is a boy of superior intellectual ability whose current reading difficulties are due to a specific weakness in visual perception. This is manifested in difficulties in visualization, in spatial orientation and direction and in differentiating and reconstructing configurations. Billy is experiencing some anxiety concerning his achievement. Billy's strengths are in the verbal area as he shows a very high capacity for verbal and experiential learning and a high level of general comprehension. Billy's enthusiasm and interest combined with his inner resources and intellectual ability provide an optimistic outlook for effective functioning.

The implications of these test findings, unfortunately, were clear in Billy's performance on school tasks. An educational evaluation painted a picture of a child having considerable difficulty in school, directly related to the memory and perceptual problems outlined in the psychological report. Reading and writing responses were characterized by sequencing and reversal errors in both letters and words and by inversions of letters. Sound-symbol relationships, particularly vowels, had not been mastered in spite of what must have seemed like a lot of instruction to Billy.

Billy was reading on almost any scale used, between 1.5 and 2 years below grade level. This was a boy with a full scale I.Q. even with low performance scores, in the Superior range! Billy always understood what he managed to read but on a level considerably below his expectancy level.

The school summed up its evaluation of Billy by stating that he had superior intellectual ability but his reading difficulties could be attributed to a specific problem in visual perception. A learning disabled child! But, also a gifted child, using Maker's definition. Renzulli (1978) in re-examining giftedness states:

> *Giftedness consists of an interaction among three clusters of human traits—these clusters begin above average general abilities high levels of task commitment and high levels of creativity. Gifted and talented children are among those possessing or capable of developing this composite set of traits and applying them to any potentially valuable area of human performance. (p 261)*

The word *capable* allows us to include Billy in this group of gifted children. However, unless Billy's handicaps are overcome he might never develop and apply these traits to their fullest.

The kinds of hypotheses and theories that have been generated by the field of information processing can provide some ground rules and guidelines for instructing Billy, that as yet uncounted and, according to Maker (1976), *"relatively neglected group of individuals—The gifted and talented who happen to be handicapped"* (p. 24). Wittrock (1979) in examining how learners process information presented during instruction proposed an active role for the learner. The critical focus is placed on how actively the learner can deal with the relation between information presented and his past experience. Wittrock proposes three possibilities: the learner is *"unlikely to generate relevant relations"* (p 10) unless the relations are made explicit; the learner *"can and will construct relevant relations....when asked to generate them"* (p 10); the learner can *"spontaneously generate relevant relations between information and experience"* (p 10).

This cognitive approach to instruction can give us some very useful and practical guidelines for working with all children, but particularly with a child like Billy. Too often, with learning disabled children in particular, we become so involved with skill deficiencies and needs and with instruction in these areas that we overlook the real strengths and aptitudes of the child. In defining strengths and aptitudes we must consider both stores or knowledge and vocabulary and how information is processed and how relationships are constructed.

Billy, like most gifted children, had substantial stores of knowledge and an impressive vocabulary, and could spontaneously generate concrete and abstract relationships between past information and experiences and new information. Both test scores and teacher observations supported the notion that Billy was using these considerable strengths in processing general information from his environment. Our immediate concern was to structure our instructional program so Billy could use these strengths in mastering reading and writing skills.

The original report from the school suggested that "Billy's reading disability involves both the auditory and visual modalities. Though the auditory channel is the stronger of the two, it cannot be considered a real source of strength. Billy does appear to gain reinforcement through kinesthetic techniques, as noted by his teachers." The program suggested should involve all of these modalities.

The approach taken by the school both in terms or diagnostic and proposed remediation focused mostly on perceptual functioning. However, if we view learning as involving the utilization cognitive skills, memory and motivation as well as perceptual skills to *organize and understand* information (Wittrock 1979), then a perceptual approach suggested appears too limited. A larger focus was needed using his stores of knowledge and vocabulary, his ability to generate relationships and to use relationships generated by others, his inquisitiveness and his dedication to complete a task. The sound symbol relationships used in reading and spelling were taught to Billy, through the use of categories and relation ships. R-controlled vowels, for example, were introduced by comparing and contrasting the auditory and visual aspects of ar and or. A word was dictated and Billy decided which of the target letter pairs the word contained and wrote the word in the appropriate column. He thought of his own words and put them in the correct category. He began to see and understand a visual and auditory pattern and became motivated to make up his own nonsense words. Billy was generating and using a relationship between information and experience. *Er, ir* and *ur* were introduced. Reinforcement took place by having Billy choose words from his lists and use as many as he could in a creative sentence.

> "*Instruction involves the stimulation of relations between the stimuli and stored memories by inducing verbal or imaginal elaborations...*
>
> *In studies testing or applying this model, sizable gains have regularly been produced by having learners generate semantic relations between information and memory.*" (Wittrock,p.9)

Every activity used with Billy in some way involved the element of meaning and the task of developing or generating relationships between new information and pervious knowledge,as well as the use of his creativity and inquisitiveness. Billy was becoming very frustrated by his inability to read words and content at an appropriate intellectual and interest level. Therefore, rather than teach him vowels and vowel combinations solely in single syllable words, we elected to use multi-syllable words that were already in his speaking vocabulary, such as anthropology. Much emphasis was placed on the use of context. Billy was taught syllabication rules which he learned to apply with multi-syllable words with little difficulty. In fact, he was intrigued with the logic of applying rules and was enormously rewarded by being able to read interesting words. We combined instruction in syllabication with the use of the meaning through cloze technique. The following is an example of a cloze passage, used with Billy in which difficult words were omitted to encourage him to use context.

"I like to read about anthropology. I like to read about _____ anthropology which is the study of how man's life is *changed by the world around him.* _____ *anthropology is the study of* _____." Billy was encouraged to verbalize his thinking process. *"How could you divide the long words into syllables? What word would go in the first blank? How do you know that? Here's the word physical. How do you know this word stands for /physical/? Can you think of another word that starts with phys? Good, write it here underneath the word physical. What do they both mean? What do they have in common? How would you spell he word cultural? What letter pairs stand for the r-controlled vowel sound you hear in the word? How can you finish the last sentence?"* Not all these questions were asked, for much of the information was volunteered by Billy. The teacher interacted with Billy in such a way as to get Billy to "construct relevant relations . . . when asked to generate them" and to have him "spontaneously generate relevant relations between information and experience"(Wittrock,p. 10).

If the sole criteria used in judging the suitability of vocabulary words and reading materials had been readability formulas, then much of the material actually chosen for Billy might have been considered inappropriate. However, as a recent study by Belloni and Jongsma (1978) indicated "students transcended their frustration levels when reading materials that were highly interesting to them"(p. 108). When passages which were two to four grade levels above the mean reading level of the sample were given to low-achieving adolescents, "the *students comprehended the* high interest passages significantly better than they com*prehended the low interest passages."(p.* 108). Billy, understandably, found almost all reading material that was at his reading level to be of very low interest. He was, however, highly motivated to read high level books dealing with subjects of interest to him, and used all the available cue systems previous knowledge and concepts, vocabulary, syllabication rules, context and probably grammar and sentence structure–to read and comprehend. Suddenly he was reading and was interested in reading. We had tapped the "motivational mechanisms" involved in learning.

Recommendations to the school included the kinds of general and specific help already outlined that Billy was receiving from us. In addition, suggestions were made to expand reading instruction to include critical reading, with an analysis of the various forms of written organization, such as enumerative, cause and effect, comparison and contrast, and sequential. We encouraged the school to have Billy both read and then write his own paragraphs, eventually working into longer units using the various forms of organization as a cue system for generating the needed relationships. In every activity the recommendation was made to encourage Billy to use a variety of questioning techniques. Billy's ability to generate hypotheses and relationships on his own must form the foundation for his overcoming and, where needed, compensate for the disabilities he displayed so clearly in the third grade.

Billy made great progress in 2 years. On the Metropolitan Achievement test given in March of Billy's fifth grade year he scored 5.4 in word knowledge and 5.9 in reading. The Spache Diagnostic Reading Scales given at the same time indicated an instructional level of 7.5 and an independent level of 6.5. The Stanford Diagnostic

Reading Test, Brown Level, administered in April of the same year, gave him scores of 8.2 auditory vocabulary, 4.8 literal comprehension, 6.7 inferential comprehension with a total reading level of 5.6. While we cannot directly compare all these scores, they do indicate much the same kind of conclusion. After two year's work Billy is reading on grade level. Spelling and writing skills, although considerably improved, remain an area of concern. The latest Learning Center report to Billy's parents states "spelling and written expression have not yielded as successfully as reading to remediation and they continue to be Billy's weak areas."

However, perhaps the most important change in Billy has been his view of himself. Bond (1979), in summarizing a body of research on self-concept and reading achievement, states "*reading failure* and low self-concept may stem initially from different causes, but the strong positive relationship between them suggests that they affect each other in a synergistic manner, each serving to fuel the other. Add to this Maker's (1977) statement that "most *gifted persons, whether handicapped or not are highly self critical and will set extremely high goals for their own performance"(p.34)*. Billy did set very high goals and consistently found himself wanting. Each attempt at reading and writing reinforced his negative view of himself as did the comparison he and others made of his performance and that of his peers. This negative self-image appears to be a common characteristic of the gifted learning disabled child (Maker, 1977, p.67).

Once Billy began to see some results of his work with us, he eagerly participated in every activity, frequently, in fact, telling us why he needed to do it. The transition to using cursive handwriting was initiated by Billy. He had observed that children who wrote in cursive were faster than he was and he had heard one of his teachers say that she had seen cursive straighten out reversals in writing. That was all he needed.

When progress became tangible and Billy was able to read independently, particularly in areas of interest to him, he requested that he come only once a week instead of twice a week. " *I know I can do it, and I need time for my own projects now that I'm doing better I had better taper off though and come once a week of a while longer*". His new found abilities and self-confidence became reflected in his school work, his peer relations and his whistling. Billy always whistled when things were going well!

The prognosis for Billy is not without some concerns, but it is considerably improved over two years. We will never know what would have happened to him if instruction had been limited to weak *auditory and visual modalities with reinforcement from kinesthetic techniques*. However, he certainly has made substantial progress, both in skills and in self-confidence by using his very special strengths, not just in knowledge and vocabulary, but also in how he is able to process information and generate relationships on his own. His ability to generate hypotheses and relationships between the known and the unknown has enabled him to overcome or compensate for many of the problems arising out of his learning disability.

Billy is, in fact, a real child. But, in addition, he represents a group of our most promising and overlooked handicapped children, that *"group of individuals—the gifted and talented who happen to be handicapped.*(Maker, 1976, p. 24). By approaching skill instruction from this perspective, not from the perspective of continual drill, ditto sheets, and drawing in sand, we can engage the very particular strengths of our gifted learning disabled children in overcoming their particular handicaps.

In teaching these children, the basic reading and writing skills they must have in order to utilize their talents, we must:

■ Provide rules and categories by means of which the student can generate relationships between past information and new information or provide examples which he can use to formulate their own rules and categories.

■ Use materials which are meaningful, interesting, intellectually appropriate and motivating.

■ Plan activities which demand an active response by the student requiring that he attend to the task, use relevant schematic and generate relationships.

References

Belloni, Loretta Frances & Jongsma, Eugene A. "The Effects of Interest on Reading Comprehension of Low-Achieving Students." *Journal of Reading.* 1978. 22. 106-109.

Bond. Frances "Self-concept and Reading Achievement." *The Allyn and Bacon Reading Newsletter.* 1979. 5. 1-2.

Maker. C. June. "Searching for Giftedness and Talent in children with Handicaps." *The school Psychology Digest.* 1976. 5. 24-36.

Maker. C. June. *Providing Programs for the Gifted Handicapped.* Reston, Virginia: Council for Exceptional Children. 1977.

Renzulli. Joseph S. "What Makes Giftedness? Re-examining a Definition." *Phi Delta Kappan.* 1978. 60. 180-261.

Wittrock. M. C. "The Cognitive Movement in Instruction. *"Educational Researcher."* 1979. 8. 5-11.

Reprinted with permission of Roeper Review, vol. IV, no. 3, 1982, P.O. Box 329, Bloomfield Hills, MI 48103.

CASE STUDIES

Susan Baum
Linda J. Emerick
Gail N. Herman
John Dixon

Described below are composite studies of individual students with whom we worked over the past four years. They provide illustrative profiles of the different kinds of gifts found in high-ability learning-disabled children and how they were nurtured.

Case Study 1: A Visual Thinker

In defending his proposal to include instruction in visual communication in the school curriculum, Howard Foster (1979) states that a visual medium such as film or video is as much a "created and controlled" form of communication as the printed word. Yet, many LD children have difficulty in dealing with the printed word and do not have the opportunity to use or communicate their thoughts in other ways. The LD child who is visually oriented has the ability and the desire to use a visual rather than a verbal or written mode to solve problems, generate ideas, and communicate those solutions and ideas. It is possible that a change of emphasis for the identification of abilities, method of instruction, and variety of learning experiences from a linguistic to a visual format will enable certain gifted LD children to display their true capabilities.

Identification. Aaron was a fourth grade student in an LD resource room program. He was noted for his disinterested, hostile behavior and short attention span. He often withdrew from activities involving group interaction and seldom completed work assigned in the resource room or the regular classroom. As part of a special enrichment project, Aaron's resource class had a guest speaker who gave an hour-long presentation on film production and animation. As the visitor prepared to begin the class, Aaron moved his chair from the second row to the back of the room. Sitting with his arms folded across his chest and a scowl on his face, he shouted to everyone that this was going to be very boring.

During the presentation on film and animation, Aaron's behavior underwent noticeable and observable changes. As the explanations and visual examples of the presentation progressed, Aaron moved from one empty chair to another until he was seated directly in front of the presenter. He showed a particular interest in the creation of special effects for movies, describing examples of scenes he had seen in films as much as three years previously. He offered suggestions for other ways in which effects could be developed and became extremely impatient with other students who were not as quick or as eager to understand the explanations or Aaron's ideas. He began sketching his ideas on the blackboard and physically tried to show the class what he wanted them to "see." The presentation ended with

Aaron following the speaker out of the classroom, continuing to ask questions as he helped carry equipment and presentation materials.

In a later conversation with the presenter, Aaron's teacher commented that she had never seen him so excited or interested before - "It was as if you (the presenter) and Aaron spoke the same language." She expressed her amazement at the original ideas Aaron had shared in class: "He was the last child I would have called creative."

Aaron displayed many of the characteristics of a child with potential for gifted behavior in the area of visual communication. Among these characteristics were: an intense interest in visual forms of communication; a preference for problem-solving and communicating using a visual mode; the ability to quickly grasp complex concepts related to the visual mode; the ability to generate a variety of unique ideas related to this area; and an exceptionally strong and accurate visual memory. The observation of these characteristics during the general enrichment activity led Aaron's teacher to recommend him for participation in educational activities directly related to his areas of strength.

Motivation. Frustrations with past educational experiences had left Aaron unmotivated to participate in school. It took special measures to reverse this attitude. Aaron was placed with a mentor with expertise in visual communication (in this instance, video production) for participation in a small group project. Aaron began the first session with the group and the mentor in much the same manner as his first encounter with the guest speaker—belligerent and defensive. His first statement to the other children and the mentor revealed this attitude: "I know why I'm here . . . I have problems no one can do anything about. I can't write and you can't make me." The mentor immediately responded by stating that Aaron was in this class because there were some things he could do well and Aaron would not need to be able to write. In fact, the mentor said, it would be better if Aaron did not write at all. Aaron's first response was disbelief followed quickly by relief and delight. He continued to seek reassurance that his inability to read and write well would not be a matter of concern for the mentor.

It was not expected that Aaron would overcome years of frustration and become motivated to participate simply because someone said his weaknesses would be overlooked and his strengths emphasized. The mentor used a second strategy, a more direct approach, to help Aaron want to develop his abilities. The mentor stated that Aaron's group had come together to form a video production company. Although the students knew nothing about making a video, the mentor assured them they would learn all they needed to know. In addition, the students were told the video was not just an exercise or class assignment—they would have five weeks in which to have the production ready for viewing by an audience made up of their classmates, teachers, parents, and anyone else who wanted to see the video. By establishing the need for a real product for a real audience, the mentor created a purpose and a relevancy that began Aaron's learning experience on a positive note. Aaron actively and enthusiastically worked with the other students to generate ideas for the story which would form the basis for the video. It was interesting to note that

Aaron, who supposedly had a short attention span, insisted on having lunch in the classroom so the group could continue to work on developing the story line.

Instructional mode: The young film-maker. Once a specific goal had been set for Aaron which was based on his strengths and interests, instruction was modified to emphasize the pictorial mode of communication he preferred. To aid him in developing and organizing ideas, Aaron was taught how to design a storyboard—a figural representation of various scenes which serves as a guide for filming. Although it was not necessary for Aaron to be an accomplished artist, it was necessary for him to be able to depict ideas he "saw" in his mind through a series of rough sketches. Aaron was given the responsibility for developing the ideas for certain scenes in the video and he eagerly went about creating the sequence, applying cinemagraphic techniques he had learned from the mentor. Although he was initially impatient with the time involved in working through the various scenes, the use of a storyboard enabled him to organize and communicate his ideas. He began to analyze and anticipate lack of continuity in the visual version before the mentor or any other group members questioned him.

In an interesting development, Aaron began to use writing to communicate and elaborate his ideas. While working on a portion of his storyboard, he asked the mentor to draw his idea for him. The angles he wanted to use were too complex for him to draw accurately. He commented that the camera person would not be able to tell exactly what the scene would need to look like. The mentor refused to draw the scene. Aaron then asked if he could write directions on the storyboard itself for the camera person. He was given permission to do this and shown a copy of a professional storyboard which showed that written directions were indeed acceptable. Aaron began laboriously writing directions, often misspelling the words.

During the next class, Aaron unfolded a piece of paper covered with handwriting. He showed the page to the mentor, explaining that he now had his directions written correctly. He had become so frustrated that he had gone home and recorded his ideas on a tape recorder. He had asked his father to "take dictation" from the tape and write down what Aaron had said. Aaron had then recopied the sentences from his father's transcription because he wanted to show the ideas were really "all" his. Aaron's negative attitudes toward reading and writing were beginning to diminish.

Case Study 2: A Spatial Thinker

Dixon (1983) describes spatial children as having spatial-mechanical thinking ability. This ability "involves the capacity to put the world together inside one's head such that all things relate to all others in precisely understood ways" (p. 9). He also states that "there are many children who are very capable in their spatial and mechanical understanding of the world around them and at the same time markedly deficient in their efforts to learn reading and writing" (p. 8). Such children seem to be absorbed in hobbies such as model building, sculpture, building and designing with materials like Lego bricks, and woodworking. The structures they create show high levels of creative talent. In fact, these students may be our future architects and engineers. Gardner (1983) attributes these abilities to individuals who demonstrate strength in spatial intelligence.

Identification. Brad, a shy fifth grader, is a spatial thinker. No one paid much attention to Brad as he appeared each day in the resource room for learning disabled students. He often forgot his homework, rarely spoke up, and in a sense, plodded along from day to day receiving assistance in understanding and completing assignments in the area of language arts. His teacher and others felt there was more ability in this child than test scores or class performance indicated. However, nothing in the classroom seemed to excite or motivate him. Nothing, that is, until the arrival of Lego bricks in the classroom. Brad built one project after another. He never ran out of ideas. Soon he was giving up lunch hours to teach other children how to build intricate designs with the Lego bricks. His projects showed creative and superior abilities in spatial design. The dramatic change in his personality from shy, passive, and withdrawn to outgoing, helpful, and excited convinced us that indeed he was a spatial thinker and needed advanced opportunities in spatial design.

Motivation. Until that time, Brad had invested little effort in school-related assignments. However, entrance into the special program changed that. The students in the program were personally invited to build models for the Lego Corporation. These models were to be exhibited in the Boston Children's Museum as part of an exhibit on transportation. Although Brad was given time to work on his project in the resource room for gifted students, extra time was available if he successfully completed classroom assignments. Not only did the quality of his academic work improve, but the time he needed to complete his assignments also decreased. Brad's mood improved markedly during the weeks he worked on his product, an 18-wheeler truck, complete with a separate tractor and trailer. The trailer was mounted on an appropriate platform and pivoted to facilitate a wide arc of movement. At the end of its two-foot-long trailer was a gate that opened and closed by means of a pulley. The design was original and he put much time and effort into each detail. Often he would become frustrated when he could not get his hands to create what his mind perceived. But, because the goal was important, he would start over (maybe a few days later) and work the problems through. In fact, he was his own staunchest critic.

Instructional mode: The young engineer. These students were given special training by an engineer from the Lego Corporation. He explained to the group how an engineer gets ideas and how designs evolve. He gave the students construction activities to teach them creative thinking skills, especially flexibility. In addition, he explained how the principles of calculus and physics were applied in the building process. Brad could not believe that engineers first "mess around" with a specific medium in order to come up with a plan. Ideas, skills, and competencies evolved from experimentation with the bricks first. Interestingly, when Brad felt that he didn't have a clear enough picture in his mind of the exact details in his creations, he insisted on more research. He spent hours studying pictures, models or actual vehicles to generate better ideas for product improvement.

118

When the Lego Corporation chose his truck for the exhibit, Brad was ecstatic. Pride in his achievements made him value the effort he expended on his finished project. Instead of viewing himself generally as a failure, he had a new respect for his abilities. In fact, one day after being reminded for the tenth time not to forget his homework, he proudly asserted, "You know, maybe I don't always remember to bring in my math assignments, but, boy, do I know how to do engineering. I can figure out how to create arches from square pieces, how to get the base to be stronger. I figure it out by trying out different ideas." The new feelings of self-worth spread to other areas of Brad's life. He would ask teachers questions when he didn't understand a concept in class. He volunteered to be in the drama club and was in charge of set design. Yes, he even began to remember his math book—on some days, that is!

Case Study 3: A Kinesthetic/Personal Thinker

Some gifted learning-disabled students may find a "home" in dramatic expression. According to Gardner (1983), actors often possess high ability in kinesthetic and personal intelligence. Kinesthetic intelligence refers to the "ability to use one's body in highly differentiated and skilled ways, for expressive as well as goal-directed purposes. . ."

The word "kinesthetic" has its roots in two Greek Words: "kinein," meaning to move; and "esthesia," a capacity for sensation or feeling (Flexner, 1987), especially of the sense organs located in the muscles, vicera, tendons, and joints which are stimulated by bodily movements, tensions, and emotions. The second part of the word has evolved into our word "aesthetic" which refers to a responsiveness to the beautiful. Literally, we can say children gifted in the kinesthetic area are able to perceive, feel, remember, and respond to the motion and emotions experienced in their environment. The personal intelligence, according to Gardner (1983) refers to the abilities to understand interpersonal relations in a social context as well as the ability to recall and use one's own "feeling life." Actors, storytellers, and mimes are often able to notice other people's moods, temperaments, motivations, and intentions. Thorndike referred to this as a "social intelligence" and Guilford called it skill with "behavioral content" (Guilford, 1970).

Students with strengths in these areas might become counselors, politicians, lawyers, probation officers, actors, social workers, supervisors, storytellers, teachers, news broadcasters, or mimes who are very capable of decoding or encoding verbal and nonverbal messages in various contexts.

Identification. Jim was a sixth grader who demonstrated talent in kinesthetic-personal thinking. His talent wasn't recognized or nurtured until his school participated in a gifted/LD project. He seemed to be "hyperactive," more energetic than most students his age. He was very knowledgeable about a wide range of subjects—from national elections to characters on TV and in movies. He would talk about why characters behaved as they did. Jim had a great deal of trouble in reading and writing skills as well as following verbal directions. For the last two years, his parents and teachers had noticed a decline in his enjoyment of school and an increase in inappropriate behavior.

Because dramatic expression was a preferred mode of communication for many gifted/LD students, an artist in residence (storyteller and mime) who was also a consultant in gifted education, trained the LD and GT teachers to spot above-average ability in dramatic expression. The artist helped teachers use activities and a behavioral checklist related to this thinking mode to identify gifted learning-disabled children. One activity used to spot dramatic talent in the kinesthetic, personal areas was "King of this Land."

In this activity, students formed a circle. One person stepped into the circle using a character walk and said, "I am king (or queen) of this land." The statement was repeated several times with eye contact and vocal variations. Then the teacher tapped a willing second person from the circle. This person tapped the first king on the shoulder and said, "Excuse me, but there must be some mistake. I am king (or queen) of this land." The first child returned to his place in the circle. The game continued. Each successive student tried to create a new king or queen character, to behave with nobility, firmness, or with great poise, etc., while stating, "I am king (or queen) of this land."

Using a dramatic expression checklist, adapted from Renzulli et. al. (1976), Jim's teacher was able to spot students who participated in "King of this Land" with enthusiasm, who volunteered, captured the group's attention when speaking or "hamming it up," or who displayed exceptional poise. The teacher noticed those who used facial expression easily, those who had a large number of original ideas, and those who could convey the mood or temperament of the character. Jim was one of those students.

In other activities, Jim also demonstrated exceptional ability in character motivation and mimetic action. He was able to isolate body parts in crisp, clear movements and to create reasons for characters' actions. We knew Jim was committed when he came in days later with a tape recording of a story idea he had created from a character he developed during the "King of this Land" identification activity. Jim had the voice of a jester and of a king clearly delineated. He also had created sound effects using his voice for the thunderstorms and kitchen utensils for sounds of battle. Continuing interest was evident. Jim created all of this outside of the school environment.

Motivation. At the first meeting of the program, the mentor explained to Jim that he was chosen because he showed talent for dramatic expression. Jim became particularly excited about the possibility of performing in the State Storytelling Festival organized by the mentor. Since Jim showed exceptional abilities in the areas of oral language, character development, and body movement, the mentor encouraged him to polish one of his stories.

120

Jim's parents said his selection to participate in the special program "did more for him than anything else in his school career." They noticed a big difference in his attitude toward school and family. He was happier and more willing to give brothers and sisters "credit" for THEIR achievements. And, they said, he wanted to go to school. But, as sometimes occurs in special programs, Jim's focus on his interest area interfered with his remedial program. When his LD teacher explained that he would have even more time to spend on it after he finished his assigned work, Jim began to respond favorably by completing work. It is important to note that the teacher never threatened to take away the student's time in his area of strength.

Instructional mode: The young storyteller. After a period of exploration with theatre games, mime activities, story starters, and experiments with percussion instruments for sound effects, Jim was encouraged to practice his chosen story in depth. Jim needed to find a method of remembering his story without memorizing it so that it could be told within a six-minute time frame and so that it would seem fresh each time he told it. Two methods which helped him were visual mapping and the incorporation of mimetic movements, facial expression, and gestures with his characterizations and narration. These techniques served as mnemonic devices. The visual map, a graphic depiction of the story's settings and important events, served as a picture in his mind's eye. The movements and gestures were kinesthetic cues which linked one emotional event with the next in the story. These helped Jim to keep the story in control. He was now ready for performance techniques.

He practiced the beginning of his story while standing, sitting, and moving around freely to find the most comfortable delivery. He practiced using eye contact and looking at the tops of people's heads to keep from becoming distracted. Since there would be a microphone at the Festival, he practiced with a microphone. During feedback sessions, Jim tried some of the other students' suggestions, discarding some while keeping others. The results showed great variety of movement and voice. Jim was acting like a practicing professional storyteller, focusing his attention, sensitivity, and creativity on the possible effect his words and nonverbal behavior might have on his intended audience.

Jim did attend the State Storytelling Festival and shared his story with students from many other schools. His devotion to his art form was evident from the amount of time and concentration he gave to it. His talent in storytelling was apparent from his sensitive delivery of the narration and his clearly delineated characters and mimetic actions. But, most importantly, his talent was expressed without ever writing or reading a word. His gifts were utilized for the first time in his school career.

Conclusion

All three case studies illustrate what can happen to gifted learning-disabled children when their talents are identified and nurtured. Results include an increased willingness on the part of the student to put forth effort to complete tasks. Unsuitable classroom behaviors that impede learning, such as disruptive tendencies, shyness, inattentiveness or short attention span, task avoidance and manipulation tactics, are greatly diminished when the children are actively engaged in creative production. But, most important to these special students is that, perhaps for the only time in their lives, they were singled out and respected for their gifts. Such attention in the long run may contribute more to their success in life than equal efforts to remediate basic skills. Although such a bold prediction is subject to empirical validation, the first step is to provide enriching programs and allow gifted learning-disabled children to create, learn, and grow! Let us remember the words of Carl Jung, "The creative mind plays with things it loves" (Lincoln & Suid, 1986).

References

Baum, S. (1988). An enrichment program for gifted learning disabled students. *Gifted Child Quarterly, 32*, 226-230.

Baum, S. (1984). Meeting the needs of learning disabled gifted students. *Roeper Review, 7*, 16-19.

Dixon, J. (1983). *Spatial child*. Springfield, IL: Charles C. Thomas.

Flexner, S.B. (Ed.). (1987). *The Random House dictionary of the English language*. New York: Random House.

Foster, H. (1979). *The new literacy: The language of film and television*. Urbana, IL: The National Council of Teachers of English.

Gardner, H. (1983). *Frames of mind: The theory of multiple intelligences*. New York: Basic Books, Inc.

Guilford, J.P. (1970). Traits of creativity. In P.E. Vernon (Ed.), *Creativity*. Baltimore: Penguin Books.

Lincoln, W., & Suid, M. (1986). *Quotations for teachers*. Palo Alto, CA: Dale Seymour.

Rabinovitch, A. (1977). Animal farm. In H. Myklebust (Ed.), *Progress in learning disabilities*. New York: Greene & Stratton.

Renzulli, J.S. (1977). *The enrichment triad model: A guide for developing defensible programs for the gifted and talented*. Mansfield Center, CT: Creative Learning Press.

Renzulli, J.S., Smith, L.H., White, A.J., Callahan, C.M., Hartman, R.K. (1976). *Scales for rating the behavioral characteristics of superior students*. Mansfield Center, CT: Creative Learning Press.

Schiff, M., Kaufman, N., & Kaufman, A. (1981). Scatter analysis of the WISC-R profiles for LD children with superior intelligence. *Journal of Learning Disabilities, 14*, 400-404.

Torrance, E.P. (1982). Growing up creatively gifted with learning disabilities. In W. Cruickshank and J.W. Lerner (Eds.), *Coming of age*. Syracuse, NY: Syracuse University Press.

Wechsler, D. (1974). *Wechsler intelligence scale for children - revised*. New York: Psychological Corporation.

Whitmore, J.R. (1980). *Giftedness, conflict and underachievement*. Boston: Allyn & Bacon.

Whitmore, J.R., & Maker, J. (1985). *Intellectual giftedness in disabled persons*. Rockville. MD: Aspen Publications.

Excerpted from the article "Identification, programs and enrichment strategies for gifted learning disabled youth", Roeper Review, vol. 12, no. 1, pp 50-53. Reprinted with permission from Roeper Review, P.O. Box 329, Bloomfield Hills, MI 48103.

TEACHING TEST TAKING SKILLS

Rosalind W. Rothman
Jill Cohen

Test-taking skills—a common problem for language impaired, learning disabled students! The issue becomes more critical for students who are mainstreamed and must perform as their counterparts do in the mainstreamed classroom. Yet, where in the school curriculum are test-taking skills specifically taught?

The past decade has ushered in a plethora of literature related to study skills, organizational skills, research skills, and writing skills (Alley, G. & Deshler, D.1979; Devine, T.G. 1981; Schanzer, S. & Wohlman, J. 1979; Slade, D.L. 1986). Yet, careful scrutiny indicates that the literature does not offer specifics related to *how* to study and *take* a test as much as it offers information related to test success and failure as affected by anxiety or motivation, alternatives to standardized test taking, untimed vs. timed tests, and culture-free tests (King-Fun, L.A. 1974; Pullis, M. 1983; Raskind, L.T. & Nagle, R.J. 1980; Zatz, S. & Chassin, L. 1985). Test fairness, reliability, and validity are questions ever debated by professionals who work with special children; yet, like it or not, at this present date, tests are a reality of our educational system, and LD youngsters must adhere to educational requirements.

Some Basic Problems

Educators are now aware of the need to teach basic study skills such as outlining and notetaking, and publishers have produced countless supplementary books in an effort to instruct students (Mann, L., Goodman, L. & Wiederholt, J.L. 1978; Mercer, C. 1987). It is known, however, that learning disabled students cannot, for the most part, generalize and have difficulty in the application of knowledge (Johnson, D.J. & Myklebust, H. 1967). As a result, we must question the efficacy of assuming that a student can make the transition from a supplementary workbook to a classroom text, to a reference book, or to notes from a specific lecture.

Success on a test includes not only an organized plan of study, but efficient gathering of material to be studied. The procedure begins with the material specifically required by the teacher, or the curriculum for the grade, or the subject matter specifically needed for accountability. Remediation, therefore, in terms of notetaking, study, lecture, and written expression skills should utilize the student's textbooks, classroom materials, and notes. Teacher's guides and current literature can offer information on how to study, but for the most part they ignore the critical element of what to study and the integration of how and what, which is most crucial for success.

Test Variation at Different Ages

Both elementary school children and secondary students take standardized tests. There is, however, a difference in the types of tests given at these levels. In elementary school, students primarily take exams based on rote memory or fill-in with word banks. In secondary school, students take a variety of exams: multiple choice, true and false, fill-in (without word banks), short answer, and essay. Students also are faced with chapter exams, unit exams, and cumulative midterms and finals. For these tests, rote memory is not sufficient.

Teachers in the upper grades may announce an exam, tell the students to study the text and their notes and to be prepared to write an essay on a given topic. Such teachers assume that the students have been prepared in the lower grades to take notes and to study correctly for the test. All too often, the teacher hands out notes on spiritmasters or writes notes on the chalkboard and may or may not review the handouts or notes the day before the exam. Rarely, if ever, are sample tests or sample test questions discussed or studied.

Preparation for Test Taking

Before beginning to work with a student, it is extremely useful to look at his previous tests. The objective is to ascertain strengths and weaknesses of the student's performance. By determining the areas of concern, a prescriptive approach to remediation and strategies can be formulated. Incorrect answers fall into typical catchment areas: (1) lack of information, (2) carelessness, (3) misinterpretation of the question, (4) material not studied, and (5) incorrect reading.

Lack of Information

Through questioning techniques it is possible to identify if the lack of information is because the student has not studied the material adequately or because his notes were not accurate for the required task.

Carelessness

If carelessness is a problem, it needs to be determined if anxiety is the cause or if lack of judgment is a common behavior that needs to be modified.

Misinterpretation

Misinterpretation of the question raises the issue of language. The term *language* in this context refers to the processing of written language, both visually and receptively. The application of information to formulate an answer is expressive language. If the student cannot interpret the meaning of the question, he certainly cannot consistently identify and answer correctly.

Material Not Studied

If too little material or possibly incorrect material was studied, again it must be determined if a language problem exists. Often a student approaches a test and exclaims, "This is not what the teacher said would be on the test!" It is possible that the teacher may have included some additional material. However, it is also possible that the student might have misinterpreted the directions or the wording and, as a result, fails to realize that the questions refer to the material he studied. Understandably, if the student misinterpreted the directions as to what would be covered on the exam, he would have studied incorrect material and possibly transcribed incorrect information during class.

Incorrect Reading

The student who historically makes decoding errors may reverse words, delete a word, insert a word, or change words (such as "and" to "but" and "all, but" instead of "all"). In the lower grades these errors may be ignored as relatively unimportant, but in the upper grades these "minor" errors are of critical significance for accurate comprehension.

Answer Analysis

If correct and incorrect answers are analyzed, a pattern of the type of question the student is and is not able to answer acceptably will emerge. If errors are due to lack of information, the first question to be asked is, "How did the student study?" For instance, the child states, "I read the notes from the text, the notes from class, and my homework assignments." If so, the next concern relates to the student's style of learning—which modality is strongest. For example, if the child has auditory strength and visual weakness, reading over the study material will not reinforce the learning. Studies have shown (Marcel, T., Katzl & Smith 1974, Marcel, T. & Rajan, P. 1975, Bryan, T. & Bryan, J. 1986) that retention of visual information is far less than a mixed modality approach. A student with auditory strength will benefit from recording the study material, playing it back and rewriting the notes, integrating auditory, visual, and kinesthetic modalities. The child with visual strength benefits from learning a note-taking method that he can visualize when taking the test.

Notetaking Technique

One notetaking technique is to ask the student to take a piece of notebook paper and fold it in half vertically. The student is instructed to write the term on the left side and the definition or facts with necessary details on the right side. At study time, the student folds the paper so only the terms are showing; he self-tests and checks to verify the answer. This process easily can be reversed from definition to term. It is suggested that the student use these notes in several ways: (1) to read over, (2) to write answers, (3) to be tested orally by a parent, sibling, or friend.

After each test, an error analysis is utilized. If, in fact, the correct material was studied and errors continue to occur, it is necessary to question further to identify the source of the problem.

Language Problems

For learning disabled students, incorrect answers on an exam frequently are a result of poor language processing skills (Hresko & Reid 1981). They simply do not understand the question; therefore, they are unable to provide an answer, (Blank, M. & White, S.J. 1986). For multiple choice questions, the student with a language deficit is likely to choose incorrectly through misinterpretation. It becomes necessary, therefore, for the teacher to teach the student how to analyze the language by reinterpreting the words, using the student's own language. One way to do this is to ask the student to read the question aloud. This clarifies the words by adding a verbal/aural component. Some children need to reword and/or redefine the question.

Essay Tests

Essay questions present different problems and the more traditional Harvard Outline lends itself to answering essay questions. When addressing this type of question, typically the student forgets one aspect of the question and loses critical points. For instance, a sample essay question reads as follows:

Directions: Write a well-organized essay of at least 200-250 words on the following:

> Characters in literature frequently must choose between right and wrong actions. From the poetry, short stories, novels, plays, and books of true expe-rience you have read, select two in which a character makes such a choice. State what choice was made by each character and discuss the consequences of the character's choice. Give titles and authors.

The results of such a question could be: The student selects two characters from one piece of literature and is so busy writing, he writes about one only, or the student may write about two aspects of one character.

Another typical error is the tendency for a student to start writing and wander far from the question at hand. Use of the Harvard Outline allows the student to organize his thinking in preparation for writing. The Outline is designed to identify the main ideas and include one or two details. Essays for social studies and English tests usually ask the student to select a topic and give two reasons either to defend or to attack. Thus, the outline helps to organize the student's thinking and affords a framework from which to work.

Math

Math tests present a different set of problems in test taking skills. In middle school and high school, many questions depend on formulas, theorems, equations, and equivalencies (Bley, N.S. & Thornton, C.A. 1981). For instance, before the student can find the circumference of a particular circle, he must know the equation for circumference. Then, if the measurements are mixed (e.g., 4 feet, 3 inches), the numbers must be converted to equivalencies before substituting numbers in the equation. To find the length of the hypotenuse of the right triangle, the student has to know the Pythagorean theorem. Some rote memorization is necessary before approaching the problem.

Error Analysis

As each problem is approached, it is important to watch the student carefully to understand his method of addressing the problem. If it is computational, then that is the area for remediation. If it is difficulty with application of a concept, then remediation will concentrate on concept formation and application. It cannot be too strongly emphasized that repetition of practice tests is invaluable to perfect math test-taking skills.

Summary

Teaching test-taking skills should be an ongoing process in the classroom. The teacher should *not* teach *to* the exam, but teach the students *how* to take the test. As described, students need to learn appropriate note-taking in the classroom and from the text. Then, they must prepare adequate study guides. Practice questions and practice tests should follow to provide a variety of testing experiences. The students then will be fairly tested and will be able to share with the teacher the actual knowledge they have acquired.

References

Alley, G. & Deshler, D. 1979. *Teaching the learning disabled adolescent: Strategies and methods.* Denver, CO: Love Publications.

Blank, M., White, S.J. 1986. A powerful but misused form of classroom exchange. *Topics in Language Disorders,* 6(2), pp. 1-2.

Bley, N.S. & Thornton, C.A. 1981. *Teaching mathematics to the learning disabled.* Rockville, MD: Aspen Systems.

Bryan, T. & Bryan, J. 1986. *Understanding learning disabilities.* Columbus, OH: Mayfield Publishing Co.

Devine, T.G. 1981. *Teaching study skills: A guide for teachers.* Boston. Allyn & Bacon, Inc.

Hresko, W. & Read, D. 1981. Language intervention with the learning disabled. *Topics in learning and learning disabilities, 1(2), pp. viii-xi.*

Johnson, D.J. & Myklebust, H. 1967. *Learning disabilities, educational principles and practices* Orlando, FL: Grune & Stratton.

King-Fun, L.A. 1974. Parental attitudes, test, anxiety and achievement motivation. *Journal of School Psychology,* Vol. 93(1), pp. 3-11.

Mann, L., Goodman, L., Wiederholt, J.L. 1978. *Teaching the learning disabled adolescent.* Boston: Houghton Mifflin Company.

Marcel, T., Katz, L. & Smith, M. 1974. Laterality and reading proficiency. *Neuropsychologia,* 12, pp. 131-139.

Marcel, T. & Rajan, P. 1975. Lateral specialization for recognition of words and faces in good and poor readers. *Neuropsychologia,* 12, pp. 489-497.

Mercer, C.D. 1987. *Students with learning disabilities.* Columbus, OH: Merrill Publishing Company.

Pullis, M. 1893. Stress as a way of life: Special challenges from the LD resource teacher. *Topics in Learning and Learning Disabilities,* 3(2), pp. 14-36.

Raskind, L.T. & Nagle, R.J. 1980. Modeling effects on the intelligence test performance of test-anxious children. *Psychology in the Schools,* 17(3), pp. 351-355.

Schanzer, S. & Wohlman, J. 1979. Homework organizer for teachers and students. *Academic Therapy,* 14:5, pp. 577-579.

Slade, D.L. 1986. Developing foundations for organizational skills. *Academic Therapy*, 21:3, pp. 260-266.

Zatz, S., Chassin, L. 1985. Cognitions of test-anxious children under naturalistic test-taking conditions. *Journal of Consulting Psychology*, 53(3), pp. 393-401.

Roslind W. Rothman, EdD, is an associate professor of special education at Southern Connecticut State University, 501 Crescent St., New Haven, CT 06515 as well as director of the Total Learning Center in Westchester, NY. Jill Cohen, ATR, MS, is a special education teacher on the Board of Cooperative Educational Services in Southern Westchester, NY.

Reprinted with permission from Academic Therapy, March 1988, Pro-Ed, 8700 Shoal Creek Blvd, Austin, TX 78758-6897.

Counseling Gifted/Learning Disabled Children

Paul R. Daniels

It would be helpful for teachers before reading this chapter to review Chapter 16 on the learning therapist. It is important to keep in mind that few teachers are trained as counselors and should not try to assume that role. However, throughout the course of every day, opportunities arise in the classroom to help children improve their self-esteem or assuage hurt egos.

One other aspect of teachers as counselors must be recognized and accepted by professional counselors, whether they be school counselors, school psychologists, clinical psychologists, or psychiatrists. The teacher has the opportunity to deal with problems immediately and in a relevant setting. These social and psychological dynamics usually are not present in an individual or group counseling session. Admittedly, these settings provide other types of opportunities to help the children. For their benefit, it is vital that all opportunities for assistance be seized.

Teacher-Therapist Communication

When a child is receiving therapy under any label outside of the classroom, the need for communication between that counselor/therapist and the teacher become paramount. The fundamental strategies and approaches to problems must be agreed upon and the procedures used by both adults must be in concert. They should hold face-to-face discussions in which specific anecdotes can be analyzed. (See Appendix 6-E on recordkeeping and daily anecdotal record sheets.)

If this type of concerted effort cannot be carried out, then the teacher must be sure to note in the child's record that the attempt was made. Many therapists prefer that their treatment be unaffected by information from other sources. It is their right to proceed in that fashion but the teacher must be covered.

A negative aspect if these adults do not work in concert is that it provides the child with an opportunity to play both ends against the middle. This is especially burdensome for the teacher since, without communication from the therapist, the child's responses, behaviors, etc., cannot be verified as legitimate. For example, a therapist may encourage a child to use physical retaliation to stand up to a bully. The teacher in the classroom is forced to deal with this retaliation as if it were aggression, using standard school procedures. Another approach might have been available if the teacher had been made aware of the therapist's goals.

Most children who have adjustment difficulties know only how to live within them. They tend not to be aware of more satisfactory modes of behavior. The role of counseling from whatever source should be fostering that perception. However, if infantile satisfaction can be obtained by pitting one adult against another: teacher-therapist, mother-father, sibling-sibling, etc., such children will do so. Uncoordinated responses and programs can only perpetuate the poor adjustment and its usual concomitant–poor learning.

Problems in Counseling

Gifted/learning disabled children present a unique problem for counseling. In effect, they are multiexceptioned and, unfortunately for some, might be multihandicapped. Other children with multiexceptionalities tend to have physical handicaps and cognitive disabilities. It is possible to have a blind/learning disabled child and many other dysfunctional combinations. In gifted/learning disabled children, both exceptionalities are nearly always cognitive and in many cases are recognized as polarities. It appears to be contradictory. It is this polarity that has led to the lack of understanding by the parents and teachers of these children and in the young people themselves. It also is the paradox that allows certain professionals to state that gifted/learning disabled children, by definition, cannot exist.

It is vital that the teacher operate with as much information as possible in dealing with these children. If possible, case history data should be obtained. It is important to know the home dynamics because these children all too frequently are the despair of their families. They are not and cannot be understood, yet they exist in the family and influence it, often profoundly.

Family data are important since such information could influence a teacher's reaction to a child or situation. Children who come from a laissez-faire household must be looked on differently from those in a home affected by academic or economic compulsion.

Understanding the Problem

The first step in teacher counseling of gifted/learning disabled children is an understanding of the problem they face. In most cases they have been told repeatedly that they are bright yet then are accused of laziness or indifference. The resolution of this paradox often is beyond the maturity or perception of most of these children. Therefore, the teacher's program must begin with basic education.

On the basis of their intelligence test scores, children can be shown what a percentile rating is and where in such a rating they stand. The teacher could ask "If we lined up a hundred children your age from the brightest to the dullest, where do you think you would fit?" In most cases gifted/learning disabled children rate themselves very low on this scale yet often add, "People say I'm brighter." These children must be made aware of this giftedness and begin to accept it.

The Learning Disability Concept

The concept of learning disability also must be understood and discussed with these pupils. However, the teacher must be sure they understand that remedial and adaptive procedures are available to deal with the disability. Too frequently, children accept the disability and turn it into a handicap that they suffer through forever. Hope must always be available with help.

It should be on the basis of these two understandings that the explanation for changes in programming, instructional techniques, books, etc., is based. It is important for these children to begin to verbalize the reasons for certain procedures. Techniques such as the modified Fernald Procedure, which tends to be a slow process initially, have to be accepted as a way of learning rather than faster procedures that produce little or no real learning. Adaptive procedures that are effective must be accepted as legitimate means for turning frustration into success.

Some Cautions Essential

Caution must be used when developing the understanding of giftedness and learning disability. In many instances there have been negative outcomes because reality has not been kept in the forefront of the children's perceptions. Immaturity is a trait easily observable in the gifted/learning disabled. These understandings can feed into this immaturity if permitted to do so. Children begin to use the exceptionalities for excuses. "I didn't do it because it was too easy for me," or "I couldn't do it because of my disability," or "You do know I am dyslexic, don't you?" become avoidance techniques for distasteful yet necessary behaviors.

In this situation, the teacher can move in at least two directions, based on the child's background. If the pupil has been hurt by failure, abrupt confrontation seldom avails anything. A better approach might be, "I know that you've tried things before and they didn't work so you need to say that not to get hurt. But know you can do the things I asked, if you try. Would I ask you to do something if thought you couldn't do it?"

The learning therapist section suggested that the teacher for a while has become the child's superego. This is just such a situation. The idea of accepting the "rightness" of the request is transferred, at least for a while, from being the child's responsibility to being the teacher's. In many cases with gifted children, positive changes in this adjustment mechanism do not come quickly or easily. Those children have lost their sense of confidence in self.

On the other hand, some may use these excuses for nearly infantile reasons. The pleasure-pain principle was never established. These kinds of children usually come from families that allowed them to excuse themselves from everything requiring emotional growth and control and in many cases to become tyrants. They get to feel omnipotent and accountable only to themselves.

The teacher in such a situation may have to take on a confrontation role. It may be necessary to say, "If it is so easy, do it for me and prove yourself right," or "So what if you are dyslexic, does that mean you can do anything you want to do to anybody at any time?" This also is the time to use the group as a focal point of reference. This highlights again the point made throughout this text: homogeneity of intelligence is needed in grouping this type of disabled child. The teacher might respond to the use of the handicapping level as an excuse with, "I don't understand that. Many of the children in this group have been called dyslexic yet they seem to be doing things. How are you different from them?"

Whenever a confrontation approach is used, it is important that the child does not interpret the action as punitive. In such situations, it is important for the teacher to get as near eye level as possible, maintain eye contact, and keep the comments personal. It will only cause further hurt if the group is used as a means of shaming or disgracing the child. There is a very fine line that must be walked in this situation. The pupil must understand, especially because of the teacher's past behaviors, that this is a supportive technique.

During this discussion the child could be asked to analyze why the teacher is behaving in that fashion. It is important for the particular pupil and for all in the group that the teacher's behavior is planned and, if observed, changes from child to child.

This particular concept is crucial in teacher counseling. The children should know that they are all different and unique and therefore are not always treated the same. Neglect of this point often causes programs to fail in all educational settings. In certain situations, everyone is treated the same, with the same demands and privileges. However, in certain other respects, different children are treated differently. This point should be made as early as possible in the program. It should be stated to the group that this is the teacher's policy and its rationale should be explained. Making the statement clearly and early eliminates concern about favoritism and indifference. This concern of children with problems in adjustment can be so pervasive that nearly all of their energies are directed to it and thus are diverted from learning. As so often happens, the educational plan then is considered inadequate or inappropriate when it never penetrated the child's comprehension.

Failure or Lack of Success

There is a point in the relationship between a student with problems and the teacher that is unique. This is the point of failure or perceived lack of success. Most gifted/learning disabled children have not enjoyed success commensurate with their abilities. In most cases this has been made very obvious to them. Some of them with good support from home and professional personnel enter remedial programs with hope for success. Others, even with the same support, start the program knowing they will fail.

Both groups can be found in remedial classrooms. Both groups have to encounter the phenomenon that education is based on–failure or lack of knowledge. Well-adjusted children see nothing wrong in error or ignorance and readily accept help. Many learning disabled children, especially those with excellent basic intelligence, view failure as the confirmation of their fundamental stupidity or as adult deceit. For teachers in these situations the counseling role is theirs alone. Therapists and counselors are not involved when a child errs or is unable to deal with an academic task.

For both types, this problem should be dealt with early, and preferably in a group situation so no child can feel singled out or stigmatized. The teacher must have at hand evidence of past successes but, most importantly, documented evidence of progress to reassure the hopeful child. When the child feels learning is hopeless, the same basic need for data is necessary but the evidence should be narrowed to those successes because such pupils often are overwhelmed by the use of progress data. They find that the idea of continuous progress seems unsustainable; this may well lead to a total halt in effort. They express the idea, "What's the use, I've got too far to go." The teacher in a counseling role must be extremely careful not to foster that attitude.

There also should be a weariness about dealing with success. (See Chapter 16 on the teacher as learning therapist.) The teacher must be aware that for many children, success brings with it failure. Quite simply, as stated by one child, "If I get this done, you're going to give me something harder." This is a statement not lacking perception. Too many teachers do not anticipate this possibility and in their enthusiasm at seeing progress forget that the child may view education as a never-ending process. Most adults know that that is true and tend to relish the idea. However, children–especially those who have found education painful and degrading–may not feel the same way.

The use of praise should be handled as carefully as reproach. As noted in the learning therapist segment, children who still need the teacher as a superego usually cannot handle praise. When this praise is elaborated into expected control and learning, these children seem only able to revert to past negative behavior or failure as if to prove that they are incapable of sustaining themselves. From an adjustment view, they probably are right.

The Role of Responsibilities

During these interpersonal relationships between the individual child and the teacher, the latter needs to have enough ego to assume responsibilities and even blame for factors for which the instructor is not truly accountable. However, it is an important aspect of the role of teacher as counselor. When things have not gone right or well, the child should be given an indication that the teacher takes responsibility: "I guess I didn't understand how you would feel about that. How could I have done it differently so you wouldn't get upset?" or "I guess I asked you to do too much. How much do you think you could have done?"

However, the teacher never should assume the role of being the cause of the problem if the child is capable of correct behavior of whatever nature but simply has chosen not to conform or mature. At that point, confrontation may be the proper approach. If the child is truly unable to handle the tasks, mutual understanding must be redeveloped. To make progress, more limited types and degrees of responsibility should be tried, as suggested in the learning therapist chapter.

This limiting of tasks, if at all possible, should evolve out of the questions the teacher asks the child: "How could I have done it better . . . ," or "How much do you think you could have done?" This type of approach gives the child the reassurance that someone will listen and try to comply. It is a minor testimony of faith in the child as a reasonable human being.

When it appears that the pupil is capable of more self-direction, the teacher should suggest small increases in responsibilities or learning, making sure the child understands that positive support will be available no matter what the youngster's decision.

Problem Child: The Attention Seeker

There is another type that can be found in all classrooms yet presents a particular problem in a learning disabilities class: the attention-seeking child, who can be one of the most difficult to deal with therapeutically. This child often is labeled attention getting, which implies the pupil was successful in obtaining what was sought.

Attention-seeking in itself demonstrates a need. In most cases the need is for self-esteem or sense of self-worth or love. These children try to use their behavior to wrest these attributes from others. Their primary need is attention and they often will pay a severe price for it.

Attention and New Needs

The problem with learning disabled children, especially bright ones, is that in many cases they have had attention. They did not recognize it since it was in the form of testing, remedial programs, special classes, etc. Their problem is compounded since in most cases the attention has not worked. They still feel worthless and useless. A caution must be noted here. Some children feel that way because of traumatic factors in early life. They should be helped at the fundamental level of development by trained psychotherapists with attending support from the teacher.

The first task the teacher as counselor must face is to develop in attention-seeking children an understanding of their behavior. Punishment will not do, as is discussed later. This is a time for direct, intimate conversation in which the beginning levels of introspection can be put in place. Simply requesting that the child try to enumerate some reasons for the behavior is a starting point. At times the teacher can make simple suggestions about possibilities that have been observed. The daily record sheet with its anecdotes can prove useful.

The second aspect for discussion should be an understanding about negative and positive attention. It is amazing the number of very intelligent children who are unable to discern this difference. The teacher should ask for some actions that the child could have used to get positive, rather than negative, attention. The concept of laugh with, rather than laugh at, is useful.

Punishment Counterproductive

These children's lack of understanding of the negative/positive attention concept is the reason that punishment as a technique often is counterproductive. When they are punished, they receive attention and in some cases all the attention of their classmates as well as of the teacher. This negative reinforcement of useless, disruptive behavior can become quite addictive to many children.

As early as possible, punishment should be moved from the hands of the teacher to the hands of the child. The concept that "you punish yourself" should be promoted. Rules should be set down so that children know the consequences, positively and negatively, of their behavior: "If you get your work finished, you would have time to play a game with your friend, or use the computer," or "If that follow-up isn't done, how are you going to get to use the computer?"

Every attempt should be made in these situations with attention-seekers for the teacher to be an arbitrator between the child and the behavior. The judge and jury roles too often play into the hands of the attention-seeking child. It is not easy for the teacher to maintain controls in these situations but it must be kept in mind that if they are not maintained, the problem only becomes worse and undoubtedly is prolonged.

Positive Attention

Examples of positive attention in many cases must be verbalized. A child can simply be asked to state some positive behaviors. In most cases it is better to start with social behaviors that have to do with individual or group acceptance. Simple techniques for positive entry into groups may have to be discussed. How does one get into a group game or group conversation? Food sharing, swapping, etc., can be helpful in moderation. These techniques must be monitored and discussed since in these situations attention-seekers often tend to go overboard and bring themselves into ridicule, which is another form of negative attention.

In some cases, frank discussions about hair, clothes, hygiene, etc., may have to be initiated since these factors can get negative attention. Older girls often become sexually provocative for no reason other than the need for attention. In these situations frank, honest observations by the teacher concerning possible reasons for the behaviors are pertinent and suggestions for changes are appropriate.

Academic negation can be handled more easily if strides have been made in the social aspects. The teacher should let the children know that making honest errors is acceptable but that deliberately failing, in order to command attention, will not be tolerated. When appropriate, the teacher should share the joy of success with the individual and sometimes with the group. Recognition from a teacher is important for most children.

The teacher in the counselor's role should conduct certain procedural aspects on an individual basis. However, a number of procedures can be handled in the group setting. The initial group effort has been discussed already; everyone is not always treated the same in all things.

A second important facet of the group procedure is the development of the nature of its members. There is a valid reason to keep their giftedness in front of them. They must accept their abilities and learn to live with the positive and negative aspects. Factors suggested for this concept with individuals are equally as valid for groups. The use of percentiles and line graphs can become concrete enough to be used as referents when an individual child begins to have troubles.

Planning on Their Own

All learning disabled children should be given time for daily initial planning and daily final evaluation. The initial planning phase is important as it should provide them with the structure they usually need. It also can be a time of sharing. However, caution must be observed in this respect.

Sharing is a particularly upsetting activity for many attention-seeking children. It can provide an opportunity for the "clowns" in the group to make fools of themselves and get the appropriate negative attention. For others, it can become a time to demonstrate their inabilities or handicaps. In some instances these children will do and say things to bring ridicule on themselves, which again provides the desired negative attention.

In both of these situations the teacher's counseling role begins before the activity. A deliberate check of a proposed sharing presentation should be made and anything inappropriate rejected, with an explanation. Suggestions for other types or degrees of participation are legitimate as well as a direct personal evaluation of the reason behind the inappropriate behavior. One child who was fanatical about dinosaurs made a fool of himself by labeling them wrong, forgetting their names, etc., and admitted doing so because "Nobody even thinks this is important so at least they laughed at me."

Show-and-tell activities at any time of the day are apt to produce problems, even if only of a subtle nature. When they are used with children having adjustment difficulties, they can be disruptive to the program and deleterious to certain pupils. Teacher monitoring is demanded. In some instances children have participated in these activities using articles that were dangerous, inappropriate, or even pornographic because the teacher did not monitor what was to be done.

The daily final evaluation in the group of the group is a crucial activity for gifted/learning disabled children. It is here that some of the best opportunities are provided for the introduction of flexibility and adaptability. Answers can be elicited from the group concerning other methods of doing things, other types of procedures, and other ways of thinking or viewing things. Too frequently, this very important element in the instructional program is excluded completely. When appropriate, during this activity, individuals can be called on to provide information, suggest courses of action, etc., and obtain positive attention.

It usually is risky for anyone not professionally trained in counseling or therapy to try to use group practices as a direct medium for individual guidance activities involving group dynamics. It is more appropriate to use the groups as a supplement to the development of the individual on a one-to-one basis. With gifted/learning disabled children, group activities do not appear to be the best approach, as suggested above.

In certain situations, especially in private schools for children with problems, professional counseling or psychotherapy is provided during the academic day. This causes problems for the teacher as counselor. Communication between the counselor/therapist and the teacher is mandatory. There is really no other satisfactory procedure if the children are to make progress academically as well as psychologically .

The type of therapy being used by the child's personal therapist also can be a problem. In most cases children returning from individual "talk" therapy might be a little morose or too exuberant but usually not to such a degree that the academic program is completely disrupted. The same cannot be said in many cases where the children are in group or play therapy. They frequently return to the classroom quite hyperactive and try to extend group therapy to the class or instructional group. They seem unable to recognize the differences in the two situations. This is another example of the flexibility and adaptability problem.

Play therapy causes the same type of behavior. Children who have sublimated or denied feelings for years find an acceptable outlet in play therapy and become almost intoxicated with the emotional release. When returning to the classroom they are reluctant to assume a more placid or conforming role. These behaviors can disrupt the educational program to such a degree that the teacher has to abandon all plans while attempting to restore an academic environment. The children must always be faced with the concept that their teacher is there first of all as an educator.

Methods of Coping

A number of ways exist to meet this problem. As was suggested earlier, teacher-therapist communication is a must. As another method, group and play therapy sessions should be scheduled so that afterward the children are through for the day or are going to lunch or to any activity other than receiving instruction. If these arrangements are not possible, the teacher must request that the therapist finish the session by reinstating some controls. The teacher should schedule the children so that the block of time in their programs to which they are returning is either independent activities or independent reading. (See Chapter 18 on classroom management procedures.) They should not be scheduled into instruction or follow-up activities.

Finally, there is an aspect of the counselor role that is particularly pertinent to the teacher. If things have gone well in the teacher-children personal relationships, an unsettling condition must be faced. Eventually, the relationships must be terminated. Eventually all contacts will cease and some piece of each individual's ego will be lost. Most teachers and nearly all the children either forget or ignore this finality. But it does occur—every year. It is important that the teachers of learning disabled children of all types keep this in mind because when the termination becomes apparent to the pupils, a rather specific phenomenon emerges: separation anxiety.

Teacher-child personal relationships often become quite close. Deep fears, longings, and loves have been shared. A confidence has been developed that for some children may have been the first and possibly the only time they have ever known that trait. Yet this relationship must end. School will close; summer vacation will begin.

To protect themselves, some pupils may revert to former childish behaviors. Others actually will show losses in skills and abilities. Still others may become sullen and even rude toward the teacher. All of these behaviors seem to be a defense that says, "See, you are not that important to me. You didn't help me. I don't need you." If individuals really are so unimportant, they cannot be missed too much; the hurt cannot be too bad.

Teachers, when dealing with this separation anxiety, must be sure to recognize what it is and not allow it to impinge negatively on their own feelings. It is important to help children deal with it individually, not in group activities, since their reactions will be unique. The teachers should provide evidences of continuing care by suggesting meetings during the coming year, exchanges of cards over the summer, and sharing of information if meetings are not possible. Teachers also must be willing to verbalize their feelings when they are genuine. They should let the children know that having warm, positive feelings for other people is a fine human trait and nothing to be ashamed of; caring and loving are what life is really about. For many gifted/learning disabled children these two relationships seem to be distorted, whether in fact or in faulty perception; which of these is unimportant, since the children believe it and operate with it. During the period of separation anxiety, the teacher's thoughtfulness in handling this reaction can make a significant positive change in a child's emotional outlook.

Summary

The role of the teacher as counselor might be summed up in a simple statement: the teacher must care about the child as a human being, not just as a student. Any situation in which an individual's own needs are intertwined with those of others always carries with it the chance for hurt. The teacher as the adult and better adjusted member of the pair must be willing to roll with the punches and see through the reasons for the behavior. The returns for caring are enormous.

Excerpted from Daniels, P.R. (1983), Teaching the Gifted Learning Disabled Child. Reprinted with permission from Pro-Ed, 8700 Shoal Creek Blvd, Austin, TX 78758-6897.

Developing Self-Esteem

Sheri Searcy

The child with learning disabilities faces new challenges each day, and the outcome of each challenge affects the child's beliefs about himself. Parents are often concerned about the self-esteem of the child with learning disabilities. They want their children to grow into healthy, happy, self-directed individuals. Self-esteem may be the most important component of this.

The purpose of this article is to describe how self-esteem develops "normally," how it suffers when learning disabilities are present, and what parents can do to contribute to a child's self-esteem. A second, underlying purpose is to alert teachers to the significant role self-esteem plays in children with learning disabilities. Many of the activities recommended for parents can easily be translated into classroom activities. In addition, teachers may want to make copies of the article available to their students' parents. (Requests for reprints should be sent to the author whose address appears at the end of this article.)

What is self-esteem?

A child's feelings about himself make up his self-esteem. High self-esteem means being satisfied with who you are, liking yourself, and respecting yourself for meeting your own standards and as a human being (Rosenberg 1985). Psychologists talk about self-esteem as something related but slightly different from self-concept. A person's self-concept is made up of the ideas he has about himself, an assessment of his skills and traits, whereas self-esteem is how much he feels he is worth. Two children may each think that they are attractive but not good in school. One child may think it is most important to look good while the other child may think that doing well in school is most important.

These two children may have very different degrees of self-esteem, because they differ in the values and attitudes they hold on school achievement and personal appearance.

There are a number of components to self-esteem. We must feel that (1) we are capable; (2) we are significant in that we matter to others; (3) we are powerful and have some say in what we do; and (4) we are unique and worthwhile in our own right (Coopersmith 1967; Schilling 1986). A child must develop in each of these ways in order to have a good feeling about himself.

How does self-esteem develop?

Children begin to form a sense of themselves from the time they are born. These early experiences are especially important because it appears that "at some time preceding middle childhood the individual arrives at a general appraisal of his worth, which remains relatively stable and enduring over a period of several years" (Coopersmith 1967). The individual's self-esteem will fluctuate with certain events, and he will have higher esteem for some aspects of himself than for others. But the child's general attitude toward himself is much more resistant to change after this early period.

Stanley Coopersmith (1967) summarized three conditions associated with the development of self-esteem:

> . . . total or nearly total acceptance of the children by their parents, clearly defined and enforced limits and the respect and latitude for individual action that exist within the defined limits. In effect, we can conclude that the parents of children with high self-esteem are concerned and attentive toward their children, that they structure the worlds of their children along the lines they believe to be proper and appropriate, and that they permit relatively great freedom within the structures they have established.

The relationship between parent and child lays the foundation for self-regard. In their early interactions, the baby learns that he can signal and engage his parent, and the parent replies with love and comfort. This helps the infant gain a sense of confidence and worth (Givelber 1983). As the parent responds to the infant's movements and expressions and shows admiration for the child, the infant learns that he is a good person who is worth loving. As the child learns to walk, talk, and play, he looks to the parent for recognition and praise. The constant attention reassures him that he is important and capable. When he asserts his own wishes, he learns the limits of what is permitted and that he has the power to make many choices within those limits.

The young child is always expanding concepts of what he is and what he'd like to be. He takes in what key people say about him and begins to respond toward himself in a manner consistent with others' attitudes toward him. The value young children assign to themselves is a reflection of how they believe others value them.

As the child masters new skills, he begins to determine what specific areas of the self are valued. The young child delights in learning new things. He will begin to recognize that there are some areas in which he excels and some in which he is deficient. His overall regard for himself will depend on the relative value attached to these areas of the self.

As the child grows older, he is more likely to filter what is said in a way that confirms his existing self-image. Nancy Cotton (1983) has explained that as the child goes through middle childhood, the impact of praise greatly depends on whether the child values the praising person and the area of self being praised. If the praise comes from someone important to him, it is more likely to be meaningful. If the praise is aimed at an area that the child thinks is important, it will also have a greater impact than praise for things that are not important to the child.

The young child defines himself by concrete abilities, achievements, and physical characteristics. The child is particularly vulnerable when defects in this "social exterior" occur (Cotton 1983). Success at school is particularly important. Erik Erickson (1959) characterized the school years by "I am what I learn." The child's specific and general self-images continue to develop as he discovers his own strengths and weaknesses according to these external standards.

However, as the child enters adolescence, he is capable of more abstract thought, which leads to introspection. He is more likely now to be concerned with internal aspects of himself like loyalty or anger. In general, early adolescence appears to be the time when the child's self-esteem is at its lowest as he comes to recognize his own imperfections. In general, younger adolescents have poorer self-concepts than older adolescents, with 12-13 years of age being the low point of self-esteem (Rosenberg 1985).

Children who mature earlier seem to develop more favorable attitudes about themselves than late maturers. Any differences between boys and girls are most visible at adolescence. Girls appear to have slightly lower self-esteem than boys during adolescence (Rosenberg 1985).

Also beginning in adolescence, the individual's sense of worth is generally regulated from within himself. That is, he is less vulnerable to others' opinions and begins to rely more on his own opinion. Even the healthiest adults will need some reassurance of worth from others at times, however. One's level of self-esteem will shift up and down throughout life, depending on how he thinks he measures up to his own standards (Brennan 1985).

How does a learning disability affect self-esteem?

Children with learning disabilities seem to be at risk for having low self-esteem. We don't yet know how widespread the problem is (Kistner et al. 1987), but we do know that it is a serious concern to parents. In addition, low self-esteem appears to extend into adulthood and is often associated with employment problems (Hoffman et al. 1987; Schmitt 1986).

The learning disability's potential effect on a child's self esteem has been described by many parents and the professionals who work with these children (Burka 1983; Kronick 1981; Osman 1982; Ungerleider 1985). Unrecognized disabilities may even affect the early interactions between mother and infant. The infant may not be able to localize and respond to its mother's voice (Jacobs 1983), or to attend to the early games parents play with their babies. As they fail or struggle to learn new skills, many children with learning disabilities are insecure in their abilities and overall feelings of self-worth. Some children with learning disabilities may feel "dumb" and suffer ridicule and defeat because of school failure, athletic ineptitude, or inability to pick up on social cues. Often they believe they cannot perform quite well enough to meet their parents' and teachers' expectations. When they fail to master even the most basic skills, their confidence in themselves is greatly lowered.

What Parents Can Do

Helping Children Feel More Capable

-   Allow the child to take on special projects for you, even if the other children might do them better or if it would be easier for you to do them yourself.

-   Help your child make improvements in just one or two areas at a time. Avoid pointing out mistakes in other things he does, so he doesn't feel that everything he does is wrong.

-   Display works of art, school papers, scouting honors, certificates of swimming achievement, and so forth on the refrigerator or some chosen showcase.

-   Ask him to teach a skill to someone else, like a younger brother or sister.

-   Assign him well-defined, simple daily chores to do. See Weiss and Weiss (1976) for help in teaching by task analysis.

-   Help him to find his own abilities and allow him time to pursue them (White 1985). If he's a good swimmer, don't neglect swimming because he's too busy with tutors.

Helping Children Feel More Significant

-   Learn to listen to your child. Without pressuring, encourage him to talk about his feelings and thoughts. Let him know that his ideas or concerns carry weight.

-   Help your child find a group to feel a part of. Participation in student government, scouting programs, school clubs, computer-user groups, and clubs can foster a sense of belonging (Chervin 1986).

-   Have your child volunteer time to help an elderly neighbor, at a hospital, day-care center, therapeutic horseback riding or swimming class.

- Don't forget to tell your child that you love him. Some times parents get out of the habit and it becomes awkward. Children with learning disabilities may have a special need to have it said.

- When he experiences a success (like making a new friend or learning to drive) celebrate to show him that his life events matter to the whole family.

- Involve the whole family in different family outings based on what individual persons would like to do, e.g., visit a doll museum for one child, go to garage sales for another, and play basketball for another.

Helping Children Feel More Powerful

- Help the child with a good sense of humor recognize the power he has to change people's mood with humor.

- Teach the child to make decisions. Start by giving two choices and gradually increase his responsibility for recognizing and choosing between alternatives (The Future Planning Project 1987).

- Have the child help set the dinner menu, select what will be in the lunches he takes to school, and order his own food at restaurants.

- Have the child make a schedule for himself with your help in determining average homework time, bedtime, etc. Allow him to determine the order.

- Let the child buy his own clothes, choose the color, or pick between two styles.

- Help the child recognize self-defeating behaviors like fear of failure and lack of motivation (Omizo & Omizo 1986). You may want to find a counseling group to help.

- Be aware of natural parent tendencies to hold your child back for his own protection. Take a look at the decisions you make for your child and carefully assess the risks of having the child make those decisions for himself.

Helping Children Feel More Worthy

- Recognize and point out the inner qualities that the child has that make him special — his sensitivity to animals, his ability to have fun, his regard for others' feelings, his playfulness, desire to understand things, ability to make others laugh, or his creativity.

- Promote hobbies, such as collections, photography, gardening, crafts, or music (San Diego City Schools 1983).

- Demonstrate respect for all people. Discuss the uniqueness of each person and point out that all have qualities to be admired.

- Help the child meet positive role models in college students or adults with learning disabilities (San Diego City Schools 1983).

- Discuss the child's problems openly with him. Emphasize the positive and let him know that trouble in school does not mean he will not do well in life (Sternberg, date unknown).

References

Brennan, A. 1985. Participation and self-esteem: A test of six alternative explanations. *Adolescence*, 20:78, pp. 445-446.

Burka, A. 1983. The emotional reality of a learning disability. *Annals of Dyslexia*, 33, pp. 289-301.

Chervin, S.N. 1986. Doubts and fears of the learning disabled. *Academic Therapy*, 21:3, pp. 331-338.

Coopersmith, S. 1967. *The antecedents of self-esteem*. San Francisco: Freeman.

Cotton, N.D. 1983. The development of self-esteem and self-esteem regulation. In J.E. Mack & S.L. Ablon (Eds.), *Development and sustenance of self-esteem in childhood*. New York: International University Press.

Erickson, E.1959. *Identity and the life cycle*. New York: International Universities Press.

The Future Planning Project. 1987. University Affiliated Facility Department of Special Education, Haworth Hall, University of Kansas, Lawrence, KS 66045.

Givelber, F. 1983. The parent-child relationship and the development of self-esteem. In J.E. Mack & S.L. Ablon (Eds.), *Development and sustenance of self-esteem in childhood*. New York: International University Press.

Hoffman, F.J., Sheldon, K.L., Minskoff, E.H., Sautter, S.W. 1987. Needs of learning disabled adults. *Journal of Learning Disabilities*, 20:1, pp. 43-52.

Jacobs, D.H. 1983. Learning problems, self-esteem, and delinquency. In J.E. Mack & S.L. Ablon (Eds.), *Development and sustenance of self-esteem in childhood*. New York: International University Press.

Kistner, J., Haskett, M., White, K., & Robbins, F. 1987. Perceived competence and self-worth of LD and normally achieving students. *Learning Disability Quarterly*, 10:1, pp. 37-44.

Kronick, D. 1981. *Social development of learning disabled persons*. San Francisco: Jossey Bass.

Omizo, M.M., & Omizo, D.A. 1986. Group counseling–It works. *Academic Therapy*, 21:3, pp. 367-369.

Osman, B.B.1982. *No one to play with*. New York: Random House.

Rosenberg, M. 1985. Self-concept and psychological well-being. In R. Leahy, *The development of the self*. Orlando: Academic Press.

San Diego City Schools. 1983. Connections: *Developing skills for the family of the young special child*, 0-5. San Diego City Schools

Schilling, D.E. 1986. Self-esteem: Concerns, strategies, resources. *Academic Therapy*, 21:3, pp. 301-307.

Schmitt, P. 1986. About the unique vocational adjustment needs of students with a learning disability. *The Directive Teacher*, 8:1, pp. 7-8.

Sternberg, W. (Date unknown). Self-esteem and your learning disabled child. *ACLD Newsbriefs*.

Ungerleider, D.F. 1985. *Reading, writing, and rage*. Rolling Hills Estates, CA: Jalmar Press.

Weiss, M.D., & Weiss, H.G. 1976. *Home is a learning place*. Avon, CT: Tree House Associates.

White, S. 1985. *Social skills and self-esteem development through drama therapy activities*. Minnetonka, MN: Susan S. White.

Sheri Searcy, PhD, is the Learning Disabilities Project Manager at the National Information Center for Children and Youth with Handicaps (NICHCY), 1555 Wilson Blvd., Suite 700, Rosslyn, VA 22209. Information in this article was developed with funding from the National Institute on Disability and Rehabilitation Research, U.S. Department of Education (Grant #G0086352048) ATP

Reprinted with permission from Academic Therapy, vol 23 no. 5.

What about College for the Gifted Student With A Learning Disability?

For most gifted students who have a learning disability, college will be an obvious and appropriate continuation of their education. They will, however, need to have some special help in preparing for this important event and some information about their options. The articles in this section present parents, students, and educators with information that should be helpful in the process of preparing for and choosing a college to attend. The process of finding the right school and program can be a time-consuming and difficult experience for any student, but for the student with a learning disability it is even more critical to make this decision after careful consideration.

We have selected articles from several valuable resource books that are available commercially. Other articles reprinted here came from magazines, journals, or private sources. These papers discuss the various college options and what questions students should ask themselves and the school so that they will be able to make an informed decision. The article written by Brown University students is especially interesting and useful because it was written by students. Finally, we would urge you to take advantage of additional sources of information on colleges listed in the **Resources** section.

Getting LD Students
Ready for College

Parents, counselors, teachers and LD students may use this list as a reminder of helpful skills and necessary steps to take as a high school student with a learning disability moves toward college.

1. Make sure psychological testing is up-to-date. P.L. 94-142 mandates this testing be done ever three years for students in LD programs.

2. Obtain all special testing records before high school graduation. Some school systems destroy these records upon the student's graduation. Colleges, as well as vocational rehabilitation offices, request these records to assist in providing special services to students.

3. Make contact with the local Department of Rehabilitation Services (DRS) office before graduation. DRS offers a variety of services to eligible LD students such as vocational assessment, job placement, etc.

4. Consider a vocational assessment as a way to amplify present and future goals.

5. Make sure the student's knowledge of study skills is adequate. In addition to high school assistance, consider special study skills classes/programs offered at community colleges, private agencies, or individual tutoring.

6. Consult with the high school to get a good understanding of how much support or special help the student is receiving. It is important to determine realistically whether minimal LD support services or an extensive LD program at the college level will be needed.

7. Help students to increase their independent living skills. Help them learn to manage their own checking accounts, do their own laundry, cleaning, some cooking, etc.

8. Encourage part-time jobs or volunteer positions. These are helpful to improve socialization skills as well as to give a better understanding of work situations and expectations.

9. Make sure students have a good understanding of their particular learning disability. They should know and be able to articulate their strengths and weaknesses as well as what compensating techniques and accommodations work best for them.

10. Help students understand how their disability is connected to social experiences with peers, families, and employers. A visual or auditory discrimination deficit, and/or and attention deficit disorder frequently lead to missed cues and inappropriate timing in conversation.

11. Encourage students to be their own advocate. A good first step is to encourage them to discuss their learning disability and needed accommodations, if any, with their regular high school instructors.

12. Learn about Section 504 of the Rehabilitation Act of 1973. This law indicates what types of accommodations must be provided and/or allowed at postsecondary institutions if a student requests them. The responsibility is on the individual to initiate the provision of services and accommodations (unlike the requirements of P.L. 94-142 which puts the responsibility on elementary and secondary schools).

13. Get information on special exam arrangements for SAT and/or ACT. Options include untimed tests, readers or cassettes.

14. Obtain two copies of all college applications (or duplicate the one received). Use the first copy to collect needed information. Type that information onto the second copy to be sent.

15. Contact the Disabled Student Services Offices of college before applying. Get information on what kinds of services and support are available, the number of LD students attending, if there are modified admissions for LD students, and if there are any special pre-admission requirements when making application (such as a reference letter from an LD teacher).

16. Visit colleges before making a definite choice. Also, look at the communities in which they are located.

17. Consider having students start college in a summer session rather than fall. Summer classes tend to be smaller and instructors tend to have more time for individual help. Students can get acclimated before fall crowds arrive.

18. Consider an appointment with a qualified optometrist. If the student has visual perception problems, there may also be functional vision problems with tracking and focusing. Sometimes these problems can be partially corrected with special lenses.

19. Encourage students to have their own memberships in LD organizations. Newsletters from ACLD, Orton Dyslexia Society, etc. can help keep them informed about new resources and special programs.

20. Make sure it is the student's choice to attend college. The most successful LD college students are those who have high motivation and a good understanding of their particular strengths and weaknesses. They

understand that it may be harder and take more time to manage college level work. They are committed to spend that extra time on studying, and to request and use appropriate accommodations when needed.

Developed by: Carol Sullivan, Counselor for LD students, Northern Virginia Community College, Annandale, Virginia; and The Staff of HEATH Resource Center, One Dupont Circle, NW, Washington, DC 20036.

March 1987
Reprinted with permission.

COLLEGE AND THE LEARNING DISABLED
UNDERSTANDING SECTION 504

Margaret Dietz Meyer, Ph.D.

The challenges of seeking admission to an appropriate college and succeeding after acceptance can be an exciting and enjoyable process for learning disabled students and their parents. The better informed families are about the governance over the process, the more straightforward it may be. This is particularly true for individuals who wish to study at a four-year college or university with competitive admission and scholastic standards.

Why Is Section 504 Important?

Section 504 of the Rehabilitation Act of 1973 (PL 93-112) directly addresses the college experience:

"No otherwise qualified handicapped individual in the United States . . . shall, solely by reason of his handicap, be excluded from the participation in, be denied the benefits of, or be subjected to discrimination under any program or activity receiving Federal financial assistance . . ."

This law protects all handicapped students, including learning disabled college students, against discrimination, but it does not mandate that colleges must have specific programs exclusively for learning disabled students. Subpart E of Section 504, Post-secondary Education, defines nondiscrimination in relation to seven important parts of the college experience:

- Admission and recruitment

- Treatment of students

- Academic Adjustments

- Housing

- Health and insurance

- Financial assistance

- Nonacademic services

159

The term "postsecondary education" is a broad one which includes education at competitive colleges, education at colleges with open admission, and vocational training after high school. Because Section 504 covers all of these options, students who wish to continue their educations through academic or technical training after high school may discover that many more opportunities are available to them than they might have expected.

Although Section 504 is certainly not the only law governing education after high school, it is one which greatly affects opportunities for learning disabled students. Competitive colleges are complying with Section 504 because it affects their receipt of Federal monies.

Given this situation, what are some basic explanations which can make the college experience more clear and straightforward for learning disabled students and their parents?

Admission and Confidentiality

Except in very specific circumstances, colleges are generally prohibited from making preadmission inquiries about learning disabilities. In addition, colleges may not set limits on the number of learning disabled students they may accept. While these and other provisions of Section 504 protect students, colleges which have a competitive admission standard are free to accept only qualified students who meet ". . . the academic and technique standards requisite to admission . . . "

After students are accepted, usually before classes begin, colleges may make inquiries on a confidential basis about needs for academic adjustments which may be necessary to make programs accessible. Student responses to such inquiries are voluntary. In practice, lack of voluntary disclosure may release the college from any particular commitment to academic adjustments. Because such inquiries and student responses to them are confidential, students should expect to assume the greater share of the role in their own advocacy.

Selection of Courses

Although this provision applies primarily to physically handicapped students, it affects learning disabled students as well. Overall, colleges cannot exclude qualified learning disabled students from taking any course or course of study they choose, and ". . . as a whole . . ." such programs must be offered in ". . . the most integrated setting appropriate." In addition, qualified students are permitted to participate in any academic programs with no extra help if they so choose.

Academic Adjustments

These may include, but are not necessarily limited to, extended time to complete a degree, alternate forms of testing, and use of tape recorders in classrooms. As is the case in the Treatment of Students provision, Academic Adjustments are to be made on "an individuals case by-case basis." For example, colleges cannot make rules which prohibit the use of tape recorders by learning disabled students who need them to take notes, but professors' rights to materials they present in class are, interestingly enough, generally protected by copyright laws; students should speak with professors before using tape recorders because some colleges may still require students to sign a waiver agreeing to use classroom tapes only for personal study, i.e., not for distribution to anyone else.

Housing, Health and Insurance, Financial Assistance

Here again, the "as a whole," "most integrated setting appropriate," and "individual case-by-case basis" terms apply. Housing includes both campus and off campus living facilities. Health and Insurance includes both campus health facility services and student health insurance policies offered to all students.

Financial Assistance is commonly referred to as financial aid. As opposed to repayable loans and other types of awards based on financial need, many colleges administer or help to administer scholarships. Some scholarships have been established through legal wills, trusts and bequests which require that some type of discrimination, such as scholastic excellence or demonstrated talent, be made in their award; this is permissible under Section 504 so long as the "overall effect" does not create less opportunity for qualified learning disabled students to receive financial aid.

Counseling–Social Organizations

Nonacademic Services include physical education, counseling and placement, and social clubs and organizations. Although colleges cannot counsel qualified learning disabled students toward more restrictive career objectives than those which are available to all students with similar abilities and interests, colleges may provide factual information about licensing and certification requirements which can be obstacles to learning disabled students in pursuit of a particular career.

Suggestions For Parents

The college experience typically begins in the junior year of high school, with visits to high school counselors, letters of inquiry to colleges, and preliminary campus visits. Students should consider their unique abilities, talents and gifts, particularly in relation to college major fields of study. It is just as important to be able to articulate one's talents clearly as it is to be frank about the nature of one's learning disability. This aids high school and college counselors in doing their best to help each individual find an appropriate college.

Teach Students to Become Their Own Advocates

Parents who are well informed about both their rights and their responsibilities as advocates under PL 94-142 of 1975, may find Section 504, especially the provision related to college admission, noteworthy. The value of teaching students to become their own best advocates and to be articulate about their special gifts should not be underestimated.

That there is flexibility in the interpretation of Section 504 should be obvious. That its implementation requires well-informed dialogue among parents, students and educators is evident.

Individually and collectively, we all have a great deal to gain from the dialogue and interchanges which must follow. One of our most precious resources should not be wasted! That resource is human talent.

Editor's Note: *Margaret Dietz Meyer, Ph.D., is an Assistant Professor of Writing at Ithaca College. She wishes to thank Arlyn Gardner, Executive Director of FCLD, for the invitation to write this article and Kay Nelson, Affirmative Action Officer at Ithaca College for providing resources.*

Reprinted for THEIR WORLD magazine with permission of the editor, Julie Gilligan. THEIR WORLD is the annual publication of the National Center of Learning Disabilities, 99 Park Avenue, New York, N.Y. 10016. Founder, Carrie Rozelle.

THE COLLEGE OPTION

College offers potential benefits for all students, including those with learning disabilities. For some, a two-year or four-year college or university program may lead to a career-entry job; for others, a college degree may lead to advanced graduate or professional training. Stretching one's horizons intellectually and socially can lead to personal growth. Experiences both in and out of classes can help to set a career course. For nearly all students, college provides exposure to new ideas and new friends and can have a lasting, lifelong effect.

In considering the college option, students with learning disabilities should not only review the levels of services, as previously described, but should know the goals and objectives of each institution and the advantages each offers to learning disabled students. (For additional help in narrowing choices, see the chapter, "Matchmaking: Selection and Admission.")

Two-Year Colleges

Public community or junior colleges differ from private junior colleges, but all of them offer students an opportunity to test the academic waters. For many students, this is a chance to prepare for further education, to learn an occupational skill, or to change careers; for others, it is a way to enhance personal development. Students who complete these two-year programs earn an AA (Associate of Arts) degree, and credits can be transferred to a four-year college or university. For courses of study in specific occupations (e.g., bookkeeping, child care, or graphics production), a certificate is usually awarded. (These courses frequently take less than two years to complete.)

Public Community and Junior Colleges

Publicly funded community or junior colleges exist in or near almost every city of the United States. These institutions are committed to serving the educational and training needs of the local communities. Open admission policies make it possible for anyone over 18 years of age to attend even if they do not have a high school diploma. However, most community colleges do require that students taking courses for credit pass a high school equivalency test (GED). Preparation for the GED is usually given on campus.

Community colleges offer liberal arts subjects as well as training in specific occupations, such as hotel management, auto mechanics, marketing, computer programming, or dental assisting. Most also have remedial or developmental courses for upgrading basic academic skills.

Community colleges are becoming increasingly responsive to the needs of learning disabled students, and many are developing excellent support services. To find out what services are available, contact the disabled student services (DSS) office.

Advantages for learning disabled students attending community colleges:

- The choice of living at home while making the transition to college.

- No admissions requirements, such as college entrance exams, grade point average, class rank.

- An opportunity to try out college by taking one or two courses.

- A chance to build a better academic record that can be transferred to a four-year college or university for which the student is qualified. A student transferring to a four-year college is not usually required to take entrance examinations, although other entrance requirements must be met.

- An opportunity to learn an occupation, to work on academic skills, or to learn ways to accommodate learning problems.

- The chance to return to school to upgrade academic and job skills and to work toward improved employment opportunities or a career change.

Private Junior Colleges

Of the approximately 200 private junior colleges in the country, most are small, residential schools that prepare students for transfer to a four-year liberal arts institution. Some offer occupational training. Upon completion of the two-year program, an AA degree is awarded. Entrance examinations are usually required, although in many cases, other criteria, such as work experience and extracurricular activities are considered.

Advantages for learning disabled students:

- An opportunity to live away from home in an intimate, supportive environment.

- Small classes in which instructors can provide individualized attention.

- Opportunities to work on improving reading, writing, and math skills.

- A chance to train for a new career after being in the working world.

Four-Year Colleges and Universities

Four-year colleges and undergraduate university programs, including four-year technical schools, vary in tradition, size, admissions criteria, academic standards, course offerings, student population, location, and cost. All grant a BS or BA degree upon completion of four years of study with a concentration in a major subject.

In most college or undergraduate university programs, students are expected to sample a variety of courses during the first two years and select their major in the last two years. Requirements for graduation differ, although most colleges require a certain number of credits in English and foreign languages.

A number of colleges are specialized, such as the Massachusetts Institute of Technology, the Juilliard School of Music, and the Rhode Island School of Design. Students are expected to be proficient in their fields but must also take courses in other fields.

Tuition varies greatly. State-supported institutions tend to be less costly. Some financial aid is usually available.

Advantages for learning disabled students:

- An extensive selection of majors. There are over 400 majors offered in American colleges and universities. With appropriate accommodations and services, learning disabled students who have the potential to do college-level work can find many subject areas that are of interest.

- Several sources of help, such as counseling services, peer tutoring, learning labs, math centers. Some departments of education, special education, psychology, or English, particularly at universities, offer diagnostic and special tutorial services.

- Opportunities to develop talents (e.g., music, art, dance) either by majoring in that field or by attending a specialized four-year college.

- Availability of DSS offices on many campuses.

Graduate and Professional Schools

Opportunities for learning disabled students in graduate and professional schools are opening up, and new and innovative support services are being developed. At Ohio State University, the Office of Disability Services is working with the colleges of dentistry, medicine, and law to tape textbooks and make provisions for accommodations in testing situations.

A pioneering program for learning disabled students is under way at the New York University College of Dentistry. The program grew out of awareness that many bright, potentially good dentists were lost to the profession because of learning disabilities and that with appropriate accommodations, these people could fulfill all professional requirements and have productive careers.

Graduate students are entitled to the same types of accommodations and services that are becoming more available in undergraduate schools. Graduate students who think they have a learning disability can take advantage of campus diagnostic, tutorial, and other support services. If there is a DSS office on campus, this is a logical place to go for assistance. Graduate students, as well as other students, should familiarize themselves with Section 504.

Financial Aid

College tuition varies greatly, with state-supported institutions tending to be less costly. There are no specific scholarships for learning disabled students, and they must go through the traditional channels of applying for grants, loans, scholarships, and work-study programs. Students who are vocational rehabilitation clients should check with their counselor to see whether tuition and/or accommodations are covered.

Any applications for funding should be obtained no later than the beginning of the high school senior year. These applications and information about funding sources are available in high school counselors' offices.

When applying to schools, remember to request information about financial aid or check the general college directories regarding financial aid policies of individual schools. These directories explain eligibility for each school's financial aid program and give application deadlines.

Information Sources

Financial aid programs are either public or private, and there are some excellent pamphlets, booklets, and organizations that have up-to-date material about these programs.

The HEATH Resource Center, the National Clearinghouse for Handicapped Individuals, has a fact sheet on financial aid and a list of state agencies responsible for postsecondary education. These state agencies are knowledgeable about financial aid as well as grant and loan programs for state residents. To get these fact sheets, write to the HEATH Resource Center, One Dupont Circle, N.W., Washington, D.C. 20036 or call the toll-free information number 800-54 HEATH.

The Federal Student Aid Programs, U.S. Department of Education, publishes an excellent, clearly written booklet, *The Student Guide—Five Federal Financial Aid*

Programs (updated annually). This guide describes and gives the application process for five major federally supported student aid programs:

- Pell Grants

- Supplemental Educational Opportunity Grants (SEOG)

- National Direct Student Loans (NDSL)

- Guaranteed Student Loans (GSL)

- PLUS loans

- College work-study programs.

To get this booklet, check with your high school guidance department or career center or write to Federal Student Aid Programs, US. Department of Education, P.O. Box 84, Washington, D.C. 20044 or call (301) 984-4070.

A new organization, National College Services, provides information and advice about financial aid, tuition plan options, scholarship searches, and other special funding sources. For a brochure, fee schedule, and any free booklets, such as *The College Financial Aid Emergency Kit,* write to National College Services, 16220 South Frederick Road, Gaithersburg, Maryland 20877, Attention, Herm Davis, President.

Another new resource, *Mortgaged Futures: How to Graduate from School Without Going Broke* (available from Hope Press; P.O. Box 40611; Washington, D.C. 20016-0611; $9.95), is a well-written, factual book on the many ways to finance a college education.

College Preparatory Programs

Some learning disabled students who have graduated from high school are capable of college-level work but still have needs in certain academic areas. For them, college preparatory programs for learning disabled students can help improve reading, math, writing, or study skills. Following are examples of specific programs; others can be found by looking in directories listed in the chapter "Matchmaking: Selection and Admission."

■ The Hilltop Preparatory School in Rosemont, Pennsylvania, offers a transitional college program. Students work on areas of academic weakness while taking a number of college credit courses at nearby schools.

■ The Landmark School in Prides Crossing, Massachusetts, a private residential school for learning disabled students, offers a one-year college preparatory course. The program provides intensive, individualized instruction in language arts, math, and study skills. Students also learn ways to cope with the challenge of organizing the demands of college life. The school offers a similar college preparatory program during a seven-week summer session.

■ Specific Diagnostic Studies, Inc. in Rockville, Maryland, is a private diagnostic and tutorial program in which students get individualized tutorial or small-group teaching in areas that need strengthening. Some students receive help while attending college; others are helped to prepare for college and to take college admission tests.

In Conclusion

Learning disabled students can succeed in all types of colleges and universities, including the most prestigious. But it is very important to be realistic about the level of support needed and to know in advance if that support is available.

Reprinted with permission from Scheiber, B. & Talpers, J. (1987), Unlocking potential: College and other choices for learning disabled people pp. 45-49. Bethesda, MD: Adler and Adler.

QUESTIONS TO ASK YOURSELF

■ What school size are you looking for? Do you want to be in an urban or rural environment? do you want to be on a large or small campus?

■ Do you want to live at home? Do you need time to be with your family while you are trying out the academic world?

■ Do your SAT and ACT scores, grade point average, courses, and class rank match the requirements of the schools you are considering? If not, do you have talents, interests, motivation, and ways of compensating for your learning problems that might be taken into consideration by an admissions officer?

■ Are you comfortable explaining the different ways that you learn and how you have coped with these differences?

■ What kinds of support services do you need?

■ What is your financial situation? Do you have to work part time? Can you get assistance from vocational rehabilitation or can you get a loan?

Questions to Ask Schools

■ What is the school's attitude toward learning disabled students? Are faculty and administrators aware of the problems and needs of learning disabled students as well as their potential for success?

■ What are the admission requirements? SAT's, ACT's, grade point average, class rank? Are there nonstandard ways to take entrance exams? Are letters of support, extracurricular activities, or personal essays considered?

■ Are there other ways to be admitted? Special admission policies, transfer, provisional admission?

■ What are levels of support services? If a school says that it has support services, what are the specific ways in which help is available, and how does a student get that help?

■ What accommodations are available (untimed tests, alternatives to taking written exams, access to taped texts, notetaker services, tutors, readers?)

- Are waivers granted to disabled students who, because of their disabilities cannot pass certain courses, such as foreign language or statistics?

- Is there a disabled student service office on campus? If so, is there someone in that office who has a special understanding of learning disabilities?

- If more intensive counseling is needed, is there a counseling service on campus?

- If tutoring is available, who does it? Is there supervision? Are tutors trained to work with learning disabled students? What is the cost?

- If this is a technical or vocational education school, does it have a coordinator of services for the handicapped or a vocational support team?

- How available are faculty members to students?

- How many credits must be taken for a student to be considered full time?

- Are special study skills courses given for credit and/or can they be counted as hours toward full-time status?

- What are the experiences of other learning disabled students on that campus?

- Is there a learning disabilities student self-help group?

Reprinted with permission from Scheiber, B. & Talpers, J. (1987), Unlocking potential: College and other choices for learning disabled people pp. 45-49. Bethesda, MD: Adler and Adler.

LIVING AND LEARNING WITH DYSLEXIA

Sarah L. Levine and Sally Osbourne

I was in the seventh grade when my teacher asked me to stand up and read. I stood up, but I couldn't recognize even one word on the page. After what seemed an eternity, the teacher got angry and told me to go into another classroom where I was to write, again and again: "I am stupid because I cannot read."

I didn't say a word. But I couldn't do what the teacher wanted, because I couldn't spell. So I just sat and waited until a friend came in at the end of the day to collect the assignment. After she had spelled it out for me, I wrote it over and over again. Then I gave it to the teacher and went home.

That was the end of it. The teacher never helped me with my reading or writing before or after that time. A couple of days later, my mother got angry enough about this incident and about my education in general that she sent me to live with my aunt in Michigan.

Today I am a graduate of Harvard University. Just saying "Harvard" makes me shiver. I remember well that sunny September day during graduate student orientation, when the dean reassured all of us that the admissions committee had not made a mistake. We did, indeed, belong there. I watched as others sat tall in their seats, and I felt myself slip down several inches in my own. I knew the dean was not speaking to me. Why would Harvard want anything to do with a learning-disabled student?

Sally Osbourne was 5 when her father died in a boating accident. The oldest of three children, Sally had a sister who was 2 1/2 and a brother who was just a year old at the time. Sally's mother was a full-time homemaker until her husband's death. Then she returned to college and became a teacher. Concerned about the potentially negative influences of city life on her young family, she moved to rural Wisconsin.

The four Osbournes stayed close together as they moved from one small community to another. Rarely did they stay in one place for more than a year. For Sally, these were times of mixed emotions.

I didn't like all the moving around, because it was hard to make friends. But it was nice in a way, because it takes a while to get to know someone, so it would be some time before people found out that I couldn't read. Actually, it really helped to keep moving.

I remember kindergarten being a lot of fun, but school wasn't fun from the first grade on. My first-grade teacher used to walk by our house every week to drop off a bunch of flash cards. My mother was supposed to go over them with me until I learned the words. But it was so hard. I'd look at a word and wouldn't know it. When my mother told me what it was, I would repeat what she said. But then we'd go to the next word, and I'd forget the first one. It was frustrating.

Sally knew very early in her school career that something was wrong. There had to be a reason why she couldn't learn when all her friends were learning. She decided there was something wrong with *her.* She decided that she was *dumb.*

Students with learning disabilities often become frustrated with their inability to learn in school. Some become behavior problems to divert attention from their academic performance; others try to behave perfectly and hope that adults won't notice them. Sally adopted the latter strategy, always smiling and pretending that she was happy. "It was much easier to make believe that everything was fine than it was to admit that I did not understand," she says.

Many people mistakenly associate learning disabilities with limited intelligence. In elementary school, when one of Sally's friends asked to have Sally sit near her she was told that Sally was retarded and needed to sit next to the teacher. And that message, reinforced many times during Sally's years in school, had staying power. Now, at age 38, with a degree from Harvard, 12 years of experience as a teacher, and with a husband and three children, Sally is just beginning to believe that she is smart.

In fact, children who have difficulty with two-dimensional work, such as reading and writing, may have a talent for working in multiple dimensions. Sally discovered that she was good in math and science as long as she steered clear of word problems.

Individuals with learning disabilities may also display a talent for adopting strategies to hide their limitations. For years, Sally conspired with friends to avoid the horror of having to read aloud. If she sat with one friend in front of her and another behind, she might be passed over when the friend protecting her from the front "mistakenly" read two paragraphs. If Sally dropped her book at just the right time, the friend protecting her from behind could quickly continue reading. Or sometimes Sally would sit in the back corner of the room while friends in front occupied the teacher with such delaying tactics as extraneous discussion. Often the class would end long before Sally had a turn to read.

What seems strange to Sally today is the fact that most adults in the schools simply ignored her. Once, when she was called on to read and couldn't, the teacher told her mother that Sally needed glasses. When that didn't work, the teacher moved Sally from the lowest reading group to the highest reading group—and never asked Sally to read again. Of course, Sally couldn't even read the book in the lowest group, but, wherever the teacher told her to sit, Sally sat and continued *not reading*.

Sally struggled through school with poor grades and consistent help from her mother, who read to her, talked her through her papers, spoke on her behalf at school, and, perhaps most important, continued to tell her that she was smart. While Sally did poorly at school, she excelled in the extracurricular activities that her mother encouraged her to try, including music and dance. Her mother would say, "Look at all the things you can do, Sally. You *must* be smart!"

In high school, Sally's guidance counselor told her that she was "not college material." But Sally's mother insisted that she was. After a heated argument, Sally was placed in the vocational track, to satisfy the guidance department—*and* in the college-preparatory track, to satisfy her mother. She had no free periods, she had twice as much work, and she was under a lot more pressure to hide her differences. From first grade through high school, Sally did not experience academic success. For the most part, teachers returned her smile but were content to ignore her learning problem. Always, her mother encouraged her. And Sally kept wondering what was wrong. Gradually, she became convinced that she was not stupid. The way she was treated and the results of all her efforts in school, however, offered powerful evidence to the contrary.

When Sally finished high school, she could not read or write at a level even close to the level expected of a high school graduate. But Sally's mother congratulated her for finishing high school and, in almost the same breath, told Sally, "Of course, you're going to college."

Sally had no idea what she wanted to do. When her mother read her a book about a teacher in Appalachia, Sally decided that she, too, would teach poor children in rural schools. Sally's mother picked out a state college for her. When the college admissions officer insisted that Sally's academic record and test scores offered little hope of success, a phone call from her mother to the governor's office secured a place for Sally.

College was a struggle from the start. I remember fighting my way through freshman registration lines, asking other students where to go. I felt ashamed because I couldn't read the signs posted on the walls or the forms I held tightly in my hand. Had anyone asked why I was having so much trouble, I was prepared to say that I was a foreign student.

When I did register, it was for classes that had oral tests, projects, or papers. I could not take a written exam.

Four years later, I earned a bachelor's degree - or perhaps I should say my mother and I earned one. She read many of the textbooks to me; she transcribed the ideas from my head onto paper; she pushed me to accept new challenges. I remember how she smiled when I received an A in a class in which she had once received a B. She danced with delight when she saw my first grade report with a B + average. She cried when my name appeared on the dean's list.

Sally graduated from college with a teaching certificate and found a job teaching first and second grades in a rural school. Sally's ingenuity paid off in the classroom. She had second-graders teach first-graders, even though some of the children refused to believe her when she said she didn't know the answers to their questions. When she read a book and came to a part she couldn't remember, she would close the book and ask the class, "What might happen next?"

Sally and her students did a lot of hands-on learning. Since they were out in the country, they could go for long walks. She used these times to demonstrate, and this is how they did math and science. Inside, they also learned by doing; they did a lot of cooking, for instance. Parents were frequently invited to visit and help with the class, and Sally had an aide who could teach the children phonics.

The test scores of Sally's students improved. And it is interesting that her alternative and expanded strategies for teaching and learning were the products of her ostensible *limitations*. Perhaps all teachers could do more for students by doing less traditional teaching. Certainly, most teachers could profitably expand their repertoire of teaching methods.

A year later, Sally agreed to take over a friend's special-needs classroom in another state. Her friend, a teacher of the learning disabled, suspected that Sally had learning difficulties and encouraged her to take the position, which would also require Sally to enroll in an intensive summer course. As Sally learned about teaching dyslexic children, her own reading and writing abilities gradually improved. For Sally, both the learning experience and the discovery that she had a learning disability were revelations.

> *It was absolutely wonderful to experience the joy of learning. And it was wonderful knowing that there was a reason I hadn't been able to read and write. What a revelation it was, learning that am not stupid. I love to say the word dyslexia. I can learn to read and write. It's going to take me longer than most people, and am going to have to work a lot harder, but it will be worth it.*

During that summer, Sally exuberantly accepted the challenge of learning. Waking at dawn, she met two of her classmates for early-morning tutoring sessions. From 8 a.m. until 5 p.m. she attended formal classes. Then, instead of relaxing after dinner, she'd seek out individuals to work and talk with her until late into the night. "Everyone thought I was so dedicated," she recalls. "They didn't realize that I was completely captivated by learning."

Not only did the world of learning open to Sally that summer, but, in the fall, so did the world of teaching. Buttressed by her nascent abilities to read and write, by her own difficult school experiences, and by an introductory knowledge of learning disabilities, she began to broaden her perceptions of her students. Sally could see herself in the children who smiled politely to avoid admitting that they didn't understand. She recognized the little boy who consistently needed to leave the reading group for a drink of water just before his turn to read. She understood the unruly children, the ones who preferred the label *troublemaker* to the label *stupid.*

Finally, there was John, a hyperactive child who squirmed at his desk, often with his feet in the air and his head on the floor. Sally told the children how she once knew some people who used a similar trick to keep their feet warm. She taped the words that she wanted John to learn under his desk where he could see them. "I felt I had to meet him where he was, rather than force him to sit like everyone else," Sally explains. Maybe he would learn better with his feet up in the air. I realized from my own experiences that everyone learns in his or her own special way."

One of Sally's enduring qualities is her tendency to set high personal standards. She is bent on proving her capabilities to the world (and to herself). After years of teaching kindergarten, she wanted a new challenge. She began by taking several graduate courses. Then she decided to go back to school full-time. She applied to the Harvard Graduate School of Education, and she was accepted.

At Harvard, Sally's insecurity about her disabilities resurfaced with fierce intensity. She did not want anyone to know that she was dyslexic, to make concessions for her, or to decide that she didn't belong. She lived by herself in a dormitory room, telling no one of her learning disabilities for the entire first term. One can only imagine how difficult it must be for someone with severe dyslexia to cope in such a highly conceptual environment, in which reading and writing are so important.

Sally started her papers months before they were due. In one course, she joined every available study group, so she could hear the readings discussed over and over again. She repeatedly turned down opportunities to go out. Her friends were limited to the students who could help her learn. She slept an average of four or five hours a night. By the start of winter, she was on the brink of exhaustion.

Only a marginal grade on a term paper drove Sally to seek help. Thinking she had failed, Sally went to an office at the university that was specially designed to help students with reading and writing. Even then, she initially told the counselor that she was seeking information to improve her teaching. Desperation—more than courage—finally motivated Sally to tell her story and agree to be tested. Two weeks later, Sally received the first official description and diagnosis of her learning disabilities: she was the most severely dyslexic student that the specialist had seen in his many years at the university.

Although there is no universally recognized definition, most professionals accept the description of dyslexia as a difficulty with learning to read and write efficiently, despite intelligence and emotional health, opportunity, and conventional instruction. Dyslexic individuals may also have difficulty with spelling, spoken communication, and organizational capacities.

In addition to being officially diagnosed as dyslexic, Sally remembers two other significant points in the diagnostic report: she did belong at Harvard, and she was entitled to support services. She was referred to an office for student services in the Harvard Graduate School of Education, where she learned that the university would pay for someone to tape her assignments, read to her, and edit her written work. She also discovered other resources: a university support group for learning-disabled students and a student organization that sponsored monthly speakers on learning disabilities.

Sally took advantage of these services. She joined the support group, attended a presentation, and accepted assistance with her writing.

> I especially appreciated the help of my student editor. She'd read my papers, circling spelling and grammatical errors and identifying paragraphs that she didn't understand. All my life, people had told me that I had good ideas but didn't express them clearly. Talking my ideas through with an editor really helped me to see where I was being unclear. With practice and feedback, I gradually learned to be more precise.

Sally decided not to take advantage of the services available to improve her reading. Instead, she received informal help with reading from her friends. "I still felt ashamed that I couldn't read," Sally recalls. "Most students seemed able to handle the reading, but many complained about having a hard time with papers. Somehow it was more acceptable to ask for help with writing."

Once her coursework was completed, Sally teamed up with a friend to read Shakespeare. The friend would read several pages aloud and explain their meaning. Then Sally would reread the pages. With practice and persistence, she proudly completed *Macbeth*. Along with all the reading she had done for her classes, this deliberate work on reading and comprehension gradually improved her skill and increased her confidence.

During her second semester at Harvard, Sally told her story—to teachers to classmates, and to friends. To her surprise, most of them were empathic. None lowered their expectations for Sally's performance, but many developed a new appreciation for diverse learning needs. Several teachers were especially helpful. One offered the services of his teaching assistants as well as his own time to read assignments, to review papers, and to discuss the readings. Sally took advantage of this offer and talked to the teacher about specific readings. Understanding Sally's preference for visual learning, this teacher made a point in class of drawing figures and diagrams on the chalkboard and pausing after a question to give students time to formulate their responses.

In a course on school law, the professor deliberately paid extra attention to cases involving the handicapped. In a course on reading and school policy, Sally was asked to serve as a resource person during the sessions on learning disabilities. In a course on leadership, Sally shared her story and led a discussion on the problems faced by teachers and leaders who have learning disabilities. At the final class session, Sally read something she had written. "It was the first time I'd ever read aloud to adults—and these were adults at Harvard! I was nervous but I did it. It felt like a wonderful accomplishment."

Not all of Sally's teachers were comfortable with her disclosure. Sally noted in one class that her fast-paced instructor consistently overlooked her raised hand, which Sally interpreted as an effort to protect her. In fact, it exaggerated her sense of isolation, of being different.

Overall, Sally found support and encouragement from teachers and friends. She also felt relieved after sharing the secret she had kept for so long.

Today, Sally believes that the services she received from the university markedly strengthened her ability to read and write, but she is convinced that the most critical factor in her growth was her enhanced feeling of self-worth. "Once I began to feel good about myself," she says, "I could start learning. And now that I'm learning, I never want to stop."

Sally graduated from Harvard with a master's degree in education. She returned to her family and to the classroom. She plans to continue teaching and hopes eventually to become an elementary school principal.

Sally's story raises some important questions: How is it possible for a student to go through school without learning to read and write with proficiency? How can educators pass over, ignore, or deny learning difficulties? Why are there so many schools in which only a very narrow range of learning styles is rewarded?

Sally's story also teaches many lessons - some of them painful, but most of them promising. Sally's gains have not been without cost. In order to keep up with her schoolwork and to keep her disability a secret, Sally distanced herself from the activities and friendships that most of us take for granted. A person who likes people, Sally found it especially difficult to maintain this social isolation.

Sally's story dramatizes the essential role of parents in personal development and in schooling. Sally's mother contributed to Sally's success in tangible and intangible ways. Without her support and encouragement, Sally would not have believed in herself or experienced success.

Sally's story also dramatizes the power of individual initiative, courage, and resilience. Despite constant obstacles Sally refused to accept defeat. In fact, the obstacles only sparked her desire to triumph.

Sally's experience at Harvard illustrates the importance of special services for learning-disabled students. It shows the positive influence of knowledgeable and understanding teachers, as well as the need to reeducate those teachers who may be unfamiliar or uncomfortable with learning handicaps.

Sally's story demonstrates that learning-disabled teachers may have special talents, including expanded strategies for working with all children and adolescents —whether or not they have learning disabilities. Learning-disabled teachers may also bring to their work higher than usual levels of motivation, empathy, and understanding, because their own experiences with schooling attune them to the learning problems of their students.

Finally, Sally's story reminds us that learning disabilities may be constructively thought of as learning *differences*. Children and adults with dyslexia and other learning handicaps often demonstrate talents in the visual arts, athletics, music, and math. Rather than dismiss learning-disabled students, teachers can identify their strengths and can capitalize on them.

When Sally began to share her story at Harvard, she was surprised to discover how many others have learning disabilities. Like her, many have taken great pains to hide their differences. As an aspiring principal, Sally recognizes that some teachers and parents, as well as children, may indeed be learning disabled. And she has come to view her own disabilities as a resource for school leadership.

Sally left Harvard determined to disclose her disabilities to the students and staff of her school, to her school board, and to her community. But her friends were concerned. Was her community ready to accept a teacher with learning disabilities? Would disclosure interfere with Sally's quest for a principalship? Perhaps many individuals and groups were not yet ready to accept the limitations as well as the strengths of dyslexia.

These questions persuaded us to disguise Sally's identity when we told her story. They also persuaded us to qualify the nature of Sally's victory—though, in fact, it is not Sally's victory that is compromised as much as it is our own triumph that is diluted. As long as we harbor negative attitudes toward learning disabilities, we run the risk of constraining the extraordinary talents of many children and adults.

Sally recognizes both the risks and the potential power of revealing her disabilities. Some people might argue that her learning differences prevent her from being a competent professional. In our view, however, such differences are to be celebrated. They help us to understand and know Sally better. They will help Sally—as an adult and as an educator —learn to recognize and honor the individual needs and complexities of others. And they illustrate the pressing need for our society to accept diversity, both within and outside of the schoolhouse.

Suggested Resources

ORGANIZATIONS

Association for Children and Adults with Learning Disabilities
4156 Library Rd.
Pittsburgh, PA 15234 412/341-1515

This national office will answer questions and send information, including a reading list and the location of state chapters. Printed materials range in price from 15 cents to $45.

Orton Dyslexia Society 724 York Rd.
Baltimore, MD 21204 301/296-0232

This organization serves as a clearing-house for information on dyslexia, including suggested readings. Staff members will answer questions and send out materials. In particular they recommend: *Readings for Educators* ($10 plus postage) and *Intimacy with Language* ($7, including postage).

READINGS

Louise Clarke. *Can't Read, Can't Write, Can't Talk Too Good Either.* New York: Penguin Books, 1973.

Susan Hampshire. *Susan's Story.* New York: St. Martin's Press, 1982.

Eileen Simpson. *Reversals: A Personal Account of Victory over Dyslexia.* Boston: Houghton Mifflin, 1979.

Priscilla Vail. *Smart Kids with School Problems: Things to Know and Ways to Help.* New York: Dutton, 1987.

The authors gratefully acknowledge Priscilla Vail for her suggestions.

Levine, S.L. & Osbourne, S. (1989, April). Living with dyslexia. Phi Delta Kappan, p. 594-598

Dyslexics at Brown:
A Student Perspective

Introduction

This booklet was written by some of the dyslexic students at Brown in order to make the Brown community — especially incoming freshmen — aware of dyslexia, its symptoms and some study strategies for coping with it. The booklet also lists some of the resources which Brown offers its student body.

In addition to writing this booklet, the students have formed a self-help group called Dyslexics At Brown (DAB). It is the first campus branch of the Orton Dyslexia Society. Its goals are to help identify other dyslexics on campus, to help dyslexics get through college successfully, and to reach out to other campuses to encourage the formation of similar groups.

Among the ways the group tries to help its members is by educating them about dyslexia and ways for compensating for its effects, and advising them of the special ways the university helps them overcome their difficulties. Also, the group is trying to make the faculty and administration more aware of the variation in learning styles of *all* students (not just dyslexics) and to encourage the use of teaching methods to accommodate them.

Many of the students struggling academically through their years at Brown will be dyslexic, but they will never learn to overcome their troubles successfully until they understand the reasons behind their difficulties. The University and DAB want learning-disabled students to leave Brown with the tools they need to succeed in their adult lives.

Definition

Dyslexic: It doesn't mean you aren't an achiever. It doesn't mean you're stupid or lazy, that you have "minimal brain damage" or severe psychological problems. What it may mean is that you have to train yourself to cope with an organizational and language disability which manifests itself most noticeably in reading and writing, but which affects your life from the most mundane task to the most crucial. The concept of dyslexia is not well-defined. Many writers differentiate among "dyslexia", "dysgraphia", "discalculia", and other learning disabilities.

At Brown we have found it useful to refer to all these information processing disorders by the single term "dyslexia", since all the different manifestations seem to have the same basic cause. Many dyslexics also have attention deficit disorder

(ADD), which affects their ability to concentrate on tasks for a sustained period of time. ADD and dyslexia are different disorders that often have similar symptoms. Most dyslexics have developmental dyslexia, which means that they have had it since birth. It is also possible to acquire dyslexia through traumatic injury.

What causes dyslexia? Recent research indicates that the brains of dyslexics differ structurally from other brains and process information in a distinctive manner.

At the moment, dyslexics cannot look forward to being "cured," but they can learn to compensate for their disability and make use of specific remedial techniques that will strengthen their reading and writing skills. They need not have lower expectations. Here at Brown, a strong and active community of dyslexic students takes the same courses and earns the same degrees as other students in a variety of disciplines, including such heavy-reading concentrations as history and English. Just to have gotten this far in their educations demonstrates that they are intelligent, highly motivated, shrewd and persistent. This means they can do what they are willing to try hard enough to do.

Still, dyslexics, no matter what the academic task may be, constantly face an insidious shortage of *time*. Everything takes longer for them, and this results in fatigue and frustration.

Though they can look forward to a period when understanding of dyslexia will be more widespread, dyslexic students know that they– and their brains– are not going to change. It is a realistic concern that their disabilities rather than their talents and strengths (they really do have strengths) may be "noticed," and dyslexics need to learn to deal with this.

Classic Symptoms

The following represents groups of characteristics found among dyslexic students at Brown University. Many students experience some difficulty in a number of these categories. However, dyslexics – for the most part– have trouble in *most* of these areas, though the exact degree varies from student to student. The most commonly recognized problem is a reading disability. In a dyslexic, this spectrum of problems is symptomatic of a constitutionally determined difficulty in processing certain kinds of information. In a "normal" person who has some of these difficulties, the problems do not reflect a larger disability.

If a student recognizes a good number of the symptoms listed below, he or she should consult Dean Shaw, who may then refer the student for diagnostic testing.

1. Reading

- slow reader
- trouble distinguishing between main thesis and supporting evidence
- can't remember what you just read
- reading literally: problems with tone, metaphors and words with more than one meaning (e.g., "there is a *fork* in the road")
- reading out of sequence and omitting words: ("the student went to see the professor" = "the student to the see professor")
- decoding problems: trouble associating letters and their sounds
- often mistaking one word for another ("for" and "from," "to" and "of")
- tracking difficulty: skipping over words or lines when reading
- commonly omitting titles, chapter headings and subheadings
- inevitably experiencing headaches or falling asleep when reading

2. Writing Difficulties

- freezing up when trying to write
- difficulty organizing thoughts and papers difficulty visualizing a paper's overall topic and formulating a thesis statement
- tendency to focus on specific parts of the paper instead of the overall picture and how each part relates to the whole
- beautiful sentences in your head vanishing before they can be set down
- "perfect draft" syndrome
- you generally don't catch all your own errors when proofreading
- professors comment that your ideas are great but your mechanics and structure are weak
- difficulty using cursive script, so you usually print (and even that may not be legible), and whether it's cursive or print, you write slowly.

3. Spelling

- reversals:"friend" = "freind", "probably" = "propadly"
- habitually dropping or adding letters and parts of words when writing: "know" = "now"
- unable to spell common, everyday words as well as more difficult words
- letters and words often come out of sequence

4. Speech: Listening and Speaking

- difficulty pronouncing words
- difficulty getting a point across on first try
- difficulty reading aloud
- stuttering, hesitancy in speech
- difficulty understanding spoken language

5. Oral and Written Word Association

- difficulty translating oral speech into written words
- problems with simultaneously taking notes and attending to what's going on in class
- orally a word means one thing, but written that same word seems to mean some thing else or nothing at all
- words are heard yet not comprehended

6. Coordination/Orientation

- difficulty distinguishing left from right
- difficulty with local geography and directions
- feeling lost in a familiar setting
- becoming confused when going down stairs or passing people– you may even miss steps or stumble despite being a good athlete
- difficulty doing simple mechanical tasks
- never can seem to organize things
- uncoordinated
- hyperactive in order to compensate

7. Memory

- difficulty with retention of "common knowledge" items, such as friends' names, names of places, your current age and even what day it is
- difficulty recalling names of things in conversation: frequent use of "this" or "that" or "whatchamacallit" rather than more precise words
- difficulty memorizing a string of numbers or letters in order
- constantly misplacing, losing and forgetting things
- always behind – you seem to live in a time warp

8. Concentrating

- marked difficulty concentrating with noise or people talking in the background
- easily distracted
- difficulty focusing attention
- get tired or overloaded quickly
- unable to do two activities at once (e.g., reading while eating)

9. Testing

- unable to complete an exam in the allotted time although material was well-understood and well-studied
- blanking out on exams
- difficulty narrowing down a multiple choice question to one correct response

- perpetually interpreting questions or directions differently from the way the professor intended them

10. Mathematics

  - difficulty understanding the wording of a problem
  - difficulty doing basic calculations

11. Foreign Language Learning

  - difficulty learning vocabulary
  - very slow in oral performance
  - no amount of hard work seems to help

12. Psychological Barriers

  - it's hard to begin writing a paper because it takes so long to get focused and get thoughts organized
  - feeling lazy, stupid or ashamed because of difficulty doing tasks which come so easily to others (low self-esteem)
  - feeling constantly behind no matter how hard you try or how much you learn
  - feeling that your own work is infantile or crude or otherwise not as good as that of others, and that it's definitely not on the same level as your thinking
  - frustrated by unsuccessful attempts to read, write, spell and speak correctly
  - feeling as if you are "faking" your education: people say you are smart, but you don't genuinely feel this is true even though you may be getting good grades
  - paranoid about deadlines
  - fear of filling out forms and applications and using the telephone
  - isolation: fear of not being understood
  - intensified self-consciousness and stress *because of* your other problems

Some students have found that as they begin to talk with other dyslexics the psychological symptoms begin to diminish. When frustration and fatigue decrease, dyslexic symptoms become less pronounced.

For a first-hand, published account of the struggle which dyslexics must persistently wage, we recommend reading either *Reversals* by Eileen Simpson or *Susan's Story* by Susan Hampshire.

Faculty Involvement

In addition to being able to identify the symptoms just noted, there are other ways faculty members can help. You may notice differences in a student's ability to interpret visual aids and complex diagrams, or to understand the style of teaching, especially if humor, metaphors, intuitive leaps or free-wheeling discussions are hallmarks of your classes. Conversations with a student may reveal that he/ she is having trouble grasping the organization of lectures. This problem may be reduced or alleviated by keeping lectures well-structured and by noting (on the blackboard, perhaps) at the beginning of a lecture just what the objectives and structure of the lesson are for that day. The explicit presentation of underlying structure and objectives will also aid students in organizing note-taking, studying for exams and preparing assignments and papers. Reviewing the main points brought up in classroom discussions can help integrate them into the overall organization you intended for the lesson.

Also very helpful are a willingness for personal contact, suggestions for specific study skills relevant to your discipline, and cooperation with a certain amount of a student's experimentation in trying to find a personal learning style for the particular course material. (These practices and attitudes will help not only dyslexic students, but *all* students.)

The Brown Curriculum

While in college, students are grappling with fresh ideas, different perspectives and new insights. Particularly at Brown, they are able to challenge themselves through self-directed learning and discover effective, personalized modes of learning. The Brown Curriculum offers multiple options to the motivated college student, many of which are especially helpful to dyslexic students.

For example, the University leaves up to you the decision of what group of courses best serves your academic purposes. You may opt to take as many courses as you wish S/NC: Satisfactory or No Credit. Thus, you can adjust the pace of your undergraduate work and take courses which otherwise you might avoid. You can also enroll in an ambitious five courses one semester and a slower paced three in another. If you wish it, you may request the CAS (Committee on Academic Standing) to put you on a reduced load of two or three courses per semester and pro-rate tuition costs.

You can design an independent concentration or participate in a Group Independent Studies Project (GISP) with some of your peers, focusing on a specific area of knowledge not covered by current course offerings.

Brown also encourages students to take a leave of absence or study abroad for a semester or more. This is a good way to help you figure out how to use the rest of your time at the university most effectively.

The openness and flexibility of Brown are part of what makes our school unique, so we urge you as fellow students to explore all the possibilities.

Study for Success

To be successful, a dyslexic student does not need *carte blanche* extensions on papers and untimed exams: he or she needs discipline – a lot of discipline. Not every student – whether dyslexic or not – learns to develop the quality of study habits that it takes to be successful in college. However, for a dyslexic student, a lack of discipline can prove fatal. The following is a compilation of suggestions from successful dyslexic students at Brown on coping with college-level work and developing various academic skills. If you find your self feeling guilty about requiring extra time on an examination or paper, remember that **school is not a race.** It is okay to take extra time if it means that you get more out of your education and your entire Brown experience.

General Study Habits

Because of the attention deficit often related to dyslexia, it is essential to find a quiet place to study (the library, a deserted classroom, etc.). It is also important to get enough sleep, eat well, exercise and take reasonable breaks when studying. Otherwise, dyslexic symptoms are likely to become more pronounced.

Scheduling

Having a large desk calendar (or wall calendar) on which to write all due dates for the semester is vital. Many people make up weekly and daily work schedules, setting realistic goals and making sure that they accomplish these objectives.

In order to make useful schedules, it is important to be able to assess accurately how long it will take you to do a given task. For instance, one student knows that she generally reads about 15 pages an hour (depending on the density of the material), writes one page in a half hour – actually, it takes her 20 minutes to write a page, with 10 minutes added for procrastination – and types three and a half pages in an hour, pacing herself accordingly.

Other scheduling skills that dyslexics must develop include limiting activities (you can't do everything that interests you), balancing courses (don't take four heavy reading courses in one semester), and most important of all, not fooling yourself by believing that you can finish that paper in the same amount of time as your non-dyslexic friends.

Taking Notes

If you have problems taking notes (i.e., you don't think your notes adequately reflect the lectures), here are a few tips:

-   Sit up front in the classroom. You can see better and it forces you to pay attention, and if you're going to bother going to classes, you might as well know what's going on. What goes along with this is leaving your previous location early enough to get a seat up front–five minutes makes a difference.

-   Develop a critical frame of mind. Don't write down everything the professor says — be discriminating.

-   Many students develop a personal shorthand of symbols, codewords or abbreviations to speed up note-taking, especially for technical terms or often repeated ones.

-   If you blank out on something, leave a space and go on. You can come back to it later when you think of it. This goes for exams as well.

-   Go over your notes right after class to make sure they make sense and add anything significant that you recall but didn't have time to write down.

-   Right after the lecture, borrow the notebooks of one or two of your non-dyslexic classmates and compare their notes with yours. While the lecture is still fresh in your mind, go over the notebooks — just to make sure that you managed to get all of the important points.

-   If absolutely necessary, tape-record the lectures — but then you have to budget time to listen to the tapes. Use the counter on your tape recorder: write down the number when you miss a part of the lecture and then listen only to those parts of the tape.

Reading Books

Before beginning an assignment, examine the book's title, the chapter and subchapter headings, and the table of contents in order to get an overview of the major ideas of the book.

Always read the introduction. It usually summarizes the book's thesis. (With technical articles, scan the abstract and summary for an overview of purpose and the significant findings.)

Read actively: take notes, write in the book's margin, and *selectively* underline and highlight (in different colored markers) while reading.

There are effective techniques for improving reading and writing skills – we don't mean speedreading, but basic reading skills. This is something you might want to work on with a trained reading therapist or tutor throughout the school year or intensively during a summer.

Recordings for the Blind has been useful for many students. This organization records educational books of your choice. You should order the books several weeks in advance to give them time to record the ones they do not already have. Information on registering for this service is available through Dean Shaw's office.

Studying for Exams

There are, of course, many ways to study for an exam. The value of memorizing your class notes from cover to cover is debatable, but many students find that reviewing notes alleviates tension and facilitates the recall of examples and details.

Flash cards and study guides serve well both as organizing and studying tools. Outlining and summarizing your notes in colored markers are great ways to study. Going over past exams can also be useful.

Many people find it helpful to get together with their classmates several days before the exam (long before anyone has seriously started studying) and talk about the exam and the topics that the course has covered in order to devise some kind of framework to aid later studying.

Teaching assistants can also help you to orient yourself for exams, especially if you seek their help well before exam time.

Writing a Paper

The hardest thing about writing a paper is getting started. Here is a little friendly advice (the easy-to-say, hard-to do kind of advice):

Don't fall into the trap of trying to make your rough draft perfect. If you're having problems getting started, just write anything, no matter how bad you think it is. You can edit it later.

Don't procrastinate: you're not going to be inspired. Eventually, you're going to have to sit down. Think it out and write it.

Many people also find it helpful to talk to someone else or themselves out loud about the paper. It can be useful just to talk into a tape recorder in order to define what you want to say and to make sure that you really know what your paper is to cover.

Developing a technique for writing and structuring a paper is a personal thing. There is, however, at least one feature that successful dyslexics have in common when facing the task of writing a paper: they all have some sort of plan. These vary from being nothing more than a list or flowchart of ideas to strictly detailed outlines, some of which even go so far as to specify how many words or sentences long each paragraph should be. The key is to consciously develop a planning format that works for you.

Lastly, deal with spelling errors. Try to identify the words that you consistently misspell and pay special attention to them when writing. Keeping a list or file of words you constantly misspell will give you an easy reference for checking yourself. Learn to double-check your spelling with a dictionary, which you keep nearby. Get a list of spelling and punctuation rules and *learn* them. Have friends proofread your paper for you or use a computer with a spelling checker.

Computer Word Processing

Many dyslexics have found a word processor to be a wonderful tool to help them master the process of writing. Since a computer has the potential of helping you with your writing for the rest of your life, you may want to consider buying your own personal computer. You may do it on your own or you may choose one of the models on sale at the Brown computer store at considerable discounts. It will be yours forever, and you won't have to wait in line to use it.

Whatever machine you use, you will find that the ability to revise and reorganize your written work is well worth the effort you spend learning how to use a word-processing program. And the spelling checker alone will greatly improve the appearance of your papers.

Administrative Policies

Brown University was one of the first institutions of higher education to formally acknowledge and try to act upon the problems of dyslexic students. Dyslexic students are not treated differently from other students here. They are expected to meet the same standards as other students, though they may require certain adjustments in the procedures they use in meeting those standards.

If an identifiable group of students requires a particular resource to succeed at Brown, the University attempts to provide it. Our services for dyslexic students are consistent with this policy. As this booklet illustrates, many services designed for all Brown students are particularly helpful for dyslexic students. In addition, certain administrative procedures have been established specifically for dyslexic students.

- Brown employs a specialist in language disorders to diagnose students who may be dyslexic and to offer advice on the particular needs of individual students.

- At the student's request, a note is sent to some or all of the student's professors, suggesting that the student might require untimed examinations, oral examinations, the tape recording of lectures, taking exams alone in a quiet place, or other accommodations in the course procedures.

- A severely dyslexic student may petition to take less than a normal load each semester, completing requirements for the degree in more than four years. In such cases, the student pays a pro-rated tuition charge each semester.

Dyslexic students are frequently at a disadvantage in a competitive college. This does not mean that dyslexia should act as a barrier to securing a liberal arts education. On the contrary, if you are identified as being dyslexic and can learn to accept and deal with it, you *can* achieve academic success. Indeed, dyslexic students often see things in a new light, which can be a definite advantage in a college that values creative thinking.

However, dyslexia is not an easy thing to detect. If you've thought in a certain way for your entire life, you learn to believe that your way is the norm. Almost every dyslexic diagnosed as an adult has initially been heard to say, "Do you mean that *most* people don't do that?" It is also not easy to accept because once you've admitted that you're dyslexic, you also recognize that you're never really going to "change."

Dyslexic students are bright, creative and capable people (and if they have gotten into Brown, they are in all likelihood highly motivated and disciplined as well). But, as a dyslexic, you have to accept that you're different—no dumber, no less competent—just different. You work at a different pace because you think in a different way.

Bibliography

Aaron, P. G., & Phillips, S. "A Decade of Research with Dyslexic College Students. " *Annals of Dyslexia,* Vol. 36, 1986, pp. 44-65.

Blue, Rose. *Me and Einstein: Breaking Through The Reading Barrier.* New York: Human Science Press, 1979.

Clarke, Louise. *Can't Read, Can't Write, Can't Talk Too Good Either: How To Recognize and Overcome Dyslexia in Your Child.* New York: Penguin, 1975.

Critchley, Macdonald and Eileen A. Critchley. *Dyslexia Defined.* London: William Heinemann Medical Books, 1978.

Duane, D. & Leong, C. K. (Eds.) *Understanding Learning Disabilities: International and Multidisciplinary Views.* New York: Plenum Press, 1985.

Ellis, Andrew W. *Reading, Writing and Dyslexia: A Cognitive Analysis.* Hillsdale NJ: Laurence Erlbaum Associates, 1984.

Evans, Martha M. *Dyslexia: An Annotated Bibliography.* Westport CT: Greenwood Press, 1982.

Farnham-Diggory, Sylvia. *Learning Disabilities: A Psychological Perspective.* Cambridge MA: Harvard University Press, 1978.

Goldberg, H. K. *et al. Dyslexia: Interdisciplinary Approaches to Reading Disabilities.* New York: Grune & Stratton, 1983.

Hampshire, Susan. *Susan's Story: An Autobiographical Account of My Struggle with Dyslexia.* New York: St. Martin's, 1982.

Johnson, D. & Blalock, J. (Eds.). *Young Adults with Learning Disabilities.* Orlando: Grune & Stratton, 1987.

Miles, T. R. *Dyslexia: The Pattern of Difficulties.* Springfield IL: Thomas, 1983.

Orton, Samuel T. *Reading, Writing and Speech Problems in Children.* London: Chapman & Hall, 1937.

Roswell, Florence G. and Gladys Natchez. *Reading Disability: A Human Approach for Learning,* 3rd ed. New York: Basic Books, 1977

Scheiber, Barbara & Talpers, Jeanne. *Unlocking Potential: College and Other Choices for Learning Disabled People: A Step-By-Step Guide.* Bethesda, MD: Adler & Adler, 1986.

Simpson, Eileen. *Reversals: A Personal Account of Victory Over Dyslexia.* New York: Houghton Mifflin Co., 1979.

Stevens, Suzanne H. *Classroom Success for The Learning Disabled.* Winston-Salem NC: John F. Blair, 1984.

Vellutino, Frank R. *Dyslexia: Theory and Research.* Cambridge MA: MIT Press, 1979.

Velluntino, Frank R. "Dyslexia." *Scientific American, Vol.* 256, No. 3, March, 1987, pp. 34-41.

Vogel, Susan A. "Learning Disabled College Students: Identification, Assessment, and Outcome." In *Understanding Learning Disabilities: International and Interdisciplinary Perspectives,* Drake Duane & C . K. Leong (Eds). NY: Plenum, 1985.

A Note of Thanks

Dyslexics At Brown members would like to acknowledge the warm support of Dean Harriet Sheridan, Dean Robert Shaw, Mrs. Helaine Schupack, Mrs. Marilyn Fox, Mrs. Clelia Heebner and many other interested members of the Brown community, including the few, rare professors who have bravely admitted to having dyslexia themselves.

We welcome inquiries of any person who would like to learn more about this language disorder or the activities of our group. Please write to: Dyslexics at Brown, Box 114, Student Activities Office, Brown University, Providence, RI 02912.

Writers

Carol Cain '84
Rafael Gasti '85
Suzanne Keen '84
Maria Lewis '87
Heather Quinn '84
Bruce Clark '70
Judith Parker, M.A. '84

Editors

Rafael Gasti '85
Heather Quinn '84
Dean Robert Shaw
Bruce Clark '70
Judith Parker, M.A. '84

Other Contributors

Margaret Elsner '86
Jocelyn Hale '85
Elizabeth Zaldastani '86
Eli Johnson '84
Caleb Tower '84
Dawn Suggs '86
Scott Graham '85
Christine Arbor '88
Deborah Prothro, M.A. '87

June, 1990 Fourth Edition. Reprinted with permission of the Office of the Dean of the College, Brown University.

Attention Deficit Disorder 6

Children who exhibit a variety of attention problems, including inappropriate attention, inability to concentrate unless they are highly interested in a task, or impulsive behavior, are often diagnosed as ADD (Attention Deficit Disorder) or ADHD (Attention Deficit Hyperactivity Disorder). This situation often causes more problems and is less understood than other kinds of learning problems. Because these children quite often display inappropriate behaviors in the classroom, can be disruptive, or highly creative they present special problems for teachers.

Because gifted students are often misdiagnosed as ADD when they are not sufficiently challenged in school, and because LD and ADD quite often occur together, we have included a section on this condition. Included are several articles that present definitions and common characteristics of children who exhibit attention problems. Since medication is sometimes indicated, two of the articles ("Current Understanding" and "A Guide for Teachers") address this issue while emphasizing the need for concurrent behavior management strategies.

Finally, we include two case studies that we believe will be informative and motivating to students, parents, and educators. The first is the story of the struggles of a young man written by his mother. The second article is about a very successful, creative, and highly respected scientist at Hopkins who just recently discovered that his puzzling struggle throughout school, as well as his creative work, was a result of ADD.

ATTENTION DEFICIT DISORDER: CURRENT UNDERSTANDING

Richard O. Elliot, M.D., F.A.A.P.

I. CAUSE

ADD is generally understood to be one of a number of organically based learning disabilities. Research has shown that ADD is caused by an intermittent deficiency of neurotransmitters, which are specific enzymes necessary for the transfer of impulses from one nerve cell to another. These occur in the frontal lobes of the brain where the **control systems of the body** are regulated. ADD occurs in families, is presumed to be inherited, and is more common in boys than girls. While prenatal and perinatal factors, such as anoxia, head injury, infection, alcohol or drug abuse, lead poisoning, and malnutrition can be a cause, these factors are considered to be infrequent.

II. INCIDENCE

The frequency of ADD is somewhere between **five and ten percent** of school-age children. A study of middle childhood revealed that 17% have learning problems, the most common being deficits in attention. ADD is often associated with other learning disabilities, in the areas of language, mathematics, and perceptual and spatial relations, all of which are considered to be neurologic in origin.

III. MANIFESTATIONS

A. **Behaviors** - The current designation of ADD is **Attention Deficit/Hyperactivity Disorder** according to the current (1987) Diagnostic Manual of the American Psychiatric Association. The following behaviors are listed in this manual.

1. A period of 6 months or more during which at least 8 of the following behaviors are present.
   a. Has difficulty remaining seated when required to
   b. Often fidgets with hands or feet or squirms in seat
   c. Has difficulty playing quietly
   d. Often talks excessively
   e. Often shifts from one uncompleted activity to another
   f. Has difficulty sustaining attention to tasks or play activities
   g. Has difficulty following through on instructions from others (not due to oppositional behavior or failure of comprehension), e.g., fails to finish chores

      h.   Is easily distracted by extraneous stimuli
      i.   Often interrupts or intrudes on others, e.g., butts into other children's games
      j.   Often blurts out answers to questions before they have been completed
      k.   Has difficulty waiting turn in games or group situations
      l.   Often engages in physically dangerous activities for the purpose of thrill-seeking e.g., runs into street without looking
      m.   Is often extremely messy or sloppy
      n.   Often loses things necessary for tasks or activities at school or at home (e.g., toys, pencils, books,assignments)
      o.   Often does not seem to listen to what is being said to him or her

2. Onset before the age of 7.

3. Not occurring only during the course of autistic disorder.

B. **Characteristics** - Children with ADD exhibit most of the following characteristics:

1. *A short attention span*, easily distracted.

2. Appears to hear but *does not register what is said.*

3. *Impulsivity* - acts before thinking, talks before thinking.

4. *Insatiability.*

5. *Hyperactivity* - not the majority - often fidgety, appears driven, usually subsides in adolescence.

6. *Sleep/awake disturbances* - easy fatigability during the day and trouble getting to sleep at night, often restless in sleep.

7. *Inconsistency* - especially in learning tasks and in learning behavior.

8. *Impersistence* - does not complete tasks.

9. *Superficiality* - unable to pursue anything in depth.

10. *Peer relationships* - difficulty in the give-and-take of getting along with other children.

11. *Inability to understand cause and effect* - tends to blame others.

12. *Disorganization.*

IV. DIAGNOSIS

A. **History** - Others in family may have similar traits, although the diagnosis was often not made in years past. The child may have been an irritable or insatiable infant or a hyperactive toddler. Symptoms of hyperactivity may be recognized in preschool or kindergarten. The child who is not hyperactive may simply be a chronic underachiever and escape identification. The diagnosis may not become apparent until adolescence, when school programs become more complicated and the child has more teachers and is expected to become more responsible for his own work. The bright child may not be identified early because his only problem may be that he does not perform as well as his IQ testing would suggest.

It is also important to find out how the child relates to his parents, siblings, peers, and teachers. Behavior check lists are useful but may be quite variable, depending upon the observer.

B. **Physical Examination** - This is usually unremarkable and is conducted to rule out other physical conditions which can affect learning and behavior. Obviously, it is important to check for vision and hearing problems, and to rule out seizure disorders, cerebral-palsy, thyroid dysfunction, and neuromuscular disorders. Considerable variation in neurologic development is normal for all variations in fine and gross motor coordination for children in general.

C. **Laboratory Studies** - These are not particularly useful and should not be considered routine. EEG, CT scan, electrical activity mapping, Magnetic Resonance Imaging (MRI), Sonography Emission Tomography (PET), etc., are currently available. Such testing for this type of neurologic dysfunction is done for research purposes and at some point in the future may have clinical value.

D. **Specialty Referral** - The child should be seen by a neurologist if seizures are suspected. He should be referred to a psychologist or psychiatrist if emotional or environmental factors are suspected. Neuropsychological testing does not usually yield new information. A referral to a pediatric neurologist who specializes in the neurology of behavior, or to a psychopharmacologist, is of value when the medical management becomes complicated by additional diagnoses, such as depression, seizure disorder, or disorders of affect. An educational specialist is helpful in making recommendations for the formulation of an appropriate educational plan.

V. COURSE

ADD is not a self limited or maturational problem. It is usually recognized by age 5 years and carries on through adolescence and into adult life. Hyperactivity usually subsides by puberty. The child who is not hyperactive may not be recognized as having ADD until junior high school age. Recent studies show that 2/3 improve and 1/3 still show significant symptoms throughout adolescence. Those who were never labeled as hyperactive have a better chance of improvement as they get into adolescence. Children who were seriously aggressive in early childhood are much more likely to become anti-social adolescents. One half of these go on to truancy, stealing, serious lying, and aggression. It has been clearly shown that anti-social behavior precedes any problem with drug abuse. We have as yet no figures to show how ADD affects adult life. Adults are usually better able to come to grips with attention problems, adjusting their lives and becoming successful in career choices that are minimally affected by these manifestations.

VI. TREATMENT

A. **Recognize the problem** - Treatment begins with the recognition that this is a malfunction of the control mechanisms of the brain, and that these children cannot just "shape up." They do not always have control over their behavior; it is not just a matter of attitude, laziness, or lack of motivation.

B. Emphasize assets - They may have superior intelligence and are often unusually creative with free flow of ideas. As a group these children are very sensitive and artistic.

C. **Reassure parents** - Parents need to be reassured that ADD is not caused by inappropriate or inadequate parenting. They need to understand that these loveable and affectionate children often suffer from uncontrollable and unpredictable mood swings of neurologic origin.

D. **Help child to understand** - The child needs help understanding the nature of this disability. It is not because he is lazy or crazy or dumb. The adolescent who said, "My brain is like a TV set without a channel selector and all the channels come in at once and I have trouble dealing with any one of them," had unusual insight. Children need to be reassured that ADD is a treatable condition and that life can be a lot easier. A deficiency of cause and effect understanding makes it difficult for many adolescents to really understand the nature of their problem. Certainly peer groups among ADD adolescents should be helpful.

E. **Help teachers understand** - School programs can help teachers understand that this is a bona fide neurologic disability, and provide suggestions for dealing with these children:

1. They need routine.

2. They need to sit at the front of the class.

3. They need as close to a one-on-one teacher/pupil relationship as possible.

4. They need directions which are given simply and clearly, preferably written and one at a time. Given three things to do, they may remember the first one.

5. They need on-going help with organizational skills.

6. They need modification of homework requirements. Homework is the biggest school problem the adolescent with ADD has. It takes them longer to do the same work.

7. They need open-ended exam opportunities.

8. They need assignment notebooks, properly supervised both at home and in school, with lots of parent/teacher coordination.

9. They need the opportunity to do written work on a computer. They may learn to type but often cannot function well in typing classes because of the distractions.

F. **Video Games** - Almost all of these children generate sustained enthusiasm for video games. This is interesting because video games require a great deal of concentration, hand-eye coordination and sustained attention. This illustrates the point that these children can do well in areas where they have intense interest, and where brain stimulation is constant and intense.

G. **Medication** - Medication is indicated in children or adolescents properly diagnosed as having ADD when manifestations significantly affect school performance, home life, or peer relationships.

1. Types of Medication
   a. *Stimulants*
      1) Methylphenidate
         (Ritalin)
         Amphetamines
         (Dexedrine)
         Pemoline
         (Cylert)
   b. *Tricyclic Antidepressants*
      1) Imipramine
         (Tofranil)
      2) Desipramine
         (Norpramine)
   c. *Tranquilizers*
      1) Chlorpromazine
         (Thorazine)
      2) Thioridazine
         (Mellaril)

2. Mode of Action and Side Effects

    a. *Stimulants* - Stimulants affect specific neurotransmitters, allowing nerve impulses to cross connectors from one neuron to another. Pulse rate and blood pressure rise slightly and increase the blood supply to the brain. There is an 80% expectation of significant improvement. Educational gains are made and maintained if stimulant therapy is appropriately and consistently continued as long as necessary. There is no maximum age for stimulant therapy. One side effect, usually temporary, is loss of appetite. If it persists, an alternative eating schedule can be used, i.e., the child can be allowed to eat more food in the evening when the medication effects have worn off. Long term studies indicate no interference with ultimate growth. Stimulants will interfere with sleep if given too late in the day or in too large a dose. Temporary emotional lability (mood swings) is occasionally reported, and stimulant medication can bring about tics in those who are prone to Tourette's syndrome. When that happens, stimulant medication is reduced or withdrawn. Stimulants as a group and Methylphenidate in particular, are among the safest of all commonly prescribed medications. Stimulants have been shown not to be habit forming when used in the treatment of ADD.

    b. *Tricyclic antidepressants* - Like stimulants, they also affect specific neurotransmitters. They have the advantage of being long-acting but are less specific in action. They can cause drowsiness, weight loss, abdominal pain, dizziness, and nausea; and in high doses may cause cardiac arhythmia and abnormal liver function and can produce seizures. Therefore, electrocardiogram and liver function tests must be done periodically to monitor the administration of these medications, and periodic blood level measurements are required.

    c. *Tranquilizers* - The mode of action in the treatment of ADD is less clear. They are certainly not specific and have only occasional use. Possible side effects are blurred vision, irritability, depression, and sedation.

H. Counseling - The ADD child often needs help with eroding self-image and with secondary maladaptive behaviors. A counselor is needed who understands the nature of ADD. Behavior modification approaches must be specially tailored because of marginal cause and effect understanding.

I. **Unsubstantiated Approaches to Treatment**

   1. Food: The effect of food upon behaviors is not yet well understood, and no caause and effect relationship has been established.

      a. Feingold diet
      b. Sugar and hypoglycemia
      c. Megavitamins
      d. Food allergies

   2. Optometric exercises

   3. Bifocals

   4. Patterning

VII. PROGNOSIS

A. **Severely Affected** - If unrecognized, those severely affected by ADD may, in early adolescence, become disenchanted with school, seeing themselves not only as academic failures but social failures as well. They may be drawn toward those generally accepted as losers. Suffering the consequences of impulsivity and lacking the ability to distinguish cause and effect, these unfortunates may drift into accident proneness, delinquency, or to drug or alcohol abuse, progressive depression, and ultimately, to suicide.

B. **Moderately Affected** - For those children moderately affected the outlook is better. They may go through school as underachievers, be deprived of a college education, go on to be chronically under-employed, and generally never be satisfied with their position in life.

C. **Minimally Affected** - Those minimally affected probably will go on to successful education and career choices. They must recognize a need to work harder, and come to grips with their impulsivity, short attention span, and so forth, but may be successful in careers that encourage creativity and minimize attention to details.

D. **Importance of Intervention** - Given the opportunity to live in an accepting and understanding home, to receive enlightened educational management, and to be provided with medication when appropriate, many children with ADD can enjoy the same expectation for success as any other child. With early intervention and careful attention to medical management even those children severely affected with ADD have a significant chance of improvement.

VIII. GOALS OF MANAGEMENT

A. **Improving Self-Image** - Aside from good health, the most important asset a child has is a positive self-image. The child with organically based learning disabilities has an extremely fragile self-image, which suffers constant, continuous, and progressive erosion. These children are continually being misunderstood and misjudged by parents, siblings, peers, and teachers, and learn to see themselves as dumb, bad, and disliked. They need understanding and desperately need success - at home, at school, on the playground, and on the athletic field.

B. **Pediatrician as Advocate** - The pediatrician should be willing to attend referral meetings and review educational plans as the child's advocate. His involvement in educational issues is a direct result of his special interest in the quality of education for all children.

C. **Team Approach** - Attention Deficit Disorder and other related learning disabilities are generally accepted as developmental in origin. The initial identification and ongoing management depend on a team effort. Mutual understanding and continued involvement of the educator, the physician, the child, and his parents are essential to success.

May 1988, Reprinted with permission from Richard Elliot, Center for Talented Youth, Johns Hopkins University.

ATTENTION DEFICIT DISORDERS: A GUIDE FOR TEACHERS

Defining Attention Deficit Disorders (ADD)

Attention Deficit Disorder is a syndrome which is characterized by serious and persistent difficulties in three specific areas:

1. Attention span
2. Impulse control
3. Hyperactivity (sometimes)

ADD is a chronic disorder which can begin in infancy and can extend through adulthood while having negative effects on a child's life at home, school, and within his/her community. It is conservatively estimated that 3-5% of our school age population is affected by ADD, a condition which previously fell under the heading of "learning disabled," "brain damaged," "hyperkinetic," or "hyperactive." However, the newer term, attention deficit disorder, was introduced to more clearly describe the characteristics of these children. There are two types of attention deficit disorder, both of which are described below.

Attention Deficit Hyperactivity Disorder (ADHD) – According to the criteria in the Diagnostic and Statistical Manual of the American Psychiatric Association, to diagnose a child as having ADHD s/he must display for six months or more at least eight of the following characteristics before the age of seven:

1. Fidgets, squirms or seems restless
2. Has difficulty remaining seated
3. Is easily distracted
4. Has difficulty awaiting turn
5. Blurts out answers
6. Has difficulty following instructions
7. Has difficulty sustaining attention
8. Shifts from one uncompleted task to another
9. Has difficulty playing quietly
10. Talks excessively
11. Interrrupts or intrudes on others
12. Does not seem to listen
13. Often loses things necessary for tasks
14. Frequently engages in dangerous actions

Undifferentiated Attention Deficit Disorder – In this form of ADD the primary and most significant characteristic is inattentiveness; hyperactivity is **not** present. Nevertheless, these children still manifest problems with organization and distractibility and they may be seen as quiet or passive in nature. It is speculated that Undifferentiated ADD is currently underdiagnosed as these children tend to be overlooked more easily in the classroom. Thus, these children may be at a higher risk for academic failure than those with attention deficit hyperactivity disorder.

Diagnosing Attention Deficit Disorders

Students who have exhibited the characteristics mentioned above for longer than six months may be at risk for having an attention deficit disorder. However, a diagnosis of attention deficit should only be made after ruling out other factors related to medical, emotional or environmental variables which could cause similar symptoms. Therefore, physicians, psychologists, and educators often conduct a multi-disciplinary evaluation of the child including medical studies, psychological and educational testing, speech and language assessment, neurological evaluation, and behavioral rating scales completed by the child's parents and teachers.

Causes of Attention Deficit Disorders

A 1987 Report to Congress prepared by the Interagency Committee of Learning Disabilities attributes the probable cause of ADD to "abnormalities in neurological function, in particular to disturbance in brain neurochemistry involving a class of brain neurochemicals termed 'neurotransmitters.'" Researchers are unclear, however, as to the specific mechanisms by which these neurotransmitter chemicals influence attention, impulse control and activity level.

Although many ADD children tend to develop secondary emotional problems, ADD, in itself, may be related to biological factors and is not primarily an emotional disorder. Nevertheless, emotional and behavioral problems can frequently be seen in ADD children due to problems that these children tend to have within their school, home, and social environments. Such characteristics as inattentiveness, impulsivity, and underachievement can also be found in non-ADD students who suffer primarily from emotional difficulties which effect concentration and effort or in those students who simply have motivational deficits leading to diminished classroom attentiveness and performance. Differential diagnosis, therefore, is an essential prerequisite to effective treatment.

Treating Attention Deficit Disorders

Treatment of the ADD child usually requires a **multi-modal approach** frequently involving a treatment team made up of parents, teachers, physicians, and behavioral or mental health professionals. The four corners of this treatment program are as follows:

Educational Planning	**Multimodal Treatment Planning**	Medical Management
Psychological Planning		Behavioral Modification

*"Hyperactivity with ADD, **without treatment**, often results in school failure, rejection by peers and family turmoil, all of which can lead to developmental delays and psychiatric complications stemming from low self-esteem and frustration."*
Jerry M. Weiner, M.D., Pres. Amer. Academy of Ch. & Adol. Psychiatry

With this downward cycle in progress ADD can lead to:

Poor social adjustment
Behavioral problems
School failure
Drop-out and delinquency
Drug abuse

Using Medication in the Treatment of Attention Deficit Disorders

The use of medication alone in the treatment of ADD is not recommended. As indicated earlier, a multimodal treatment plan is usually followed for successful treatment of the ADD child or adolescent. While not all children having ADD are prescribed medication, in certain cases the proper use of medication can play an important and necessary part in the child's overall treatment.

Ritalin, the most commonly used medication in treating ADD, is a psychostimulant and has been prescribed for many years with very favorable results and minimal side-effects. Other psychostimulant medications which are used to treat ADD are Cylert and Dexedrine. In the past several years antidepressant medications such as Tofranil and Norpramine have also proved successful in treating the disorder. All these medications are believed to effect the body's neurotransmitter chemicals, deficiencies of which may be the cause of ADD. Improvements in such characteristics as attention span, impulse control and hyperactivity are noted in approximately 75% of children who take psychostimulant

ADD student may take as teachers need to work closely with the child's parents and other helping professionals in monitoring medication effectiveness.

Medication side effects such as appetite loss, sleep difficulties, and/or lethargy in the classroom, among others, can often be controlled through medication dosage adjustments when reported by the child's parents or teachers.

Teaching Students With Attention Deficit Disorders

The most effective treatment of ADD requires full cooperation of teachers and parents working closely with other professionals such as physicians, psychologists, psychiatrists, speech and educational specialists, etc. In the coordinated effort to ensure success in the lives of children with ADD the vital importance of the teacher's role cannot be overestimated. Dennis Cantwell, M.D. claims, "Anything else is a drop in the bucket when you compare it with the time spent in school."

Recommendations for the Proper Learning Environment

1. Seat ADD student near teacher's desk, but include as part of regular class seating.

2. Place ADD student up front with his back to the rest of the class to keep other students out of view.

3. Surround ADD student with "good role models," preferably students that the ADD child views as "significant others." Encourage peer tutoring and cooperative collaborative learning.

4. Avoid distracting stimuli. Try not to place the ADD near: air conditioner, high traffic areas, heater, doors or windows

5. ADD children do not handle change well so avoid: transitions, physical relocation, changes in schedule, disruptions (monitor closely on field trips)

6. Be creative! Produce a "stimuli-reduced study area." Let all students have access to this area so the ADD child will not feel different.

7. Encourage parents to set up appropriate study space at home with routines established as far as set times for study, parental review of completed homework, and periodic notebook and/or book bag organization.

Recommendations for Giving Instructions to Students

1. Maintain eye contact with the ADD student during verbal instruction.

2. Make directions clear and concise. Be consistent with daily instructions.

3. Simplify complex directions. Avoid multiple commands.

4. Make sure ADD student comprehends before beginning the task.

5. Repeat in a calm, positive manner, if needed.

6. Help ADD child to feel comfortable with seeking assistance (most ADD children won't ask).

7. These children need more help for a longer period of time than the average child. Gradually reduce assistance.

8. Require a daily assignment notebook if necessary.
   a. Make sure student correctly writes down all assignments each day. If the student is not capable of this then the teacher should help the student.
   b. Parent and teachers sign notebook daily to signify completion of homework assignments.
   c. Parents and teachers may use notebook for daily communication with each other.

Recommendations for Students Performing Assignments

1. Give out only one task at a time.

2. Monitor frequently. Use a supportive attitude.

3. Modify assignments as needed. Consult with Special Education personnel to determine specific strengths and weaknesses of the student. Develop an individualized educational program.

4. Make sure you are testing knowledge and not attention span.

5. Give extra time for certain tasks. The ADD student may work more slowly. Don't penalize for needed extra time.

6. Keep in mind that ADD children are easily frustrated. Stress, pressure and fatigue can break down the ADD child's self-control and lead to poor behavior.

Recommendations for Behavior Modification and Self-esteem Enhancement

Providing Supervision and Discipline

    a. Remain calm, state infraction of rule, and don't debate or argue with student.

    b. Have pre-established consequences for misbehavior.

    c. Administer consequences immediately and monitor proper behavior frequently.

    d. Enforce rules of the classroom consistently.

    e. Discipline should be appropriate to "fit the crime," without harshness.

    f. Avoid ridicule and criticism. Remember, ADD children have difficulty staying in control.

    g. Avoid **publicly** reminding students on medication to "take their medicine."

Providing Encouragement

    a. Reward more than you punish in order to build self-esteem.

    b. Praise immediately any and all good behavior and performance.

    c. Change rewards if not effective in motivating behavioral change.

    d. Find ways to encourage the child.

    e. Teach the child to reward him/herself. Encourage positive self-talk (i.e., "You did very well remaining in your seat today. How do you feel about that?"). This encourages the child to think positively about him/herself.

Other Educational Recommendations Which May Help Some ADD Students

1. Some ADD students may benefit from educational, psychological and/or neurological testing to determine their learning style, cognitive ability and to rule out any learning disabilities (common in about 30% of ADD students).

2. Private tutor and/or peer tutoring at school.

3. A class that has a low student-teacher ratio.

4. Social skills training and organizational skills training.

5. Training in cognitive restructuring (positive "self-talk," i.e., "I did that well.").

6. Use of a word processor or computer for school work.

7. Individualized activities that are mildly competitive or non-competitive such as: bowling, walking, swimming, jogging, biking, karate.
Note: ADD children may do less well in team sports.

8. Involvement in social activities such as scouting, church groups or other youth organizations which help develop social skills and self-esteem.

9. Allowing the child to play with younger children if that's where they "fit in." Many ADD children have more in common with younger children. The child can still develop valuable social skills from interaction with younger children.

Suggested Reading and References

Books and Pamphlets

Barkley, Russell. *Hyperactive Children*. New York: Guilford Press, 1981.

Canter, Lee & Canter, Marlene. *Assertive Discipline for Parents*. Canter & Associates, Inc., 1553 Euclid St., Santa Monica, CA 90404.

Freidman, Ronald. *Attention Deficit Disorder and Hyperactivity*. Educational Resources, Inc. 1990 Ten Mile Road, St. Clair Shores, MI 48081.

Garfinkel, Barry. *What is Attention Deficit and How Does Medication Help?* Division of Child and Adolescent Psychiatry, Box 95 UMH&C, Harvard Street at East River Road, Minneapolis, MN 55455.

Parker, Harvey C. *The ADD Hyperactivity Workbook for Parents, Teachers, and Kids*. Impact Publications, Inc., 300 Northwest 70th Avenue, Suite 102, Plantation, FL 33317.

Phelan, Thomas. *ADD-Hyperactivity*. 507 Thornhill Drive, Carol Stream, IL 60188.

Silver, Larry. *The Misunderstood Child*. McGraw Hill, 1984.

Wender, Paul. *The Hyperactive Child, Adolescent and Adult*. Oxford University Press, 1987.

Other References

Diagnostic and Statistical Manual III-R. American Psychiatric Association, Washington, DC, 1987.

A Report to U.S. Congress. Prepared by Interagency on Learning Disabilities, 1987.

Sunday Gazzette Mail, *Inaccuracies about Ritalin*. John Wender, M.D. January 10, 1988, Charleston, West Virginia.

Acknowledgments

"Attention Deficit Disorders: A Guide for Teachers" was prepared by members of the Education Committee of CH.A.D.D., November, 1988.

CH.A.D.D. would like to thank and encourage all who are involved with the important task of education. Let us work together today to ensure a bright tomorrow for our children.

For more information on ADD write to:

CH.A.D.D.
Children With Attention Deficit Disorders
1859 N. Pine Island Road, Suite 185
Plantation, FL 33322
(305) 792-8100 or 384-6869

Or contact your local CH.A.D.D. Chapter

Reprinted with permission from CH.A.D.D.

John Adam Hartley: An ADD* Story

Donna T. Hartley

This is just one story of *Attention Deficit Disorder. It's not finished and won't be for awhile. John, who had been so unfortunate in those early years, partly from what we didn't know and partly from what we and the school system were unable to provide, had his life turned around by a type of school and teaching staff that is desperately needed in this country today. The numbers of these children are legion and their talents are wasted by our inability to educate them. The psychologist who first accurately diagnosed John explained it beautifully when he told us, "these kids normally go to jail, but given the right environment they can go anywhere."

About 12 years ago I was asked to tutor some English students at a community college in Hawaii. Each had reading and writing comprehension difficulties. Because I had two boys with attention deficit disorders, they were considered learning disabled and it was decided that I might be helpful in understanding older students with this and similar learning problems. As part of the assignment the teacher requested that I view some video tapes that would lend insight into the type of student being dealt with here. In those days information on this type of student was fragmented and I took what ever I could get for my own use.

One video came out of DeAnza College in California. DeAnza had set up a program helping these students and was discovering a lot of intelligent people who had been shuffled about in the schoolrooms of their respective pasts. One young man, who was 20 years old, told of being in and out of special education programs all of his life. He'd been classified a slow learner, mildly retarded, an irritation in the classroom, and so forth. He had nevertheless decided to try college and had wound up at DeAnza where he was put into this program and was experiencing some very solid successes. The interviewer droned on for a bit and after a moment's pause shot the final question. "Would you care to mention the group of people that you are now affiliated with?" Softly, the young man replied, "I belong to the Mensa Society."

I have two boys: John, now 21 years and Brian, now 18 years of age. Both displayed early hyperactivity, short attention spans, and quick minds. They were tested and diagnosed as having what we now call Attention Deficit Disorder (ADD). I've lived with it and worked with it for about 18 years since my son's preschool teacher desperately tried to put her finger on it. I've attended classes on it, worked with private therapists, my sons, and a lot of teachers during this time. Some days were very good, others were very tough and I've blown it as badly as anyone could, simply because ADD requires more patience than I've had.

The early years were the worst. No one knew enough about ADD and some of those that didn't had a hard time accepting this. I've learned over time to respect the professionals: teachers, psychologists, social workers, and others who would simply say, "We don't know enough about this yet" or "we're still learning ourselves." Mostly, their getting through to these children was a result of a personal upbeat attitude, a sense of humor, and a certain flexibility or open-mindedness when it came to teaching them. There is still no well that I know of where you can draw the waters of information on how to teach them. We have, however, come a long way and there is some pretty good reading material now available for parents and professionals who deal with this type of child.

It was 1972 when John at the tender age of 3 1/2 years proceeded to drive his preschool teacher crazy. She said she had heard of hyperkinesis and she kindly suggested that I look into some testing for him. I took him to a child psychiatrist. This "professional" immediately proceeded to attack, becoming rude and indignant. He claimed that the teacher was probably a nut and that I was probably a bad mother because John fidgeted constantly and most likely needed more discipline at home. I was soon to learn that not all child-care experts are created equal.

Later, another teacher at John's preschool took me aside for a chat. "I won't claim to know a lot of answers," she said, "but I know certain things work. His preschool teacher reads the students stories, talks to them, and expects them to sit still. In my class John walks in, picks a project, keeps his hands busy, and behaves very well. I talk and read and while he's absorbed he hears everything. I know this is true because he gives it back to me with correct answers to my questions. I had him while his teacher was out sick and you simply have to keep his hands and mind going to be effective." At the time this was called a Montessori classroom.

John began first grade at a parochial school because I thought that we needed to try a firmly-structured classroom approach. That didn't last long. His teacher, a tiny sweet-tempered nun, was quick and observant. "This is a bright child but I think this is the wrong type of classroom for him. I think we're stifling him," she said.

John moved then to the local public elementary school in our neighborhood in Hawaii, and from there things spiraled downwards. I didn't notice this progression at first but the doctor he had gave him Ritalin in the first and second grades. She had labeled John a "developmental hyperactive" and although the Ritalin quieted his hyperactivity, he never showed great progress with it. He never completed assigned work and never seemed to be happy with school. Always thin, the Ritalin exacerbated the problem by killing his appetite somewhat, and he never gained weight. I dropped it one day never to use it again. (John's type of attention deficit hyperactivity disorder was later determined not to be helped by the medication used then.)

In the fourth grade I was called into John's school one fine spring morning. His teacher had discovered that he had stolen small items from other class rooms and had shoplifted successfully in a local store between school and our house. Although it took me by surprise I sat there thinking that I should have seen this coming.

John had expressed his vehement hatred for his school, teachers, and classmates. For awhile, every night he cried and mornings he refused to get out of bed. I had to physically drag him out and hadn't been able to get him to dress and leave without nagging him or hitting him. His grades were a disaster of Ds and Fs with his math teacher claiming that he couldn't master subtraction and addition at the fourth-grade level. In English he read and wrote nothing.

The other children shunned or taunted him saying that he was weird. He had no friends. He stayed alone at all times. He prowled the library at recess and lunch or at any moment that he could slip in there. I had John tested through the school for learning problems, but each time the results came back the same. John was called bright, a child who should have been ahead of his classmates but who must have been bored.

Since he was smart, the school maintained that he was ineligible for any special educational considerations. His teacher took it one step further. "If he's bored," she said, "that's tough." The school recognized through their testing that John had an attention problem but they claimed that his high IQ should have compensated for it. I was to learn later that this assertion was erroneous in many cases.

The school psychologist told me that she couldn't read John at all. Although he seemed like a nice, polite boy, she couldn't withdraw any information from him. She claimed that she didn't have the training of a private clinical therapist, so she recommended names and told me to get some outside help. I got on the phone fast.

Before I go into what happened next I must describe the other John, the boy at home. There, John was a child who loved to be read to. There were children's books but he didn't seem to care for them for long. I had discovered very early that he loved geography, science, natural history, and anything pertaining to evolution. They held his attention and he retained them very well. National Geographic and Jacques Cousteau's documentaries fascinated him. He peppered his father and me constantly with questions on weather, geography, geology, electronics, laser beams, electricity, and anything else that came to his mind. I regularly put him in front of the television for Carl Sagan's Cosmos and James Burke's Ascent of Man series, and he sat attentively through them both.

He was a very verbal, stubborn, argumentative, and inquisitive child whose questions had to be answered immediately. I took him to the public library where he loaded up on books, running up and down the aisles feverishly to get everything he wanted. I figured that if I waited long enough, the intellectual and school paths would finally merge.

The school had done me a favor with their recommendation of a private child psychologist. After an initial consultation, the psychologist sent John to get a complete physical with a doctor who specialized in hyperactive children. The physician said that John showed no real physical traits of being a true hyperactive and that he would not recommend medication, but he did recommend alternative schooling. He contacted the psychologist who had the results waiting when we returned to his office. John was then given a battery of personality and intelligence tests, and when that was over the psychologist called us back again.

He told us that John was an angry child with low self-esteem. He was frustrated with too many failures and he would start therapy immediately with another doctor there in the clinic. He said John was intelligent, in fact, very gifted, but had what they called learning disabilities. He described it as a short circuit in the nervous system or a short attention span. He then told us that no one knew enough about it yet or what caused it, but he was sure they could help him. His problem was largely centered around school and the doctor told us that something was very wrong there.

The psychologists in this clinic had a direct line to a private school in Hawaii. You could only gain entrance to this special school if you had a learning disability. The doors opened through special testing or a psychologist's referral. John's tests labeled him learning disabled gifted (LDG). (They were not using Attention Deficit Disorder, as this term apparently hadn't yet come into usage.) The ASSETS* school at Pearl Harbor in Honolulu, Hawaii notified us that John's case was reviewed and he was eligible to enter.

John entered ASSETS for summer school prior to the fifth grade and there the reversals started at once. Academically John had tested reading at the high school level so ASSETS gave him an individual reading program parallel with his interests. This child who could barely add moved into long division and when he was found to be capable of structured geometry it was added to his program. His progress soared and so did the reports. One progress report read that "John's use and understanding of the microscope is exceptional as he has a remarkable understanding of bacteria and virus and has furthermore contributed a great deal to his science class."

ASSETS contract with their students to do a certain amount of individual work and when a student such as John has the ability, extra contract work is added. If they find the child does not write easily, a test or a book report is required verbally and all additional efforts and interests are strongly encouraged.

John was in the LDG class where there were nine students who, like himself, were all considered gifted. Along with the nine boys, there were two certified teachers, one of these fulfilling the role of assistant teacher. The head teacher informed me that teaching this type of child was her choice. They were she claimed, the most exciting of all children, because they possessed the most uncommon gifts and the most unusual minds.

The floor was carpeted for quietness and the children often sat on it. Individual carrels were provided at the back of the room for the student having trouble blocking out distracting noises and movement. Peace and orderliness prevailed. Discipline was a finger point from a teacher whereby the student left and turned himself in at the office. Once in the history of the school a child ignored a point and much to his surprise the teacher pointed to the rest of the class, which then rose and deserted him to continue class on the front lawn. The student then went to the office.

ASSETS at the time, occupied an old renovated marine barracks on the Pearl Harbor Naval Base and had only a few Apple computers for state-of-the-art equipment.

One of the unusual things about John's class was that the boys were not of one age group. The school had children from 7 to 14 years of age and John's class was a mixture of those ages. The gifted, ASSETS had decided, communicate among themselves quite easily. Putting them into individual age segments was of little value. John got along well with younger and older boys quite smoothly now. Three months after entering ASSETS the psychologist who was seeing John dropped him, informing me that he had become a happy child and that his problems had been largely school related. We never had a recurrence of his thefts or any other serious problems. He had become open and honest in his dealing with everything that we could observe.

John went to school summer and winter during these years simply because he couldn't seem to get enough of ASSETS. He had friends. Sometimes they came to spend a weekend, or he went to their homes. Many of these boys had no doubt experienced the same problems John had.

John joined the Cub Scouts in our area and also made friends there. His Sunday school teacher sought me out within a month after he started ASSETS and told me he had made a remarkable change. When she asked him why he seemed so happy, he told her about his new school. His self-esteem seemed to have risen very quickly.

ASSETS seemed to be happy to have John and delighted with his abilities. The principal informed me that she had given a type of informational test to the boys to see how much general information they had acquired. It was geared to go on until it was over the students' heads, or in other words until they found a ceiling on the information that the boys possessed. John and one other boy had blown the top off of this test, as they hadn't found a ceiling on the information either of them had. They'd simply stopped testing when it had proceeded beyond a certain time frame.

Discipline problems didn't seem to exist for John at this school. He was too busy enjoying himself.

A couple of years rolled by like this and at the beginning of the seventh grade I sensed that somehow John had really grown capable in many ways. It had not gone unnoticed. The principal called me in and proceeded to tell me about an incident that had occurred at school. She said, "A slow child with audio-dyslexia entered school today and was being taunted by another new student in the school yard. Before a teacher could move, John had appeared out of nowhere. *What do you think you're here for?* he asked loudly. The taunter, shocked into silence, backed away. The nearby teacher never moved. "We encourage our children to be strong and independent, to face this sort of thing," she said. "John is, without a doubt, ready to face mainstreaming. This is his last year with us."

At the end of John's seventh grade, my husband retired from the Navy and we moved to Colorado Springs.

John entered the seventh grade again. I had always been uneasy that he was a little socially and emotionally young for his designated peer group in regular schools. I didn't want him to enter high school before I felt he was really ready. He would now be in a large public school with no special attention focused on him and this would be an ideal time for the switch in grades. He protested a little but once school started and he began to make friends, he seemed content. I felt that no one needed to know his past history unless circumstances specifically called for it, so I gave the school no information. When the principal asked me why he was repeating seventh grade I told him that it was purely a gut feeling of mine that this was the proper peer group for him. He graciously conceded the point without further question.

John's middle school years were normal and without any school problems. His grades were average, not spectacular. He was now back into the sequential learning type of atmosphere not wholly fitted for John's learning style but he coped well. He was still a reader and did well in math. He had friends, continued with the Boy Scouts, and now faced the next big step which was high school.

John spent 2 years on the honor roll. His math teacher stopped me one day. John and his best friend, a boy called Jim, who seemed to share every part of these years, were constantly under the man's imposing and amused eye. A retired Air Force pilot and former ROTC instructor, I had no doubt they made his classroom a little noisier and livelier than usual. Bracing myself for a word about John's tendency towards wisecracks and mischief I was surprised when Mr. Runyon told me that John was a born engineer and should never be allowed to choose anything else. He also informed me that if John would like to go to a service academy, especially the Air Force Academy or seek an ROTC scholarship, he'd be happy to write the letter of recommendation. He was also quick to add that indeed John wasn't the quietest kid in the world, but the twinkle in his eye told me he could handle the pair of them.

During his sophomore year, John won a third-place award at Colorado College in a district-wide contest sponsored by the college's German department.

This led to John receiving a German dictionary with a letter from the school saying that he was being honored as the outstanding foreign language student of the semester.

We received a letter from his biology teacher for a project John worked on. The Public Education Coalition for the Pike's Peak Region in conjunction with the Hewlett-Packard Corporation awarded a grant to the biology teacher to build a sophisticated rodent research residence. It contained a volumeter and manometer, equipment for testing respiration and body gas changes. The project, the teacher said, was built by John and his friends. He worked on it after school and in class for

about 7 months. It was photographed by Hewlett-Packard and District Twenty's administration.

John's summers were mostly spent working at Boy Scout Camp teaching ecology, weather, and insect life.

During his 16th summer he went to Finland as a foreign exchange student on a summer program. He lived with a Finnish physician and his family, toured the country, and sailed the Baltic. In order to go, he had agreed to maintain high grades and learn to speak German decently enough to get along in case of a problem in traveling. I wanted him to have one other language he could communicate in.

On his 16th birthday John became an Eagle Scout. His Eagle project was to organize a workforce of friends to lay 80 railroad ties at Wolford Elementary School in Black Forest. Erosion was moving onto the school ground and needed to be stopped.

He was Lutheran youth group director in Black Forest for about a year and organized dances and outings for the high school and junior high school grade levels. He went to Albuquerque, New Mexico twice as a delegate to their youth conventions.

When he came home complaining that there was no volleyball for boys at his high school, I told him to do something about it. He pestered the administration until they let him have a coed team, then played there until he and his friend Jim moved on to the U.S. Volleyball Association.

John finished Rampart High School in Colorado Springs in June 1988 with a 3.3 GPA. Upon graduation, John went to work at McDonald's, bought his own car, and paid his own insurance. He also babysat and painted houses to supplement his wages.

On March 18th, 1989 John went into the Naval Reserve. He graduated from boot camp as the lead petty officer recruit from an honor unit and was one of six young recruits given a meritorious promotion. He is now an E4 and has the requirements for an E5 as a Navy petty officer. John, according to his reserve post, has been the most quickly promoted reservist that they can remember. He finished his Navy technical school as the honor graduate with a 98% and was at the top of his class. While still a reservist John finished a civilian technical school after 18 months with an Associates Degree in optoelectronics. He graduated in July 1991 with a 3.9 GPA and in August 1991 entered the electrical engineering department at Colorado State University in Fort Collins, CO.

* For additional background ASSETS, the reader is referred to E.S. Hishinuma, *The Gifted Child Today,* 1991 September/October pp. 36-38 and 1993, January/February pp. 30-33.

A RADICAL EVOLUTIONARY

Lisa Libowitz

Paleobiologist Steve Stanley is a man of bold ideas, whose research, says one colleague, "is all over the map." Not until age 46 did Stanley discover the secret behind his unusual - and sometimes unsettling – approach to science.

Once upon a time, Hopkins professor Steven Stanley decided to get up close and personal with clams. He scuba dived to observe them. He scrounged them from the bottom of boats. He built an aquarium and tried to determine just what would make his clams happy. He was fairly desperate about it, because his life—or at least his livelihood—depended on these clams. He was a graduate student, and they were his thesis.

"I stared at clams for hours, willing them to burrow. I even learned how to make them burrow. If you put a clam on its side on a hard substrate, it never sticks its foot out. But if you tilt the shell so the foot can come into contact with sediment easily, it'll burrow."

The story has a happy ending: Yale University awarded him a doctorate.

"I can say now that I think like a clam.. Of course, that's not saying much. Clams don't have a head."

Winston Churchill once described Russia as "a riddle wrapped in a mystery inside an enigma." So, in many ways, is Steven Stanley.

Stanley, a lanky, soft-spoken man, isn't the type to make such dramatic comparisons. Talk to him for a while, however, and he will reveal a life filled with contradictions. He's the kind of scientist who will start talking about a great new idea – and be unable to remember the name of a basic organism. The kind who can lose a slip of paper three times in a day, then find in an instant a thin, yellowing volume he has owned since age 8 –*The First Book of Stones*.

Stanley has puzzled others throughout his life, and puzzled himself more. Outwardly sunny, usually popular, Stanley has led an enviable life. He can point to one success after another, from the time he was selected to lead the school play in sixth grade, to his promotion to full professor at the young age of 32.

Behind all of the successes, though, has lived an often frustrated and privately confused man, a scientist who collected accolades the way some people collect green stamps—yet worried about whether he would run out of ideas.

Stanley's career has been stable and unpredictable at the same time, much like the man. He joined the Department of Earth and Planetary Sciences in 1969 and began by focusing primarily on the evolution of bivalve mollusks: clams, scallops, mussels, and oysters. He collected a massive body of information about how their way of life has influenced their shape over millions of years. For many scientists, that narrow line of research would have been enough to occupy the rest of their careers. Not for Stanley.

"I could have kept going in the same direction, but I would have been studying smaller and smaller details", Stanley says. "I wanted to branch out."

So, while part of his time was dedicated to making tens of thousands of measurements from sea shells, his mind ventured into terra incognita.

After more then two decades of studying mostly clams and their cousins, Stanley veered into human evolution. His background in biology included four college courses. What it didn't include was courses in human evolution, anthropology, or vertebrate paleontology. Armed with *none* of those, a few years ago Stanley proposed a striking new theory about how humans developed their big brains.

One roadblock to the development of a baby with a big brain is something known as juvenilization—the smarter the baby, the more helpless it is at birth. Ape babies, unlike humans, can feed themselves, hang on to their mothers, and even swing from limb to limb early in their lives.

Stanley knew, then, that our ancestors must have come down out of the trees and walked upright before they developed big brains. Why? Because big brained babies couldn't be clinging to a mother. Nor could a mother hold onto a baby and swing herself. Yet the evidence – the famous "Lucy" and other hominid remains – showed millions of years of walking upright with little brain development. He puzzled over that.

"Then I found out, in the late 1980s about new evidence showing that our ancestors were partly arboreal," Stanley recalls, eyes gleaming with excitement. "It all came together. I realized that climate changes – the Ice Age — would have forced them out of the trees, as forests turned to grassland. Only then would survival pressures have favored individuals with bigger brains." So far, his theory has found tentative support among both biologists and paleontologists.

"Much of my work has not been by design," Stanley says, sitting in his Olin Hall office cluttered with books, photographs fossils and shells. "I happen to read something or see something, and I have an idea. A lot of what I've done I've had no background to do. I develop the background as I develop the idea."

That unorthodox approach makes some of his peers distinctly uncomfortable. Over the years, his ideas have ranged along the border where paleontology meets biology, sort of a no-man's land in a world of strict disciplines.

"Working on the fringes of two fields, Steve is admired but also resented," says Bruce Marsh, a professor of Earth and Planetary Sciences. "He examines a lot of people's dearly held beliefs, and some times he rejects them." Stanley was one of the first scientists, - along with Harvard University's Stephen Jay Gould, to challenge the grand old man himself Charles Darwin. Darwin believed that evolution occurred gradually; that natural selection worked as individuals were born with new traits that better enabled them to survive.

Stanley and Gould argued that most evolutionary changes occur suddenly, with the creation of new species. Species selection, as well as individual selection, ruled nature, they insisted.

Stanley took the argument two steps further. First, he tackled a question long bothering biologists: why is sexual reproduction more common than asexual reproduction? Because, Stanley proposed, sexual reproduction favors much more rapid creation of new species.

Second, he spent two years recording more than 43,000 measurements from clam fossils to demonstrate that some species never change much. If, as Darwin believed, evolution occurred gradually within species, over 3 million years the clams should have evolved.

"Steve's a wonderful combination of ideas and hard work," says M. Gordon "Reds" Wolman, professor of Geography and Environmental Engineering and former provost. "He has these ideas that are — I guess you would say, bold. Beyond accepted beliefs. And he has the ability to marshall the evidence to support them.

Take the neuron, for example. The neuron, the basic building block of the brain and nervous system, is a complex cell. Neuroscientists devote their entire careers to studying it. Never having studied it and with only a smattering of cell biology in his formal education, Stanley recently proposed a new theory about the neuron: He believes it played a central role in all animal evolution.

For hundreds of millions of years, animals remained single-celled organisms. Then, about 500 million years ago, multicelled organisms began to evolve and multiply quite rapidly, geologically speaking – an explosion of new life within only a few million years.

What happened to trigger the change? The commonly accepted theory views the lack of oxygen as a barrier to evolution. According to the theory, oxygen levels were too low to support higher animal forms until shortly before the Cambrian Period. But once enough oxygen had accumulated in the atmosphere, new species could survive.

Stanley was skeptical. So he began to piece together a new theory from research he dug up – at the library. There he discovered recent evidence undermining the oxygen theory: analyses of soils and limestones nearly 2 billion years old that suggest the existence of quite a bit of oxygen in the atmosphere even then – more than enough, Stanley says, to support complex animal life. He began to think the key to the mystery was biological, not environmental. Then came The Idea: that complex animal life couldn't evolve until the neuron did.

The neuron is nearly identical in almost all animals, from jellyfish to humans, and neurons provide animals with two important skills: the ability to move and to feed themselves. To Stanley, it seemed logical to compare the development of a neurological system in animals with plant life's development of vascular systems, networks of hollow cell structures known as tracheids. These cells enable plants to transport nutrients from roots to stems and leaves.

"Everyone has recognized for years that tracheids were critical for plants to move onto land and evolve," Stanley says. "I think I was the first to propose that neurons were just as critical for the explosion of animal life."

He presented the idea to fellow paleontologists at the Geological Society of America's annual meeting in Cincinnati last October. Since then, he has discussed his theory with other groups, including biologists.

"I had the feeling they would jump all over me and tell me I was wrong," he recalls. He pauses, awkward for a moment, staring out his office window at Wyman Park's bare trees. "They didn't do that. And I'm still amazed. I'm always amazed when people take me seriously."

That is an astonishing statement. This man's most important book on evolution, *Macroevolution,* won praise from supporters and critics. He's won a medal from the Maryland Academy of Sciences as Maryland's outstanding young scientist, membership in the American Academy of Sciences, a Guggenheim Fellowship, an American Book Award nomination—how can he be tormented about his own intelligence?

One June morning five years ago, Stanley had an important doctor's appointment to keep. He sat in the doctor's office, heard the results of a dozen tests, shook his head, and left.

"I remember every detail of that morning," he says. "It was a Thursday. The sky was unbelievably blue. And it was hot; almost 100 degrees. I looked up at the sky and I thought, I've never known who I am."

At 46 years old, Stanley learned his IQ for the first time. Standing in the doctor's parking lot beneath a perfect summer sky, he clutched a notebook full of papers declaring him a genius – and something else, he learned.

"Then I drove back to campus, and I got a headache that lasted for a week and a half."

Stanley has his routines, like most professors. Most of his colleagues can point to one or two. He is the only person in the department to wear a coat and tie every day, for instance.

But there is one habit, begun five years ago, that only a few friends know about. He faithfully takes 7.5 milligrams of a drug called Ritalin every morning.

On the same day Stanley learned his IQ, he also was diagnosed as learning-disabled. Ritalin is the brand name for a drug used to treat a learning disability known as attention deficit disorder.

Attention deficit disorder, or ADD, is a difficult condition to describe and treat. Doctors admit they do not fully understand it. It involves an inability to concentrate, to focus on a task at hand. In children, it is related to hyperactivity – an inability to be still – but it isn't the same thing. Although some children with ADD are hyperactive, others can sit for long periods, yet be unable to focus on one thing for more than a few minutes. ADD is like hyperactivity of the brain.

Children with ADD can suffer tremendous anxiety and pain if their disability goes unnoticed. Many are mistakenly labeled slow, lazy, or careless. If a child is also hyperactive, there's a good chance he'll be called a troublemaker as well.

Steve Stanley earned all four labels.

"In the first grade, I was the worst kid in school for fights," he remembers. "My teachers didn't know what to do with me. Usually they would punish me by making me sit at my desk at recess, which just made me worse."

ADD has been linked to controversy in recent years. Both parents and teachers have expressed concerns that too many children are diagnosed as learning disabled merely because they learn at their own pace. They fear children will be given drugs simply because they are boisterous. And in some cases, fears of abuse have been justified.

For Stanley, however, the diagnosis and the drug have transformed his life. For as long as he can remember, he had a nagging sense that all of his good fortune must be a mistake.

"When I was diagnosed, [the doctor] said to me, 'How did you do it? How did you survive?' I nearly burst into tears. Right at that moment, he understood me, and I understood myself for the first time. And we were the only two people in the world who did."

Gates Mills, Ohio, looks like a New England village abducted by aliens and set down in the Midwest. Sundays, city folks from Cleveland drive out to see its picket fences and quaint church. It's a town that still has parades on July 4th.

Stanley grew up there with a mother who loved to watch birds, a businessman father who hunted, and a big brother whose teasing spurred Stanley to become a good wrestler. He grew up with horses and vegetable gardens. He loved collecting rocks, and he'd travel to a museum in Cleveland to learn more about minerals. He spent endless summer days climbing trees. He lived, in other words, a fairly normal life for a middle-class American child in the 1950s.

In grade school, he was an above-average student. He went to a small local school, and he could keep up without much effort. He was good at sports, and he loved to build things. Once, interested in ancient Roman weaponry, he built a catapult. He hated to read, but no one made him read much. He was captain of the safety patrol. He excelled in sports, and the little girls began to pay attention to him. By sixth grade, he was getting love notes.

His life changed drastically in seventh grade, when his parents decided to send him to a private school with high academic standards. "I worked very hard to get a B average," he recalls. "By the time I was in the upper grades, I was spending five and a half hours a day studying.

"I hated school. The thing that took so much time was reading and memorizing. I could read something and five minutes later be unable to remember what I had read. Nothing I read would stick."

The first year, he had to read four novels in English class. The title of each despised book is still etched in his mind today: *Kidnapped. Huckleberry Finn. Johnny Tremaine. Ocean Gold.* "That course was traumatic for me. Here I was, in this school with these sophisticated, bright kids, and I was supposed to be able to keep up. I would discover that I missed things everybody else picked up on. I was frightened."

He struggled just as hard with math courses, but no matter how much time he spent on his assignments, they were riddled with mistakes. "I'd get Cs in arithmetic just by being careless," he says.

Sports were part of his salvation. Stanley was captain of the soccer team. He joined the school's swim team, which won the state championship. He ran the quarter-mile in track. And the girls liked him. High school was where Stanley met Nell, his wife of now 23 years.

His struggles were a secret; Stanley says none of his classmates ever suspected how much time he devoted to earning good grades, nor how exhausted that effort made him. All they saw was a bright, popular teenager. "I don't want people to think I was strange," Stanley says, recalling his high school years. I was like a golden boy. I even won the big award at graduation, the one for leadership and citizenship.

"Nobody knew about the problems under the surface. I earned more As than Cs. I just never understood why it was so hard for me to do what seemed to come easy to other people." There was one class, however, that gave Stanley hope: geometry. He excelled in geometry, which emphasizes logic rather than memorization. And the teacher built the boy's self-confidence by calling on him frequently for help. "I began to think of myself as a flawed student with potential," says Stanley.

He took the SATs his junior year as practice, and as he had hoped, his math score was high. His score on the verbal test, though, wasn't nearly as good, although it was above average. "I never read, so of course I didn't have much of a vocabulary. I spent the next year memorizing words. Hundreds of words."

The next time he took the test, both scores were high. High enough, the school was notified, that Stanley had won early admission to Princeton University. "When the head of my school saw the scores, he called me in to his office. Then he chewed me out. Why, he wanted to know, hadn't I been getting all As? I didn't know what to say. He thought I was lazy. I thought the test scores must be wrong.

Once Stanley arrived at Princeton, his private school experience repeated itself. However, in college, he had a little more control over which courses he took; whenever possible, he tried to avoid those requiring extensive memorization. His study skills had improved, as well. But the work still seemed excruciatingly difficult. He got a C in chemistry. Remembering equations always tripped him up. And German he found impossible. "The professor would assign us a 30-line poem to memorize, and I wouldn't do it. I knew I could spend 30 hours trying, and still not have it memorized. So I didn't even try."

The turning point of his college career, he says, came in his junior year with a course on mineralogy. The course was legendary for destroying the grade point average of even the best students. Stanley was a geology major, however; if he was to make it as any kind of geologist, he needed to study minerals.

"At first, the professor really had his doubts. He would say, 'Steve, are you with me? Do you understand?' He kept it up until the midterm...Then I took the test, and it was easy for me – because the questions required us to reason. It wouldn't work to just memorize facts and regurgitate them.

"I got a 99. And a 98 on the final."

With that success under his belt, Stanley turned to the last challenge of his college career, his senior thesis. For his thesis, he decided to write about evolution in the Key Largo limestone, a coral reef off the coast of Florida. The summer between his junior and senior year, he headed south to study the reef first-hand.

That experience taught him two things: that he could do research as well as many graduate students, and that he *loved* doing research.

The following spring, he graduated *summa cum laude* from Princeton. Graduate school at Yale – and a life of outstanding research – lay ahead.

"I never thought of myself as smart," Steve Stanley says today. "When I was told my IQ was off the chart, too high to measure, it was a total shock. Still, when they told me I had ADD, I was surprised. I didn't want to think of myself as having a disability.

"But even as an adult, I could see the signs. My work was going well, but I was tired. I was often losing and forgetting things. Whenever I was careless, my childhood came back to haunt me. 'Remember the time Steve set out for school without his shoes?' someone in my family would say. They didn't know what to make of me. Often, I wouldn't even realize I had done something wrong."

When doctors made it clear to Stanley that his symptoms fit a condition suffered by thousands of other people around the country, he felt both relief and anger. "All my life, I had a sense that I was better than I was able to show people. But every day was still a struggle."

Although he had learned to compensate for his disability, Stanley says the Ritalin has made a tremendous difference. "The doctors don't understand how it works," he explains. "All I know is, it's like a memory pill. After I started taking Ritalin, I'd look at an equation and wonder an hour later whether I could remember it – and I could. It was astounding. And now it's no effort to read the paper in the morning – just to sit down and read the newspaper without effort! For me, Ritalin's a miracle."

And the ADD itself was not *all* bad. Today, Stanley credits his disability for shaping his thinking processes to a large degree; he might never have had those radical ideas, he says, if he had not had ADD. "I lived and died by logic," he explains. "I never could memorize details, so I also never got bogged down by them."

"I began very early to develop broad, conceptual knowledge," Stanley adds. "I know a huge amount in a skeletal way. And today, even though with Ritalin I can memorize things, I prefer to deal with patterns and concepts. So my ADD still shapes how I work. I'll get one piece of a puzzle stuck in my mind, and I'll keep looking until I find the others."

Reprinted with permission from the Johns Hopkins Magazine, February 1993.

Centers, Associations and Organizations

Association for Children and Adults with Learning Disabilities (ACLD)
4156 Library Rd., Pittsburgh, PA 15234
(412) 341-1515.

Children with Attention Deficit Disorders (C.H.A.D.D.)
499 NW 70th Avenue, Suite 308, Plantation, FL 33317
(305)587-3700

Council for Exceptional Children (CEC)
Division of Learning Disabilities,
Center for Special Education Technology
The Association for the Gifted (TAG)
1920 Association Drive, Reston, VA 22091
(703)620-3660

Learning Disabilities Association of America
4156 Library Road, Pittsburgh, PA 15234
(412)341-1515

National Association for Gifted Children (NAGC)
1155 15th Street NW, Suite 1002, Washington, DC 20005
(202)785-4268

National Center for Learning Disabilities (NCLD)
381 Park Avenue, Suite 1420, New York, NY 10016
(212)545-7510

National Dyslexia Learning Foundation
P.O. Box 81318, Wellesley Hills. MA 02181
(617)239-0723

The Orton Dyslexia Society (National)
724 York Rd. Baltimore, MD 21204
(410)296-0232

Parents of Gifted/Learning Disabled Children
6222 Broad Street, Bethesda, MD 20816
(301)986-1422

> NOTE: Parents of Gifted/LD Children is offering a special advocacy service for its members. Patty Eisen, former president of the organization and counselor by training, can assist parents in negotiating the special education process. She is available for consultation and attendance at school meetings at a reduced fee for members. For further information contact: Patty Eisen, M.Ed., 13712 Castle Cliff Way, Silver Spring, MD 20904 (301)236-0399 or (301) 384-2261

The United Way (check the telephone directory to find your local chapter) can refer you to agencies and organizations (for example, Boy Scouts, Girl Scouts) that mainstream LD youth in their programs.

Select Samping of Schools for the Learning Disabled

Assets School
1 Ohana Nui Way, Hololulu, HI 96860
(808)423-1356
Full day program for gifted/dyslexics ages 5-14.

Brandon Hall School
1701 Brandon Hall Drive, Atlanta, GA 30350
(404)804-8821
College preparatory boarding school for males (ages 10-19) who are bright but experiencing academic difficulty.

Brush Ranch School INC
HC 73 Box 33
Tererro, NM 87573
(505)757-6114
Boarding school in the Sangre de Cristo mountain range for students ages 10-18 with learning differences.

Calvert Hall College High School
8102 LaSalle Road, Baltimore, MD 21286
(410)825-4266
Special program for learning-disabled students at the school, rather than a specialized school.

Chelsea School
711 Pershing Drive, Silver Spring, MD 20910
(301)585-1430
Co-ed private school for students with specific learning difficulties.

The Dominion School
Dominion Center
Seven Corner Professional Park
6408-B, Seven Corners Place, Falls Church, VA 22044
Emotional, learning, and behavior problems.

The Forman School
12 Norfolk Road, Litchfield, CT 06759
(203)567-0140
Boarding school, grades 9-12. Language training program for dyslexic students.

The Gow School
26-33 Emry Road, South Wales, NY 14139
(716)652-3450
College preparatory boarding school for young men (grades 7-PG) with a language disability or dyslexia.

Jemicy School
11 Celadon Road, Owings Mills, MD 21117
(410)653-2700
Serves students with dyslexia in grades 1-8.

Kingsbury School
1809 Phelps Place NW, Washington, DC 20008
(202)232-1702
School for students (ages 5-11) with special learning needs.

The Lab School
4759 Reservoir Road NW, Washington, DC 20007
(202)965-6600
Learning disabilities, D-12 and adult services.

Landmark School
PO Box 227, Prides Crossing, MA 01965
(508)927-4440
School for students with learning disabilities ages 8-20; non-graded.

Long Island School for the Gifted
165 Pidgeon Hill Road, Huntington Station, NY 11746
(516)423-3557
Day school, grades K-9, program at school for learning-disabled students.

Pine Ridge School
1075 Williston Road, Williston, VT 05495
(802)434-2161
Boarding school, ages 12-18.

Robert Louis Stevenson School
24 West 74th Street, New York, NY 10023
(212)787-6400
A coeducational day junior and senior high school for promising adolescents with unrealized potential.

Windward School
Windward Avenue, White Plains, NY 10605
(914)949-6968
Day school, K-12, for learning disabled (produce Shakespearean play each year).

The Winston Preparatory School
4 West 76th Street, New York, NY 10023
(212)496-8400
Day School, ages 12-19.

Woodland Hall Academy
4745 Centerville Road, Tallahassee, FL 32308
(904)893-2216
School for average/above average dyslexia or ADD students (grades 1-12)

The Vanguard School
Dept. ATP-D, 2249 Highway 27 North, Lake Wales, FL 33853
(813) 676-6091
An academic and social setting for the student of good educational potential (ages 9-12) who is experiencing learning problems and related adjustment difficulties.

Programs

*For additional information, CTY Publications & Resources publishes **Program Opportunities for Academically Talented Students: A Guide to Over 450 Programs in the U.S. and Abroad**. Please contact us for ordering information at: CTY Publications & Resources, Johns Hopkins University, 3400 N. Charles St., Baltimore, MD 21218 (410) 516-0245.*

Basic Educational Skills Training Program (B.E.S.T.)
PO Box 1002, Millersville University, Millersville PA 17551
(717)872-3745
Saturday mornings; individualized instruction for reading problems.

Disability International Foundation
P.O. Box 1781, Longview, WA 98632
(206)577-0243
Promotes educational and consultational opportunities to benefit individuals with disabilities.

Eagle Hill School
Old Persham Road, Hardwick, MA 01037
(413)4776000
  Six-week residential summer program for LD students 8-18.

General Federation of Women's Clubs
1734 N Street NW, Washington, DC 20036
(202)347-3168
  Many local chapters have current projects on LD; contact the national office for
  futher information.

Generations Together
121 University Place, Suite 300, University of Pittsburgh, Pittsburgh, PA 15260
(412)648-7150

Project Soar
P.O. Box 388, Balsam, NC 28707
(704)456-3435
  Outdoor adventure experiences for LD and ADD youth.

Publications

Academic Therapy
Pro-Ed
8700 Shoal Creek Blvd., Austin, TX 78758
(512) 451-3246

Exceptionality
Lawrence Erlbaum Associates
365 Broadway, Hillsdale, NJ 07642
(201) 666-4110

Gifted Child Quarterly
National Association for Gifted Children
1155 15th St. NW, Suite 1002, Washington, DC 20005
(202) 785-4268

Gifted Child Today
Prufrock Press
P.O. Box 8813, Waco, TX 76714-8813
(800) 998-2208

Journal of Learning Disabilities
Pro-Ed
8700 Shoal Creek Blvd., Austin, TX 78758
(512) 451-3246

Learning Disabilities Quarterly and **LD Forum**
Council for Learning Disabilities
P.O. Box 40303, Overland Park, KS 66204
(913) 492-8755

Learning Disabilities Research & Practice
Lawrence Erlbaum Associates
365 Broadway, Hillsdale, NJ 07642
(201) 666-4110

Roeper Review
P.O. Box 329, Bloomfield Hills, MI 48303
(313) 642-1500

TESTS

NAME	FORMS	AGE/GRADE	ASSESSES	PUBLISHER	ADM. TIME
Wechsler Intelligence Tests:* WPPSI — WISC-R — WAIS	3	4-6.5 yrs 5-16 yrs 16+ yrs	Verbal I.Q. Performance I.Q. Gen'l Intellectual abilities	Psychological Corp.	1.5-2 hrs
Ravens: Regular; Advanced; Colored;	3	6+ yrs 11+ yrs (above avg) 5-11 yrs (mentally impaired)	Nonverbal I.Q.	Psychological Corp.	45-60 min
Detroit Tests of Learning Aptitude	1	6-18 yrs	Aptitude-Gen'l Cognitive Processes	AGS; Pro-ED	1-1.5 hrs
Woodcock-Johnson Psycho-Educational Battery: Ability	2	2+ yrs and up	Aptitude; Basic Cognitive Processes	DLM	1 hr
Bender Motor Gestalt Test*	1	8+ yrs	Visual Motor Perception	AGS; Psychological Corp.	30 min
Differential Aptitude Test	2	8-12 grade **	Aptitude Battery	Psychological Corp.	3 hrs
School & College Ability Test (SCAT)	2	3-12 grade **	Verbal/ Quantitative Reasoning	College Board (ETS)	2.5 hrs
Scholastic Aptitude Test (SAT)	N/A	11-12 grade **	Verbal/ Quantitative Reasoning	College Board (ETS)	2.5 hrs
Woodcock-Johnson Psycho-Educational Battery: Achievement	2	3-Adult	Achievement: Reading, Math, Written Language, Knowledge	DLM	1 hr
Stanford Diagnostic Reading Test	2	8-12 yrs	Reading Comp: literal and inferential, vocab, word parts, phonetic analysis, structural analysis	Psychological Corp.	1 hr
Test of Written Language (TOWL)	1	7-17 yrs	Written Language: Vocab; word usage; style; handriting, spelling	DLM; PRO-ED	60-90 min
Peabody Picture Vocabulary Test-R	2	2.5-Adult	Receptive Language	AGS	10-20 min
Woodcock Reading Mastery Test	2	5-Adult	Reading Skills	AGS	40-60 min
Key Math	2	K-9 grade	Math Concepts and Applications	AGS	35-50 min

* Restrictions on accessibility and who can administer
** Can be used for in-level and out-of-level testing

Test Publishers

American Guidance Service (AGS)
Publisher's Bldg.
P.O. Box 99, 4201 Woodland Rd.
Circle Pines, MN 55014-1796
(800) 328-2560

DLM Inc.
1 DLM Park
P.O. Box 8500
Allen, TX 75002
(800) 442-4711

Pro-Ed
8700 Shoal Creek Blvd.
Austin, TX 78758-6897
(512) 451-3246

Psychological Corporation
Harcourt Brace Jovanovich
P.O. Box 839954
San Antonio, TX 78283-3954
(800) 228-0752

For information on the SCAT and SAT, including special provisions for learning disabilities, contact:

ATP Services for Handicapped Students
P.O. Box 226, Princeton, NJ 08541-6226
(609) 771-7137

Recommended Reading

Barton, J.M. & Starnes, W.T. (1988). Identifying distinguishing characteristics of gifted and talented/learning disabled students. *Roeper Review, 12(1),* 23-29.

Baum, S. (1984). Meeting the needs of learning disabled gifted students. *Roeper Review, 7(1),* 16-19.

Baum, S. (1988). An enrichment program for gifted learning disabled students. *Gifted Child Quarterly, 32(1),* 226-230.

Baum, S., Emerick, L.J., Herman, G.N., & Dixon, J. (1989). Identification, programs and enrichment strategies for gifted learning disabled youth. *Roeper Review, 12(1),* 48-53.

Baum, S. & Kirschenbaum, R. (1984, Winter). Recognizing special talents in learning disabled students. *Teaching Exceptional Children.*

Baum, S. & Owen, S.V. (1988). High ability/learning disabled students: How are they different?. *Gifted Child Quarterly, 32(3),* 321-326.

Baum, S.M., Owen, S.V. & Dixon, J. (1991). *To be gifted and learning disabled: From identification to practical intervention strategies.* Mansfield Center, CT: Creative Learning Press.

Bireley, M., Languis, M., & Williamson, T. (1992, November/December). Physiological uniqueness: A new perspective on the learning disabled/gifted child. *Roeper Review,* 101-107.

Boodoo, G.M., Bradley, C.L., Frontera, R.L., Pitts, J.R., & Wright, L.B. (1989). A survey of procedures used for identifying gifted learning disabled children. *Gifted Child Quarterly, 33(3),* 110-114.

Borkowski, J.G. & Day, J.D. (1987). *Cognition in special children: Comparative approaches to retardation, learning disabilities, and giftedness.* Norwood, NJ: Ablex.

Brown, S.W. (1984, Sptember). The use of WISC-R subtest scatter in the identification of intellectually gifted handicapped children: An inappropriate task?. *Roeper Review,* 20-22.

Copeland, E.D. & Love, V.L. (1991). *Attention, please!* Atlanta: SPI Press.

Cordoni, B. (1987). *Living with a learning disability.* Carbondale, IL: Southern Illinois University Press.

Cruickshank, W.M. (1955). *Psychology of exceptional children and youth.* Englewood Cliffs, NJ: Prentice-Hall.

Cummings, R. & Fisher, G. (1991). *The school survival guide for kids with LD: Ways to make learning easier and more fun.* Minneapolis: Free Spirit.

Cummings, R. & Fisher, G. (1993). *The survival guide for teenagers with LD.* Minneapolis, MN: Free Spirit.

Dockrell, J. & McShane, J. (1992). *Children's learning difficulties: A cognitive approach.* Cambridge: Blackwell.

Ellston, T. (1993, Jan/Feb). Gifted and learning disabled. . . A paradox. *Gifted Child Today,* 17-19.

Fall, J. & Nolan, L. (1993, Jan/Feb). A paradox of exceptionalities. *Gifted Child Today,* 46-49.

Fox, L.H. & Brody, L.E. (1983). Models for identifying giftedness: Issues related to the learning disabled child. In Anonymous (Ed.). *Learning disabled / gifted children: Identification and programming* Austin, TX: Pro-Ed

French, J.N. (1982). The gifted learning disabled child: A challenge and some suggestions. *Roeper Review, 4(3).*

Friedrichs, T.P. (1990). *Gifted handicapped students: The way forward.* Richmond: Virginia Department of Education.

Ganschow, L. (1985). Diagnosing and remediating writing problems of gifted students with language learning disabilities. *Journal for the Education of the Gifted, 9(1),* 25-43.

Gargiulo, R.M. (1985). *Working with parents of exceptional children.* Boston: Houghton Mifflin.

Gunderson, C.W., Maesch, C., & Rees, J.W. (1987). The gifted/learning disabled student. *Gifted Child Quarterly, 31,* 158-160.

Hannah, L.C. (1989). The use of cognitive methodology to identify, investigate and instruct learning-disabled gifted students. *Roeper Review, 12(1),* 58-64.

Harwell, J.M. (1989). *Complete learning disabilities handbook: Ready to use techniques for teaching learning handicapped students.* West Nyack, NY: Center for Applied Research in Education.

Hegde, M.N. (1991). *Introduction to communicative disorders.* Austin: Pro-Ed.

Hevesi, D. (1991, August 4). Learning disabled for a day. *New York Times.*

Hishinuma, E.S. (1991, Sep/Oct). Assets school: Serving the needs of the gifted/learning disabled. *Gifted Child Today,* 36-38.

Hishinuma, E.S. (1993). Counseling gifted/at risk and gifted/dyslexic youngsters. *Gifted Child Today,* Jan./Feb., 30-33.

Kamhi, A.G. & Catts, H.W. (1989). *Reading disabilities: A developmental language perspective.* Boston: College-Hill Press, Little, Brown and Company.

Karnes, M.B. (1984). A demonstration/outreach model for young gifted/talented handicapped. *Roeper Review, 7(1),* 23-26.

Karnes, M.B., Amundsen, J., Cohen, T. & Johnson, L.J. (1992). *General programming: detective,inventor and judge thinking activities.* Urbana-Champaign, IL: Institute for Child Behavior and Development.

Karnes, M.B., Amundsen, J. & Johnson, L.J. (1985). *Talent programming*. Urbana-Champaign, IL: Institute for Child Behavior and Development.

Karnes, M.B., Johnson, L.J. & Amundsen, J. (1985). *Talent identification*. Urbana-Champaign, IL : Institute for Child Behavior and Development.

Kirk, S.A. & Gallagher, J.J. (1989). *Educating exceptional children*. Boston: Houghton Mifflin.

Krippner, S. (1968). Etiological factors in reading disability of the academically talented in comparison to pupils of average and slow-learning ability. *The Journal of Educational Research, 61(6)*, 275-279.

Landrum, T.J. (1989). Gifted and learning disabled students: Practical considerations for teachers. *Academic Therapy, 24(5)*, 533-544.

Levey, S. & Dolan, J. (1988). Addressing specific learning abilities in gifted students. *Gifted Child Today, May/June*, 10-11.

Lipkin, M. (1990). *Guide to colleges with programs or services for students with learning disabilities*. Belmont, MA: Schoolsearch.

Lyon, G.R. (1989, October). IQ is irrelevant to the definition of learning disabilities: A position in search of logic and data. *Journal of Learning Disabilities*, 504-512.

Mendaglio, S. (1993). Counseling gifted learning disabled: Individual and group counseling techniques. In L.K. Silverman (Ed.). *Counseling the gifted and talented* (pp. 131-149). Denver, CO: Love Publishing Company.

Messerer, J., Hunt, E., Meyers, G., & Lerner, J. (1984). Feuerstein's instrumental enrichment: A new approach for activating intellectual potential in learning disabled youth. *Journal of Learning Disabilities, 17(6)*, 322-325.

Miller, M. (1991). Self-assessment as a specific strategy for teaching the gifted learning disabled. *Journal for the Education of the Gifted, 14(2)*, 178-188.
Minner, S. (1990). Teacher evaluations of case descriptions of LD gifted children. *Gifted Child Quarterly, 34(1)*, 37-39.

Minner, S., Prater, G., Bloodworth, H., & Walker, S. (1987). Referral and placement recommendations of teachers toward gifted handicapped children. *Roeper Review, 9(4)*, 247-249.

Moller, B.W. (1984). Special techniques for the gifted LD student. *Academic Therapy, 20(2)*, 167-171.

Nielson, M.E. & Mortoff-Albert, S. (1989). The effects of special education service on the self-concept and school attitude of learning disabled/gifted students. *Roeper Review, 12(1)*, 29-36.

Pledgie, T.K. (1982). Giftedness among handicapped children: Identification and programming development. *The Journal of Special Education, 16(2)*, 221-227.

Rief, S.F. (1993). *How to reach and teach ADD/ADHD children.* West Nyack, NY: Center for Applied Research in Education.

Sah, A. & Borland, J.H. (1989). The effects of a structured home plan on the home and school behaviors of gifted learning-disabled students with deficits in organizational skills. *Roeper Review, 12(1)*, 54-57.

Scheiber, B. & Talpers, J. (1987). *Unlocking potential: College and other choices for learning disabled people–A step-by-step guide.* Bethesda, MD: Adler & Adler.

Schiff, M.M., Kaufman, A.S., & Kaufman, N.L. (1981). Scatter analysis of WISC-R profiles for learning disabled children with superior intelligence. *Journal of Learning Disabilities, 14(7)*, 400-404.

Siegel, L.S. (1989). IQ is irrelevant to the definition of learning disabilities. *Journal of Learning Disabilities, 22*, 469-486.

Silverman, L.K. (1989). Invisible gifts, invisible handicaps. *Roeper Review, 12(1)*, 37-41.

Singh, N.N. & Beale, I.L. (1992). *Learning disabilities: Nature, theory, and treatment.* New York: Springer-Verlag.

Stuart, M.F. (1988). *Personal insights into the world of dyslexia.* Cambridge, MA: Educators Publishing Service, Inc.

Suter, D.P. & Wolf, J.S. (1987). Issues in the identification and programming of the gifted/learning disabled child. *Journal for the Education of the Gifted, 10(3)*, 227-237.

Taylor, R. & Sternberg, L. (1989). *Exceptional children; Integrating research and teaching.* New York: Springer-Verlag.

Thompson, L.J. (1971). Language disabilities in men of eminence. *Journal of Learning Disabilities, 4*, 39-50.

Tobin, D. (1988). Learning disabled gifted students: Is their day dawning?. *Their World: A publication of the Foundation for Children with Learning Disabilities, 14.*

Toll, M.F. (1993, Jan/Feb). Gifted learning disabled: A kaleidoscope of needs. *Gifted Child Today*, 34-35.

Torgesen, J.K. (1989). Why IQ is relevant to the definition of learning disabilities. *Journal of Learning Disabilities, 22*, 484-486.

Vail, P.L. (1988). Conundrum kids. *Independent School, Winter,* 7-10.

VanTassel-Baska, J. (1991). Serving the disabled gifted through educational collaboration. *Journal for the Education of the Gifted, 14,* 246-266.

Vaughn, S. (1989). Gifted learning disabilities: Is it such a bright idea?. *Learning Disabilities Focus, 4(2),* 123-126.

Waldron, K.A. (1991a). Teaching techniques for the learning disabled/gifted student. *Learning Disabilities Research & Practice, 6,* 40-43.

Waldron, K.A. (1991b). Teaching techniques for the learning disabled/gifted student. *Learning Disabilities Research and Practice, 6,* 40-43.

Waldron, K.A. & Saphire, D.G. (1990). An analysis of WISC-R factors for gifted students with learning disabilities. *Journal of Learning Disabilities, 23,* 491-498.

Waldron, K.A., Saphire, D.G., & Rosenblum, S.A. (1987). Learning disabilities and giftedness: Identification based on self-concept, behavior, and academic patterns. *Journal of Learning Disabilities, 20,* 422-432.

Weill, M.P. (1987). Gifted/learning disabled students: Their potential may be buried treasure. *The Clearing House, 60,* 341-343.

Whitmore, J.R. (1981). Gifted children with handicapping conditions: A new frontier. *Excep.Children, 48,* 106-114.

Yewchuk, C.R. (1985). Gifted/learning disabled children: An overview. *Gifted Education International, 3,* 122-126.

Yong, F.L. & McIntyre, J.D. (1992). A comparative study of the learning style preferences of students with learning disabilities and students who are gifted. *Journal of Learning Disabilities, 25,* 124-132.

CTY Publications & Resources

Lighting the Way for Optimal Education

CTY's Publications & Resources service was established in 1989 in response to thousands of requests for information for the benefit of academically talented students, their parents, and educators; and to permit CTY's distinctive educational vision to have the broadest possible impact on public policy and practice.

Identifying and Cultivating Talent in Preschool and Elementary School Children was designed to address questions from parents and educators on the identifcation of talent, and provide a blueprint for educational planning.

Additional information exists on some of the topics covered in this publication. If you would like to read more about acceleration, ability grouping vs. cooperative learning, or the gifted/learning disabled student, please contact Publications & Resources. We have a publication for each of these issues.

Popular publications such as *College Bound, Educational Resources for Academically Talented Adolescents,* and *Program Opportunities for Academically Talented Students* assist families with educational planning. Curricular materials (including a two-volume science set developed by retired Chief Scientist for NASA, Dr. Samuel Katzoff), and research on current issues are also available.

Please call or write if you have any questions or comments. We'd like to hear from you!

CTY Publications & Resources
Johns Hopkins University
3400 N. Charles St.
Baltimore, MD 21218
(410)516-0245   FAX (410)516-0108

You can also access information 24 hours a day through CTY's Gopher server on Internet. If you don't have a local Gopher, but you do have access to Telnet, try TELNET JHUNIVERSE.JHU.EDU. You may also telnet to the main Gopher (134.84.132.4 or consultant.micro.umn.edu) or another public Gopher. Once you are connected, go to Other Gopher, Information Servers, North America, USA, Maryland, Johns Hopkins University, Center for Talented Youth. Please send any comments or questions about our Gopher (or CTY) to GIFTED@JHUNIX.HCF.JHU.EDU.